SOCIETAL DYNAMICS AND FRAGILITY

NEW FRONTIERS OF SOCIAL POLICY

Societal Dynamics and Fragility

Engaging Societies in Responding to Fragile Situations

Alexandre Marc, Alys Willman, Ghazia Aslam,
Michelle Rebosio, with Kanishka Balasuriya

THE WORLD BANK
Washington, D.C.

© 2013 International Bank for Reconstruction and Development / The World Bank
1818 H Street NW
Washington DC 20433
Telephone: 202-473-1000
Internet: www.worldbank.org

Some rights reserved

1 2 3 4 16 15 14 13

ISBN (paper): 978-0-8213-9656-8
ISBN (electronic): 978-0-8213-9708-4
DOI: 10.1596/978-0-8213-9656-8

Cover photo: istockphoto.com

Library of Congress Cataloging-in-Publication Data has been requested.

NEW FRONTIERS OF SOCIAL POLICY

In many developing countries, the mixed record of state effectiveness, market imperfections, and persistent structural inequities has undermined the effectiveness of social policy. To overcome these constraints, social policy needs to move beyond conventional social service approaches toward development's goals of equitable opportunity and social justice. This series has been created to promote debate among the development community, policy makers, and academia, and to broaden understanding of social policy challenges in developing country contexts.

The books in the series are linked to the World Bank's Social Development Strategy. The strategy is aimed at empowering people by transforming institutions to make them more inclusive, cohesive, resilient, and accountable. This involves the transformation of subjects and beneficiaries into citizens with rights and responsibilities. Themes in this series include equity and development, assets and livelihoods, citizenship and rights-based social policy, and the social dimensions of infrastructure and climate change.

Titles in the series:

- *Assets, Livelihoods, and Social Policy*
- *Building Equality and Opportunity through Social Guarantees: New Approaches to Public Policy and the Realization of Rights*
- *Delivering Services in Multicultural Societies*
- *Inclusive States: Social Policy and Structural Inequalities*
- *Institutional Pathways to Equity: Addressing Inequality Traps*
- *Living through Crises: How the Food, Fuel, and Financial Shocks Affect the Poor*
- *Social Dimensions of Climate Change: Equity and Vulnerability in a Warming World*
- *Societal Dynamics and Fragility: Engaging Societies in Responding to Fragile Situations*

CONTENTS

The report in this book has been prepared by a team led by Alexandre Marc, Lead Social Development Specialist, and comprising Alys Willman, Ghazia Aslam, Michelle Rebosio, and Kanishka Balasuriya. Research support was provided by Benjamin Petrini, Megumi Makisaka, and Shonali Sardesai. The team was assisted by Joyce Chinsen. Lauri S. Scherer provided editorial support. The work was carried out under the general direction of Cyprian F. Fisiy and Elisabeth Huybens.

The team was advised by a panel of experts comprising Ozong Agborsangaya-Fiteu, Ian Bannon, Christina Biebesheimer, Anna Bjerde, Nora Dudwick, Paul A. Francis, Varun Gauri, Bernard Harborne, Deborah Hannah Isser, Markus Kostner, Stephen N. Ndegwa, Vijayendra Rao, Caroline Mary Sage, Radhika Srinivasan, Graham Teskey, and Michael Woolcock.

Many others inside and outside the World Bank provided helpful comments, wrote background papers and other contributions, and participated in consultation meetings, including Mary Amuyunzu-Nyamongo, Edward Aspinall, Gary Barker, Patrick Barron, Pilar Domingo, Deval Desai, Barry Hart, Dirk Kohnert, Kathleen Kuehnast, Sabine Kurtenbach, Elham M. Manea, Louis Herns Marcelin, Roland Marchal, Jennifer Olmsted, Beatrice Pouligny, Paul Richards, and Ashutosh Varshney.

External review was provided by Frances Stewart. Internal peer reviewers were Christina Biebesheimer, Anna Bjerde, and Vijayendra Rao.

The study team gratefully acknowledges the contributions of the German Development Cooperation, both during the analytical phase and by providing operational experiences from the field, which has been made possible through the kind support of Claudia Pragua of the German Ministry for Economic Cooperation and Development. Much of the background research was supported by several generous trust fund grants from the Dutch, Finnish, and Norwegian governments.

The team undertook a wide range of consultations for this book, which included workshops in Banda Aceh, Bangui, Monrovia, Port-au-Prince, and Sana'a. The participants in these workshops included academic researchers, development specialists, and staff of nongovernmental and private sector organizations.

The team wishes to acknowledge the tireless efforts of several local consultants in conducting the fieldwork for the study, including Marzi Afriko, Sam Gotomo, Khaled Hariri, Faouzi Kilembe, Lemu Makain, Hisham Nagi, Khairil Razali, and Simpson Snowe.

The support of several World Bank regions and country offices was essential for the in-country workshops and the community-level field research. In this regard, the team benefited greatly from the support of Benson Ateng, Sabine Beddies, David Craig, Muslahuddin Daud, Xavier Devictor, Coleen Littlejohn, Adrian Morel, Ohene Nyanin, Blair Palmer, Jelena Pantelic, and Renaud David Rodier.

ACRONYMS AND ABBREVIATIONS

CDD	Community-Driven Development
CIDSS	Comprehensive and Integrated Delivery of Social Services
CPIA	Country Policy and Institutional Assessment
DDR	Disarmament, Demobilization, and Reintegration
DFID	Department of Foreign Investment and Development
FSP	Fragile States Principles
GAM	Free Aceh Movement
IDP	Internally Displaced Persons
INURED	Inter-university Institute for Research and Development
KDP	Kecamatan Development Program
NGO	Nongovernmental Organizations
OECD	Organization for Economic Cooperation and Development
UNDP	United Nations Development Program
UNRWA	United Nations Relief and Works Agency

Overview

Over the last two decades, concern has risen over "fragile" states and situations. These areas—now home to at least a quarter of the world's people—experience some of the worst development conditions. Most fragile countries fall far behind on achieving the Millennium Development Goals, and they often generate spillover effects, such as trafficking in illegal goods and persons and corruption, that threaten the stability of neighboring countries (World Bank 2011; OECD 2005). Responding to these situations has become a top priority for the international community. The World Bank established support to fragility as one of its six strategic priorities and devoted the *2011 World Development Report* to the topic.

The label "fragile" is applied to a diverse range of contexts, from conflict-affected countries such as Afghanistan and Somalia, to weak institutional settings such as Haiti and Guatemala. Recognition is also growing that pockets of fragility can exist even where overall state capacity is solid, such as in slum areas in middle-income countries (OECD 2008; DFID 2010; World Bank 2011).

No consensus exists on a specific definition of fragility, nor is there an agreed-on list of fragile states or situations. Yet, generally speaking, most donors define fragility as a problem of weak state capacity, legitimacy, or will to deliver basic services (OECD 2010; DFID 2010; USAID 2005). Because fragility is seen in this way, the dominant policy response to fragile situations has emphasized state-building—increasing the capacity of the state to fulfill core functions.

The study reported in this book departs from the dominant approach in that it views fragility as *not only* a problem of state capacity, but also one of relationships in society. In other words, although some elements of fragility emanate from the state, others are deeply rooted in *societal dynamics*—the way individuals and groups interact and the relationships that form out of their interactions. This includes the relationships between groups in society and the state.

Seen in this way, fragility is not a static condition, nor is it an all-or-nothing experience. Fragility can best be understood as a continuum: societies can experience extreme state failure and violent conflict at one end and varying degrees of fragility at other points along the continuum. The continuum does not imply a linear process, as societies can jump around to different points as societal dynamics shift. Viewing fragility in this way allows one to recognize that all countries experience fragility, although to different degrees.

The study sought to understand the nature of the fragility continuum to offer insights for interventions that can help prevent societies from slipping toward greater fragility and violent conflict. It is argued that where a society falls on the fragility continuum is directly influenced by the degree of social cohesion—understood as the overall quality of relationships across groups. More cohesive societies enjoy higher levels of trust and collaboration, which provide the framework for groups to interact constructively on common goals and avoid, or move away from, the lower end of the fragility continuum.

Method and Approach

This work is based on collaboration among experts on fragility, violence, and social dynamics. It comprised three phases. First, the study team convoked a variety of practitioners, academics, and donors to assess the state of research and policy and develop lines of inquiry. Next, the team commissioned five background papers on relevant themes, to understand the relationships between particular societal dynamics and fragility.

The analytical phase was followed by in-country work in five places: Liberia, Central African Republic, Yemen, Indonesia (Aceh), and Haiti. The countries were selected to reflect varying degrees and experiences of fragility and to provide regional balance. A political economy analysis was conducted for each country to examine the different societal dynamics at play and to design the fieldwork. In each country, a national-level workshop was held with experts on the topic as well as the country context. Finally, focus groups and key informant interviews were conducted in selected communities to explore how different dynamics played out in practice and to understand grassroots perspectives on the dynamics that were considered most relevant.

Key Findings

Building Social Cohesion is Crucial for Reducing Fragility

Viewing fragility as partly a result of dysfunctional relationships in society changes the way the role of the state is envisioned in fragile situations. The state is clearly a primary actor in all contexts, including those that are fragile. However, the state is not the only actor, and it may not always be the most powerful actor. The state is formed by interactions with members of society, who bring their own ideas, meanings, cultures, interpretations, and priorities to the state. When the state is seen as embedded within society, it becomes evident that to address fragility, one has to look not only at the state and its capacities, but also at the quality of relationships between groups in society. Addressing fragility means putting social cohesion at the center of development efforts.

The term "social cohesion" has varying definitions, but all coincide on the idea that it has to do with the quality and nature of connections between people and groups. At its essence, social cohesion embodies a *convergence across groups* that provides an overarching structure for collective life and helps ensure predictability and certainty, even if it does not guarantee that all groups will agree on all issues. At a minimum, convergence across groups offers the incentive for groups to coexist. As the degree of convergence builds, and groups see their interests mesh with those of others, they become more connected to other groups and ultimately have more incentive to collaborate. Convergence across groups thus serves as an essential element for collective action.

To build convergence across groups requires certain conditions. For groups to converge, they need to believe that it is better to collaborate than to compete. They need to trust in the fundamentals of the system in which they operate, even if they still distrust the motivations of other groups. Convergence across groups also needs to persist over time: although groups may converge in the short term, for example, when fighting a war or overthrowing a dictator, that type of short-term convergence does not result in social cohesion. Similarly, a convergence that is too narrow—that does not include a large number of groups—is unlikely to persist for long. A convergence that is not sufficiently inclusive may create grievances that cause those excluded to react, creating negative effects on fragility. Finally, convergence has to be based on some common understanding of the (often subconscious) rules that determine how a society functions—what this study refers to as *intersubjective meanings*. If the points of convergence include various qualitatively different or competing concepts, the convergence will be short-lived.

Social Cohesion Is Often Weakened by Perceptions of Injustice Between Groups

A key finding of this work is that social cohesion is greatly weakened when groups in a society perceive that their situation is unfair or that they have not been treated fairly in the past, compared to other groups. Such perceptions of injustice are a critical factor in the success or failure of development interventions. A project or policy outcome may result in equal distribution of resources by objective measures, yet still be perceived as unfair by different groups. In part, the reason is that groups differ in their conceptions of fairness; that is, the same development outcome can be perceived as fair or unfair by different groups because they apply different criteria to assess fairness. Fairness as respect, fairness as a process, and fairness as inclusion and voice are often as important as fairness as equity, or more so.

Certain contextual factors exacerbate perceptions of injustice. Perceptions of injustice have more negative effects when groups have rigid identity boundaries. Rigid boundaries can also contribute to the internalization of injustice and stigma by marginalized groups. Perceptions of injustice can provoke groups to coalesce inward, defining their identity more narrowly and in opposition to other groups. Elites or other actors may also be able to mobilize groups with rigid boundaries more easily, especially if those boundaries are hardened by perceptions of injustice.

Events in history, and specifically incidents that have caused trauma, seem to have a particularly important effect on perceptions of injustice. Colonization, for example, has shaped the relationships between citizens and between citizens and the state in a large number of countries around the world. In other countries, a history of state oppression has made it very difficult for certain groups of citizens to trust the state. Events causing trauma, such as forced displacement, can harden distinctions between groups, creating an "us-versus-them" mentality that exacerbates intergroup divisions.

The Quality of Interactions Among Different Institutions Appears Strongly Related to Overall Social Cohesion

Much attention has been devoted in development policy and research to the strength and effectiveness of institutions. The study reported here probed that issue and found that, in general, people were less affected by the effectiveness of individual institutions than they were by the quality of interactions between them. That was particularly the case regarding interactions between customary and state institutions. In many cases, a particular institution may be quite effective in serving its own function, yet be unable to interact constructively with the state system. Such unconstructive interactions have a cumulative effect in reinforcing divisions between different groups in society.

Several problematic interactions were observed in the five field sites. In Liberia, the existence of two parallel systems of customary and state law provoked confusion about which system to use and reinforced the disadvantage of marginalized groups, who did not clearly understand the workings of the formal system. The problem of "forum shopping" was also observed, as people chose to take a dispute to the system most likely to rule in their favor, often resulting in competing rulings.

In Yemen, problems of the loss of accountability were observed, resulting from the co-optation of customary leaders into the formal state system. In this case, tribal sheikhs were brought into the formal system and awarded stipends, access to land, and other privileges in exchange for their loyalty to the central government. The sheikhs were effectively converted into representatives of the state in their communities, whereas previously their power had derived exclusively from the support of their constituents. This dynamic had the effect of isolating the sheikhs from their communities and reinforced divides between the state and social groups.

In Aceh, both positive and negative effects of the interactions between customary and state institutions were observed when the customary institutions (adat) were formalized. First, communities saw an increase in the transfer of resources and an expansion of the jurisdiction of adat institutions, both of which were welcome. At the same time, there were trade-offs in the loss of discretion in decision making when customary laws were codified into formal law. It was perceived that much of the customary leaders' discretion in decision making would be lost in that process because formal law would have to apply standard rules for offenses, instead of allowing for considerations such as the relationship between the parties in a dispute or the harm done to the community by a particular action.

Finally, the collapse of both customary and state institutions was observed in the Central African Republic and Haiti, leaving people without recourse for resolving disputes, obtaining basic services, and other needs. In both cases, the weakness of state institutions stemmed from the legacy of slavery and a history of a predatory, extractive state presence in much of the country. In the Central African Republic, the resurgence of the use of witchcraft was seen as a consequence of inefficient formal institutions and weakening informal institutions, such as the *nganga*, that previously had been able to keep the predatory use of witchcraft in check. In Haiti, a general avoidance and distrust of the state was observed as people sought to protect themselves. In addition, the social organization, which consists mainly of vertical, bilateral patronage relationships, was ill-suited to build a convergence across groups.

Rigid Relationships in Society that Cannot Adapt Sufficiently to Rapid Social Change Can Hinder the Building of Social Cohesion

Globalization, urbanization, and technological innovations are just a few of the factors creating rapid changes in contexts around the world. The speed of the change caused by some of these emerging forces can affect relationships between groups, potentially impairing social cohesion. Rapid change seems to affect some types of relationships more than others. For example, rapid change is often also linked to migration, whether it be forced migration or displacement, or economic migration. Migration itself changes the societal dynamics in a context, putting together groups of individuals who may have not interacted in the past. As groups start to interact, they may or may not share common understandings or ideas about where their community should be headed or about the rights and responsibilities of people living in a specific place. The new interactions can (at least initially) create perceptions of injustice or unfairness, as local populations expect things to remain as they were and new populations have different expectations. The interaction between these different groups can also create demands that existing institutions may not meet, either because of a lack of capacity or because of a lack of mechanisms for the institutions to serve the needs of different populations.

Rapid changes also affect the relationship between youth and elders. In traditional settings especially, the roles and expectations of people in different age groups are largely predefined. Socialization processes can be rigid and based on local norms. As a context changes and exposure to outside influences increases, however, youth may change their expectations and may want different roles in their communities. That can create rifts between young people and elders, as elders believe that the young still have to pay their dues and follow the rules, while young people demand change and may even decide to take action to make those changes possible. It is particularly problematic when youth decide to participate in alternative forms of socialization that are harmful to the overall society. Young people, for example, sometimes join gangs or other armed groups in an effort to make the transition into adulthood in alternative ways.

Just as with generational power relationships, rapid social changes often deliver powerful shocks to existing gender power dynamics. In many fragile situations, the structures governing gender norms are too rigid to adapt effectively to rapid social change. In such contexts, the rules that regulate how men and women interact are in flux or are directly challenged, and that can be disruptive for society. In some cases the reason is that the economic role of men as providers is challenged by shifts in the global economy. In others, the challenges come from exposure to other systems of gender norms, as people travel more and are exposed to other cultures through the expansion of global communication technologies.

These challenges to gender roles create important opportunities but also leave men and women vulnerable in different ways. The growing economic empowerment and independence of women can be a huge achievement for families and societies. In many cases families adapt smoothly to the shifting power dynamics. However, if women's economic and social empowerment is perceived to come at the expense of men's economic and social status, it can provoke a sense of injustice in men against women and potentially fuel a backlash.

Operationalizing the Findings: Recommendations for Putting Social Cohesion at the Center of Development Efforts in Fragile Situations

Recognition of the centrality of societal dynamics has strong implications for development policy and practice. The overall approach to social development must be adapted to place social cohesion as a clear objective of development policies. Resumption of growth and reducing poverty are important but not sufficient, and policies to support growth and poverty reduction will not succeed if they do not also contribute to improved cohesion. Many governments and donors still do not articulate social cohesion in their strategies to deal with fragility. Working toward improved social cohesion requires a good understanding of societal dynamics, as well as adaptability in policies and programs, as societal dynamics evolve and change rapidly. The change will include ensuring that perceptions of injustice and unfairness are addressed, as well as creating space to facilitate constructive connections among institutions, especially customary and traditional structures, state structures, and often-nascent civil society institutions.

The focus on societal dynamics needs to be grounded in contextual research. Research in fragile environments is understandably challenging, given unreliability of data and other difficulties. Understanding the dynamics at play will require asking other questions than are normally asked, to focus on the fundamentals of how a society works. That means asking questions about the elements that divide people or bring them together in society and the historical factors that have created or worsened their relationships. It requires looking at the state as one actor among many in the society, instead of using the state as a point of departure. Answering these questions will necessarily draw on a variety of tools from political and social analysis, as these dynamics occur at the intersection of the two fields. Combining political and social analysis can be especially useful in understanding the motivations, incentives, and perceptions of different actors in fragile contexts and applying the understanding to projects and policies.

The findings of the study reported in this book indicate the need to go beyond the sectoral approach employed by many donors to a more integrated approach that can accommodate the ways that societal dynamics operate. Different dynamics intersect and overlap in complex ways that may not be visible to practitioners who focus on one sector only. It is important for practitioners and policy makers to be able to step back and take a macro-level view of the complexity of societal dynamics to fully understand the whole picture.

In the area of justice and fairness, policies can address the distribution of investments and services and look at the way that the distribution affects various groups in society, not only individuals. Overall, the book recommends a problem-oriented approach that starts with the issues that people are facing every day and adapts good practice interventions to offer sustainable solutions. That may involve adjusting service delivery to address perceptions of injustice or to build cohesion across groups. For example, intergroup tensions between refugees and internally displaced persons and host communities can be eased through area development plans.

Policies and programs to address injustices and heal trauma can be invaluable in healing intergroup tensions. Dealing with trauma experienced by a particular group often requires compensation to restore livelihoods, in addition to recognition of the harm done by perpetrators. Resolving conflict and providing justice at the local level require dealing with existing local justice mechanisms, as modern justice system reform will often take a very long time. Improving the effectiveness of local conflict resolution systems is therefore important to reduce fragility. Attention should also be given to more complex issues related to perceptions of fairness, including the management of cultural diversity and recognition of the characteristics and needs of various groups, while at the same time ensuring that human rights are respected.

Creating positive interactions between institutions requires a variety of measures. It requires that spaces be created for mediation and voice. The space should allow various institutions to connect positively and in ways that lead to positive collective action. Opening space for mediation is not easy. It requires time and imagination. It is often necessary to rethink approaches to local governance and community-driven development, so that they contribute directly to improved interactions between various types of institutions. For example, this may require focusing less on delivery of services and much more on strengthening local governance and supporting the local-level institutions that matter to people with respect to conflict management, local decision making, and other issues. Finally, it requires supporting civil society, which has an essential role in strengthening people's sense of citizenship and improving the state-society relationship.

It is important that the focus on societal dynamics not remain simply a conversation among donors, but that it be taken up by governments and civil society. This book is only a first step in applying the lens of societal dynamics to work in fragile situations. More empirical research will be needed to assess the applicability of the framework presented here to different contexts. Governments and other national and local actors will need to take the agenda forward to develop the specific solutions that will work in varying contexts.

References

DFID (U.K. Department of Foreign Investment and Development). 2010. "Building Peaceful States and Societies: A DFID Practice Paper." London: Department of International Development. http://reliefweb.int/report/world/building-peaceful-states-and-societies-dfid-practice-paper.

OECD (Organization for Economic Cooperation and Development). 2005. *Paris Declaration on Aid Effectiveness.* Paris: OECD.

———. *Accra Agenda for Action.* 2008. Accra, Ghana, September 4. http://siteresources.worldbank.org/ACCRAEXT/Resources/4700790 1217425866038/AAA-4-SEPTEMBER-FINAL-16h00.pdf.

———. 2010. *Monitoring the Principles for Good International Engagement in Fragile States and Situations: Fragile States Principles Monitoring Survey-Monitoring Report.* Paris: OECD.

USAID (U.S. Agency for International Development). 2005. *Fragile States Strategy.* Washington, DC: USAID.

World Bank. 2011. *World Development Report: Conflict, Security and Development.* Washington, DC: World Bank.

CHAPTER 1

Understanding Fragility

At least a quarter of the world's population now lives in what are deemed "fragile" situations, where they face some of the most dire development conditions.[1] Fragile situations span a vast range of contexts. They include chronically troubled nations as diverse as Afghanistan, Haiti, and Somalia, where governments have struggled to build legitimacy and establish basic functions after prolonged conflict, with limited measurable success. More recently, the "fragile" label has been applied to Middle Eastern political regimes that appeared stable, at least from the perspective of economic growth, but then crumbled under social pressures. Recognition is also growing that even where a stable and functioning government exists, pockets of fragility can persist, for example, the urban slum areas in many middle-income and wealthy countries.[2]

Countries designated "fragile" consistently rank worst on all development indicators. People living in the most extreme fragile situations—where fragility has given way to violent conflict—are more than twice as likely to be malnourished, more than three times as likely to be unable to send their children to school, twice as likely to see their children die before age five, and more than twice as likely to lack clean water. Not a single low-income country mired in those circumstances has been able to achieve even one of the Millennium Development Goals (World Bank 2011). In addition, the spillover effects of fragility, such as human trafficking, corruption, and drug and arms trafficking, compromise the stability of neighboring countries and regions (OECD 2005).

How to intervene effectively in fragile situations has long vexed policy makers and development practitioners alike. There is no single definition of fragility, nor is there a consensus list of fragile states.[3] Generally speaking, most donors view the problem of fragility in relation to the state and address it by building state capacity. Fragile situations are variously defined as those where the government lacks the willingness or capacity to deliver basic services (OECD 2008; DFID 2010), where it possesses little or no legitimacy in the eyes of its citizens (USAID 2005), or where it is unaccountable to the international community (U.S. Bipartisan Policy Center 2011). Most donors recognize the need to adopt some form of specialized response to the challenges of fragility, such as those set out in the OECD Principles for Fragile States and Situations.[4] In most cases, interventions have focused on building state capacity, based on the premise that the state either is the primary source of fragility or at least is the central actor in moving the society out of fragility.

Recently, however, more emphasis has been placed on the need to look beyond the state in assisting societies as they move out of fragile situations. The OECD (2010) posits that "a state's fragility is a function also of the strength of civil society and the extensiveness of social capital" (14); among its Fragile States Principles are the needs to understand the social context and to promote social cohesion in fragile situations. The understanding of fragile situations is also evolving within the World Bank. The *2011 World Development Report,* subtitled *Conflict, Security and Development,* defines "fragility" and "fragile situations" as "periods when states or institutions lack the capacity, accountability, or legitimacy to mediate relations between citizen groups and between citizens and the state, making them vulnerable to violence" (World Bank 2011, xvi). The report advocates for more attention to such institutional weaknesses. That would include, among other interventions, building state capacity not only to deliver basic services but also to engage groups in society.

The study reported in this book responds to a growing demand for interventions that address the social dimensions of fragility. The book is written for practitioners and policy makers who have been struggling to address such contexts with limited tools. It does not promise comprehensive solutions, rather a more nuanced view of fragile situations, and it suggests operational responses. This report is a first step in a potential research agenda, and a new mode of development practice, that emphasize the relationships across groups in society as a foundation upon which to build the capable institutions and productive state–society relationship necessary to exit fragile situations.

Approach of the Study: Seeing Fragility from a Societal Perspective

This report thus views the problem of fragility as one not only of state capacity but also of societal relations. Fragility is not a function of state capacity alone. Rather, fragility reflects dysfunctional relationships in society that do not allow a state to be built or sustained. It does not minimize the importance of building state capacity to observe that it has become more and more evident that the central problem in places from Somalia to Afghanistan extends beyond the state to particular dynamics rooted in society that simply do not allow groups to come together to work cooperatively toward development goals.

Fragility is understood here not as a static condition but as a dynamic continuum. Along that continuum, societies can experience varying degrees of fragility, with state collapse and violent conflict at the extreme.[5] Conceptualizing fragility in this way need not imply a linear process; indeed, the experiences of most countries entering or exiting situations of fragility have been anything but linear. Countries do not move only upward or downward but can experience a range of situations along the continuum. Viewing fragility in this way is also useful in that it allows one to recognize that all societies experience some elements of fragility, but those elements are stronger in some societies and at some times than others. The quality of the relationships within it ultimately determines where a society falls along the fragility continuum at a given time.

Fragility can be understood as a problem not only of state capacity, but also of dysfunctional relationships across groups in society, including the relationships of different groups with the state. Rather than a static condition, fragility is better conceptualized as a dynamic continuum, along which societies can experience extreme state failure and violent conflict at one end and a more cohesive society moving up continuum. The continuum need not imply a linear process, as societies can move up and down the continuum as they respond to shocks or opportunities.

Viewing fragility as a problem of relationships among groups in society calls for a focus on the particular ways that groups interact and the dynamics that influence whether their interactions will be productive or destructive. Such *societal dynamics* describe how people interact with one another, how they form collective efforts, and the material and nonmaterial exchanges that result from those relationships. They include, among many other elements, the ways that people and groups mediate across different social identities; gender and generational relations; and interactions between formal and informal institutions. The importance of societal dynamics in fragile situations is often recognized long before the state fails or violent conflict erupts but largely left unaddressed when appropriate interventions are being formulated. As a result, state-building efforts, however technically sound they may be, are often disconnected from broader dynamics in society, with the risk that they will be without the social foundation necessary to sustain them. Observers of Egypt and Yemen, for example, had long warned that deep social cleavages had the potential to topple the state. Yet for years a large part of the development community's efforts remained narrowly focused on technical solutions, which only further isolated the state from societal processes. Similarly, more than a decade of efforts to sustain a functioning government in these two countries have fallen fall short of expectations and in some cases, left communities even more divided.

> The term **societal dynamics** refers to the ways that people interact with one another and across groups, how they form groups and other collective efforts, and the material and nonmaterial exchanges that result from the interactions.

This book suggests that fragility can be reduced significantly by fostering *social cohesion,* that is, the nature and quality of the relationships that connect people and groups to one other. As the following chapters will describe, the degree of cohesion in a society is a key influence on where it stands along the fragility continuum at a given moment. More cohesive societies are better able to engage in productive exchanges across groups and thus to move away from or avoid fragile situations. Chapter 3 is devoted to a much broader discussion of the concept of social cohesion and how it relates to fragility.

It is suggested that an essential element of building social cohesion is the ability to mobilize groups around a *convergence across groups* in society. Such convergence provides an overarching structure for collective life that helps ensure predictability and certainty, even if it does not guarantee that all groups will agree on all issues. Put another way, when groups see their interests as converging with those of others, they become more connected to other groups and ultimately have more incentive to collaborate. Convergence thus serves as an essential element for collective action.

Because the state is embedded in society, the state-society relationship is also part of this overall convergence, such that more cohesive societies tend to have higher-quality relationships between the state and groups in society. The study viewed the state as one actor among many in society, and one whose legitimacy is formed and transformed by interactions with society. In particular, this book departs from the assumption that the Weberian ideal of state structure and function is an appropriate goal in fragile situations; that idea underpins much of the literature on fragility and many state-building interventions today. The Weberian ideal of state bureaucracy sees the state as a self-contained, autonomous organization that operates separately from societal processes and that is capable of leading change in society. In contrast, the state is understood here as a product of its interactions with different groups in society, with which it shares power and responsibilities. Indeed, the state is often not the most powerful actor in fragile situations, and recognizing that is central to designing effective ways to intervene. The study argues that applying Weberian categories as goals for state building is neither realistic nor desirable in fragile situations.

The term **social cohesion** describes the nature and quality of relationships among people and groups in society, including the state. The constituency of social cohesion is complex, but at its essence social cohesion implies a **convergence across groups** in society that provides a framework within which groups can, at a minimum, coexist peacefully. In this way, social cohesion offers a measure of predictability to interactions across people and groups, which in turn provides incentives for collective action.

Finally, the study's approach emphasizes relationships among groups over those among individuals. That focus is appropriate given that group dynamics have the potential to generate effects that are more socially disruptive than individual-level dynamics. That is true for several reasons. First, actions taken by groups have more impact than actions by individuals in most cases, simply because groups are bigger. Second, group actions to correct perceived injustices tend to be aimed at fundamental changes in society and thus have the potential to alter power relationships between groups, as individual actions usually do not (Vanneman and Pettigrew 1972).

Third, individual behaviors are themselves driven by interactions with others, which form collective behavior through social norms. In other words, individual behavior is the product of "interactive relationships with others typically resulting from some form of linked and interdependent preferences, information transmission technologies, or strategic interactions" (Rao and Walton 2004: 14). As Gauri, Woolcock, and Desai (2011: 6) note, individual behavior is strongly driven by the *intersubjective meanings* that arise from interactions within and across groups. These intersubjective meanings consist of "concepts, arguments, beliefs, and judgments that cannot be attributed to individuals; rather, they are the shared property of groups of human beings." They emanate not from the individual, but from the particular rules that govern social behavior in a society. These meanings and norms are "out there in the practices, practices which cannot be conceived as a set of individual actions, but are essentially modes of social relation, of mutual action" (Taylor 1985: 36). They emerge from collective action, and they also drive collective action. Given this interdependence of individual and group behavior, focusing on group dynamics is essential to understanding the elements of fragility rooted in societies.

Study Methodology

The objective of the study reported in this book was to understand how societal dynamics can be mobilized toward a convergence across groups in society and thus toward greater social cohesion overall. The team began with an extensive *consultation phase* to identify some key societal dynamics that seemed important in understanding fragility. The German Development Cooperation (GIZ) was a key partner in the study, providing support to the analytical phase in the form of a background paper, and technical advice throughout the preparation of the report. Practitioners, academics, and policy makers with diverse experience in fragile states were also consulted. Appendix 2 gives a detailed list of individuals and organizations consulted for the exercise. The team continued to consult with these experts throughout the fieldwork and the writing of the book.

Five themes were selected for analysis by means of these consultations: identity and citizenship; interactions among institutions; trauma and resilience; gender and generational relationships; and intersubjective meaning systems. In the *analytical phase* of the project, the team commissioned leading theoreticians on the five topics[6] to prepare background papers, which reviewed the literature and analyzed the arguments regarding how the different dynamics interact with fragility. The content of the background papers is cited throughout the book, and it formed the basis for the in-country work.

The *in-country fieldwork* for the study examined how different societal dynamics interact with fragility in five places: Central African Republic,

Haiti, Indonesia, Liberia, and Yemen. The case studies were selected to represent differing experiences with various forms and degrees of fragility. As a starting point, all five countries face substantial development challenges. With the exception of Indonesia (specifically Aceh, the focus of the case study), they are among the poorest in the world, facing difficult economic challenges while the social and human indicators are also low. Haiti, for example, is the poorest country in the Western Hemisphere; it ranks 149th out of 182 countries on the Human Development Index and 168th out of 180 on the corruption perception index. Similarly, Central African Republic ranks 179th on the Human Development Index. In Yemen, half of the population lives on less than two dollars a day, unemployment hovers around 35 percent to 49 percent, and 46 percent of children are malnourished. Liberia's per capita GDP is the third-lowest in the world, and it ranks 162nd on the Human Development Index (IMF 2011).

Aceh, Indonesia, represents a different trajectory, as a society that experienced deep trauma and conflict but managed to maintain pockets of cohesion and resilience, which are being mobilized today. Aceh was reasonably prosperous prior to the conflict and even in its early stages, but it then suffered significant development setbacks. In 1996, before the effects of the conflict were readily apparent, Aceh's poverty rate was 12.7 percent, compared to 17.7 percent for Indonesia overall. By 2004 the figures had reversed, with 28.5 percent poor in Aceh against 16.7 percent in Indonesia as a whole (BPS 1996; 2003). The impact was compounded by the Indian Ocean tsunami in 2004. Yet signs are being seen that Aceh is emerging from fragility, and so it appears here as an example of the mobilization of societal dynamics toward greater resilience.

The in-country fieldwork was not designed to establish causal relationships or to obtain nationally representative results, rather it was intended to provide rich and context-specific illustrations of how various societal dynamics operate and affect situations of fragility. The work comprised three phases. First, a thorough *political economy analysis* of each of the five countries was commissioned to give a national-level view of the importance of the five themes selected from the background papers in that country and to identify any other dynamics that appeared to merit further attention. The political economy papers were prepared by established experts on the five countries.

Second, the team conducted *national-level workshops* with expert practitioners and policy makers, developed in consultation with World Bank country teams and local consultants. Workshop participants were selected based on their deep knowledge of the country and their expertise on the themes of the study. The workshops provided a venue to discuss how the societal dynamics under study play out in the particular context, to narrow the topics to be discussed in the community-level fieldwork, and to select communities for that fieldwork.

Third and finally, the team implemented *focus groups and qualitative interviews* in a number of urban and rural communities. This qualitative work was aimed at understanding a more narrow set of dynamics identified as the most relevant to that context. Thus not all dynamics were covered in all communities.[7] Because the topic is a sensitive one, measures were taken to ensure the confidentiality of the data wherever possible, and participants were informed that they could refuse to answer questions or terminate their participation at any time.

Country reports based on the data gathered were prepared by local researchers in close collaboration with the project team. The team used the country reports to further engage the World Bank country teams for each country and received feedback that was used in the preparation of the full report. GIZ country teams were also consulted for their feedback on the findings in the case study countries. The internal advisers, as well as the outside partners, were also consulted on the country data in the development of the full report.

Organization of the Book

This book reports a study about societal relationships in fragile situations. Drawing on relevant literature and fieldwork in five countries, it suggests that fragility, violent conflict, and state failure are functions not only of state inability or unwillingness to perform core tasks, but also of dysfunctional relationships in society that do not permit a state to be formed or sustained.

The present chapter has introduced the problem of fragility and suggested that seeing fragility as a problem of relationships in society can lead to more effective interventions in fragile situations. Chapter 2 turns to a key area of societal relations, the state–society relationship in fragile situations. It discusses the shortcomings of one of the key assumptions underlying much policy and programming in fragile situations today—the assumption of an autonomous state capable of directing social processes. The chapter offers evidence to conceptualize the state instead as an entity embedded within society, whose power is determined only in relationship to other groups. It is suggested that increasing social cohesion—building higher-quality relationships in society—also contributes to a more productive state–society relationship.

Chapter 3 begins a conversation about social cohesion in fragile situations. It suggests a critical element of social cohesion: a convergence across groups in society. The characteristics of this convergence are discussed, drawing on the fieldwork in the five study countries. The description of *convergence* is meant to inform a richer understanding of social cohesion and how it can be supported in fragile situations.

Chapters 4 and 5 turn to two factors that emerged from the fieldwork as particularly important in influencing the degree of social cohesion in society. Chapter 4 discusses how perceptions of injustice across groups can deepen divisions and hinder coexistence and collective action. Many times such perceptions can be even more influential than measurable differences across groups (such as income inequality) in fomenting resentment and division. Chapter 5 then takes up the issue of interactions between institutions in fragile situations. It is suggested that social cohesion contributes to more constructive interactions among institutions, increasing their capacity to realize development goals.

Chapter 6 shifts the focus to certain relationships in society that are particularly important for social cohesion. It discusses the relationships between migrants (both internal and international) and host communities; between younger and older generations; and between women and men. It is argued that these relationships are particularly instrumental in influencing overall fragility in a society, particularly in the face of rapid social shifts caused by shocks.

In chapters 7 and 8, the operational implications of an approach to fragility emphasizing societal dynamics are discussed in detail. Chapter 7 describes an overall approach to policy and programming, including how to conduct research and develop knowledge from this perspective. Chapter 8 offers specific orientations for adapting existing tools and instruments to address the societal bases of fragility.

Notes

1. According to World Bank's estimates, almost 400 million people live in fragile situations. The World Bank does not espouse a formal definition of fragility or

fragile situations. For resource distribution purposes, the World Bank categorizes fragile states as ones having either (a) a composite World Bank, African Development Bank, and Asian Development Bank Country Policy and Institutional Assessment (CPIA) rating of 3.2 or less; or (b) a United Nations or regional peacekeeping or peace-building mission (e.g., African Union, European Union, NATO), other than border monitoring operations, in the country during the past three years. CPIA ratings are based on measures of state effectiveness, including economic management, structural policies, policies for social inclusion and equity, and public sector management and effective institutions. This report does not propose a new technical definition. Rather, it aims to add nuance to the ways the problem of fragility is conceived and addressed.

2. For example, see OECD 2008; DFID 2010.

3. For reviews of donor definitions in particular, see Stewart and Brown 2010; and Engberg-Pederson et al. 2008.

4. The Fragile States Principles (FSP) were adopted by OECD ministers in 2007 (OECD-DAC 2007). A complete list of the principles can be found at www .oecd.org. Monitoring surveys of the principles were conducted in 2009 and 2011 in 13 countries.

5. The idea that fragility is not a static or all-or-nothing concept, but exists to varying degrees, is now part of many donors' and international organizations' approaches to fragility (see for example DFID 2010; OECD-DAC 2007; Stewart and Brown 2010). It is also implicit in many of the indexes of fragility employed by research institutions and donors. The indexes can be used to rank countries on the degree of fragility, and they are generally used to identify those that are sliding down the fragility continuum (see, for example, Goldstone and Marshall 2007).

6. Each paper author was paired with several advisers from different perspectives. Appendix 2 details the names of the lead authors and peer reviewers of each background paper.

7. Please refer to Appendix 2 for the field guide, which lists the issues that were explored in each country, explains the criteria by which the communities were chosen, and describes other details of the fieldwork (how the participants were chosen, the guidelines for the discussion in the focus groups). Appendix 1 provides a complete time line of the phases of the study.

References

BPS (Badan Pusat Statistik). 1996. *Statistik Indonesia: Statistical Yearbook of Indonesia 1996*. Jakarta: Badan Pusat Statistik.

——. 2003. *Statistik Indonesia: Statistical Yearbook of Indonesia 2003*. Jakarta: Badan Pusat Statistik.

DFID (U.K. Department of Foreign Investment and Development). 2010. "Building Peaceful States and Societies: A DFID Practice Paper." London: DFID.

Engberg-Pedersen, Lars, Louise Andersen, Finn Stepputat, and Dietrich Jung. 2008. "Fragile Situations: Background Papers." Copenhagen: Danish Institute for International Studies.

Gauri, Varun, Michael Woolcock, and Deval Desai. 2011. "Inter-subjective Meaning and Collective Action in 'Fragile' Societies: Theory, Evidence and Policy Implications." Background paper for *Societal Dynamics and Fragility: Engaging Societies in Responding to Fragile Situations*. Washington, DC: World Bank.

Goldstone, Jack, and Monty Marshall. 2007. "Global Report on Conflict, Governance, and State Fragility 2007: Gauging System Performance and Fragility in the Globalization Era." *Foreign Policy Bulletin* 17 (1): 3–21.

IMF (International Monetary Fund). 2011. *World Economic Outlook: Slowing Growth, Rising Risks*. Washington, DC: IMF.

OECD (Organization for Economic Cooperation and Development). 2005. *Paris Declaration on Aid Effectiveness*. Paris: OECD.

———. 2008. *Accra Agenda for Action*. Accra, Ghana, September 4. http://siteresources.worldbank.org/ACCRAEXT/Resources/4700790-1217425866038/AAA-4-SEPTEMBER-FINAL-16h00.pdf.

———. 2008. *Service Delivery in Fragile Situations: Key Concepts, Findings, and Lessons*, OECD/DAC DISCUSSION PAPER, Journal on Development 2008, Vol. 9, No 3.

OECD-DAC (Organization for Economic Cooperation and Development–Development Assistance Committee). 2007. *Encouraging Effective Evaluation of Conflict Prevention and Peace-Building Activities: Toward DAC Guidance*. Paris: OECD-DAC.

Rao, Vijayendra, and Michael Walton. 2004. *Culture and Public Action*. Palo Alto, CA: Stanford University Press.

Stewart, Francis, and Graham Brown. 2010. "Fragile States: CRISE Overview 3." Oxford: Centre for Research on Inequality, Human Security and Ethnicity.

Taylor, Charles. 1985. "Interpretation and the Sciences of Man." *Philosophy and the Human Sciences: Philosophical Papers* 2: 15–57.

USAID (U.S. Agency for International Development). 2005. "Fragile States Strategy." Washington, DC: USAID.

U.S. Bipartisan Policy Center. 2011. "A Stitch in Time: Stabilizing Fragile States." Washington DC: U.S. Bipartisan Policy Center. http://www.bipartisanpolicy.org/sites/default/files/FS_Final.pdf.

Vanneman, R. D., and T. Pettigrew. 1972. "Race and Relative Deprivation in the Urban United States." *Race* 13: 461–86.

World Bank. 2011. *World Development Report: Conflict, Security and Development*. Washington, DC: World Bank.

CHAPTER 2

Understanding State–Society Connectedness

Today a general consensus prevails that sustainable development and security rely on legitimate and effective governments that can provide basic services to their populations and be held accountable both to their citizens and to the international community. In fragile situations, where state capacity is weak or has broken down, the international response in most cases has been *state building*—increasing the capacity of the state to provide core services, including security and justice.

The international agenda with respect to fragile states and fragile situations is permeated by the Weberian ideal of state structure and function, based on monopoly of force, legitimate authority, and clear boundaries between state and society, public and private, and the civilian and military spheres (Engberg-Pedersen et al. 2008).[1] The central assumption underlying state building is that, given appropriate support, all states will eventually converge toward the Weberian ideal of western liberal democracy. That is, given adequate capacity, the state will be able to provide public services effectively through rule-based, meritocratic, and politically accountable public agencies. According to this logic, a capable state objectively assesses the needs of its citizens from a set of predetermined criteria for what it deems good for the population and identifies and applies a technical solution.[2] The work of the international community, then, is to provide technical assistance to build a capable state.

The majority of instruments available for use in fragile situations assume the appropriateness of the Weberian ideal state and are built around working with the state as the central actor in development. But when the state–society relationship is weak and the reach of the state constrained, those instruments are seriously limited. In practice, technical solutions to build a state where the state is absent or ineffective have often been applied too quickly and superficially. In what has been termed "jumping straight to Weber," state-building efforts often aim too quickly to set up institutions that, at least in form, resemble the efficient, hierarchical bureaucracies of the West (see Pritchett and Woolcock 2004; Woolcock 2007 for a fuller discussion).

This chapter contests the application of a Weberian ideal of state function as an appropriate goal for interventions in fragile situations. In particular, it disputes the relevance of the goal of a clear-cut distinction between the state and social processes. Instead, it presents the state instead as engaged in a dynamic and interdependent relationship with society. The quality of the relationship fundamentally affects the ability of the state to govern and thus the development trajectory of the society. The following sections describe this relationship, with a focus on the often-troubled nature of state–society interactions in fragile situations.

State Building and Citizenship

A growing body of literature has questioned the Weberian ideal of an autonomous state disconnected from societal dynamics. Although no one contests that the state is pervasive—there are not many communities in the world today where state has not penetrated in one way or the other (Migdal 1988)—many scholars argue that the state is not able to, and should not strive to, exercise power in an unadulterated and coherent manner independently from society. States may have "unmistakable [administrative] strengths in penetrating society . . . [but they are] surprising[ly] weak in effecting goal oriented social changes" (Migdal 1988: 9). More recently, North, Wallis, and Weingast (2009) have made the same argument. They suggest that it is wrong to assume the existence of a stable state, as the organization of each society and state–society relationships are fundamentally different from one context to the other. Moreover, the assumption of a stable state does not explain how it derives its coercive power and how it survives. It is only through exploring how social order comes about that we can reach a more fundamental understanding of the relationship between state and society and how a state can be sustained.

Recognition is growing that the state is entwined with society in a mutually dependent relationship, and the quality of the relationship determines the state's ability to direct change. Scholars across a range of disciplines and theoretical perspectives assert that groups in society offer fundamental elements of support to the state, and, likewise, the state provides critical elements for collective action in society (Kohli 2002; Migdal 2001; Evans 1995; Sellers 2010). Indeed, Weber himself insisted that a state needs legitimacy in the eyes of its citizens to be able to perform its function and that legitimacy needs to be ingrained in the beliefs of the citizens. In other words, state legitimacy is embedded in the social infrastructure rather than in the mechanics of bureaucracy (Seabrook 2002).[3]

The idea that the state and society are interdependent underlies the concept of citizenship. The citizen–state relationship implies mutual responsibility between the state and citizens and provides certain norms for how citizens should treat one another. The state is the bearer of the rights of citizens. The state promises to provide legal standing to all citizens and basic services, including security, while citizens promise to remain loyal to the state and abide by the laws of the state. Citizens also feel an affiliation with a broader community and accept certain responsibility for the collective good.[4]

The idea of citizenship formed in Western Europe over a long period of time and as a result of specific sociopolitical developments. This idea was transported outside Europe as European colonizers transferred aspects of their own experience to the colonized world "anxious to create modern mechanisms for rule-making, categorization and control" (Ayubi 1995).[5] The postcolonial states were founded within frontiers drawn by the former colonial regimes, and they acquired sovereignty without the imported forms of state organization having taken root in a national identity or collective consciousness that could transcend regional differences. In these cases, "artificial" states had to be first "filled" by nations (Habermas 1998: 398). That top-down approach created states only in what Jackson and Rosberg (1982) call the "sociological" sense and not in the ideological sense.

Under those conditions, a sense of citizenship and common identity failed to take root in many colonized countries. The people effectively acquired the legal status of citizens, but the "jump from legal status of citizen to emotionally laden identity of member of the nation [was] not an easy one to negotiate" (Watts 2004). Today a common problem across fragile situations, many of which endured colonization, is that the sense of citizenship and collective consciousness that can form the basis for a social contract with the state never really took hold. That may be the case at the national level but can also be true at the regional or even the micro level, for example, in slum areas where state presence is weak.

Some states have intentionally tried to create a sense of collective consciousness. That process often involves assimilating multiple identities under a common national identity. Pakistanis used Islam to coalesce different ethnic groups into one nation (Jalal 1995). Other countries have tried to create a unified national identity based on particular ideologies regarding development. The movement to create an African socialism, exemplified by Mobuto's "Zairization," and the Ujamaa model of development put forth by Tanzanian president Julius Nyerere are examples.

Most states must deal with multiple cultural identities in one way or another. In many states, if not most, various groups subscribe not to a single, common identity but to multiple identities based on markers such as ethnicity and religion. In those cases, it is nevertheless possible that the citizens accept and recognize the state's monopoly of violence and the principle of rights and obligations between the state and the citizens. Kymlicka (2010) argues that citizens can have a strong cultural identity that coexists with a sense of broader, national citizenship, as in the examples of India, Canada, and Spain.

State–Society Interactions

When the state is viewed as embedded in society, a range of interactions becomes visible. As already discussed, the state does not operate separately from society but is embedded in a network of relationships with a multiplicity of actors. When one shifts the focus from the state to the relationship between state and society, four main modes of interaction are evident.

The State Evolves in Relationship with Society

The form of the state, its capabilities and scope, are not determined in isolation but evolve through interactions with different groups in society. Berman and Lonsdale (1992), studying the formation of the state in Kenya in the late nineteenth and early twentieth centuries, argue that "state power is the fruit of an experience . . . made of tensions and compromises between different actors and social groups. This experience which takes place unconsciously and heterogeneously, is what forms the state" (quoted in Hibou 2004). A wealth of literature comparing development trajectories in different countries has shown how different forms of governance, themselves a result of relationships between state and society, have given rise to widely divergent development outcomes under very similar conditions (see Rodrik 2003 for various comparisons). For example, in Europe two different types of states emerged—the centralized nation-state, represented by France, and the city-state exemplified by Italy—depending on the historical configuration of the society, the expectations of the citizens, and the organization of communities (Anderson 1996). Similarly, Vu (2010) argues that since World War II, in societies where coherent social classes and status groups existed, a more cooperative state has emerged. A fragmented society can also be associated with a predatory state that capitalizes on divisions in society.

Conflicts among elite groups exert a particularly powerful influence on state evolution, as the groups struggle over resource distribution and political power. Such elite conflicts affect the resultant form of state to such an extent that Migdal (1988; 2001) has called the process of state formation "political survival" of state and localized elites. North, Wallis, and Weingast (2009) argue that all societies in their "natural" state are political arrangements among elites. They call these states "limited access" orders, as only elites have access to economic and political resources.[6] It is only in the "mature natural state" that institutions allow open access to both political and economic organizations and the form of the state is not entirely based on pacts among elites. However, the movement of societies from limited access to the open access system is not spontaneous or automatic. Some societies have progressed from closed to open access systems, but others have regressed. More recently, some have suggested that the "inclusive enough" pact among elites can be the first step toward transformation of state institutions (World Bank 2011a).

The State and Forces in Society Share Power and Responsibilities

State authority is often fragmented and contested by a variety of actors in society. Various actors, including the state, compete for power and authority in setting rules of behavior, meeting the needs of the population, and exerting a monopoly on violence, among other functions. Nonstate actors—for example, tribal leaders, religious authorities, and civil society organizations—exercise varying degrees of political power over local populations. The power may emanate from religion, the structure of resource distribution, culture, or the ability of the actor to provide basic social services. These informal sources of power may regulate behavior in every facet of life, in some cases even market behavior. Every kind of social actor that holds power in this way must negotiate that power with the population. For example, gangs or other armed groups cannot operate for long in territories without some negotiation with the population there.[7]

The range of actors competing for power and sharing power with the state is increasing with global trends. Privatization creates an economic sector with competing authority over parts of the economy. With globalization, big strides in communication and transport give rise to international organizations that exert influence on the state at various levels.

An explosion of civil society groups in many countries has created numerous alternative sources of power that can influence the state. In developed countries, such associations are important in the delivery of services. Professional associations, for example, significantly contribute to the regulation of professions and organizational change (Greenwood, Suddaby, and Hinings 2002). In his work on Italy and later the United States, Putnam (1993; 1995) has shown that "features of social organization, such as networks, norms and trust that facilitate coordination and cooperation for mutual benefit" (1995: 67), are directly correlated to the extent of civic engagement and government performance. In Africa also, voluntary associations historically have been important participants in the political landscape.[8] Even today "a rich and vibrant associational life has developed in many African countries independent of the state" (Diamond, Linz, and Lipset 1988: 23). Similarly Azarya (1988), in discussing civil society associations, asserts that "[i]nfluence and authority are not exclusive domains of the state"; instead, "various segments of society manage to maintain patterns of behavior which are at variance with the state code." In addition to relatively structured associations, Hyden (1983) argues that ad hoc arrangements with indigenous roots, such as rural savings societies and groups of elders, have undertaken fundamental development tasks, such as accumulation of capital, distribution of resources, and conflict prevention in African societies.

In many cases, its interaction with civil society groups has helped improve the state's efficiency and accountability. Analyses of social capital in the United States, India, and Italy demonstrate how participatory, organized civic groups have improved the quality of service delivery (Putnam 1993; Varshney 2002). Similarly, Ostrom's (1990) work on collective organization to address the problem of the commons demonstrated the effectiveness of engaging local cooperatives to govern common spaces, such as grazing land or forests.

Through emerging forms of joint governance, local nonstate groups may also take over some key responsibilities of the state, as is evident in such practices as participatory budgeting and planning processes, which can involve a variety of societal actors. Nonstate groups may actually take over provision of specific services, ranging from governance of natural resources and dispute resolution to security.[9] Migdal (1988) suggests that such fragmentation of social control and responsibility stems from the fact that individuals use many strategies for daily survival, not all of which are dependent on the state. Consequently, the entities that provide citizens with strategies for daily survival are able to exert political power over them. That power does not come without negotiation, however. Even the most authoritarian armed groups and gangs must share some power with the populations where they operate. For example, armed groups in Jamaica have long provided basic services, from education to electricity, in poor slums in exchange for votes for particular political parties, from which they also draw power and resources. The support of the population in the slums where they operate has been critical to such groups' survival (Harriott 2003).

Even where states were presumed to have been pervasive and domineering, their reach has been limited. For example, Lonsdale and Berman (1979) have argued that the colonizers' ambitions to transform African societies were so much compromised by the power wielded by indigenous authorities that they sought to rule through manipulation, distortion, and incorporation of local elites within the government structure.

States Operate through Individuals, Whose Behavior Is Affected by Societal Dynamics

States operate through individuals. Multitudes of bureaucrats, civil servants, and politicians make key decisions. They act as self-interested individuals within the constraint of the law formulated and enforced by the state. The decision-making process within the state and the design and objectives of state interventions are thus best understood as the product of interactions among the actors who reside in a society. In other words, the state should not be conceptualized as a homogenous institution aspiring to maximize the common good, whose stated objectives public servants carry out (Bates et al. 1998; Buchanan and Tullock 1962).[10] Rather, governments should be understood as collectives of individuals—bureaucrats who strive to advance their careers, politicians who seek to win reelection, and local elites who aim to increase their own political power and wealth.

The social influences on the behavior of public servants include belief systems, culture, conceptions of identity, and power structures within society.[11] Those factors also affect what the society expects from them, which may be in contradiction to their officially defined role. For example, favoring family members in employment decisions could be viewed in a modern state as a conflict of interest, but supporting your family and members of your community is also very important in many cultures. In Yemen, participants in the fieldwork suggested that inheriting a job in the civil service from one's father is not seen as incompatible with civil service rules but as normal, at least in the more tribal North of the country.

The State Influences Societal Processes

In addition to the fact that societal dynamics have a formidable effect on the workings of the state, the state also influences society in significant ways. Migdal (1988) argues that no society can be called "stateless" in the modern world, as almost all societies exist under the influence of a state in some way.

The state influences society most directly through the distribution of resources. Through its policies of distribution, a government can favor some groups and classes over others, and that has significant ramifications for citizens' perceptions of social justice. Extraction of resources through taxation is a fundamental form of state intervention that can have significant consequences for the structure of the society. Government decisions to allocate collected revenue to certain geographical areas or groups, as well as the distribution patterns of various goods and services, have significant economic and political implications.

In extreme cases, a predatory state demands resources from the population without offering substantial benefits in compensation. In those cases, predatory states can contribute to the degradation of relations across groups in society, becoming themselves important drivers of fragility.[12]

Similarly, the state regulates behavior in the public sphere, and sometimes also in the family and individual sphere, through its laws and statutes. Even when the rules are not followed (for example, when the enforcement capacity of the state is low), they change the incentive structure of all the actors involved just by virtue of being formulated and written. In addition to coercion through rules and enforcement mechanisms, the state also has at its disposal an infrastructure (for example, news media) that it can use to persuade citizens of the world views preferred by the individuals who are part of the decision-making process. Many scholars have argued that the ability of the state to mobilize society for war beyond the actual capacity of the state's agents indicates the effect that the state can have on society's motivations (Migdal 2004).

Social Cohesion and the State–Society Relationship

This chapter has presented the state–society relationship as one of mutual interdependence. The state is not an autonomous authority, rather it is a social actor in constant evolution through its interactions with groups in society. Various interactions are possible: the state can prey on different social groups; the state and society can collaborate productively on some issues; an authoritarian state can leave little space for society to influence governance; and so on. When the state is viewed in this way, it becomes clear that effective state institutions are the product of a high-quality state–society relationship.

The relationship between quality institutions and desired development outcomes is now well established. The literature on the role of institutions in promoting economic growth is vast (Acemoglu and Robinson 2006; see Aron 2000 for a review). Strong evidence also associates effective institutions with lower risk of conflict. Fearon (2010), using governance indicators to measure rule of law, respect for human rights, and corruption, found that countries with more capable institutions had a 30 percent to 45 percent lower risk of civil conflict in the subsequent five to 10 years than countries with lower governance indicators. Countries with more capable institutions also had lower levels of criminal violence, as measured by homicide rates. The *2011 World Development Report* takes up this idea as a central thesis, arguing that capable institutions are needed to ensure that countries can weather the effects of internal stresses (such as intergroup conflict) and external shocks without violence.

What is less understood is exactly how the state–society relationship translates into more effective institutions. Which factors matter most in improving the quality of the relationship, such that it translates to better institutions? What types of societal dynamics can derail progress in building good institutions?

No simple formula exists for improving the state–society relationship, but solid evidence indicates that building social cohesion is a critical component. Using data from a large sample of developing countries,

Rodrik (1999) found that more cohesive societies (defined as those with less income inequality and fewer ethnic divisions) responded better to the global economic recession of 1974 than less cohesive societies. He suggests that the connection works through the conflict management institutions present in society; that is, external shocks, such as those provoked by the global recession in the latter part of the 1970s, trigger distributional conflicts within society. Where social cohesion is strong, institutions are better able to mediate those conflicts and ensure that the burdens of adjusting to the shocks are perceived to be fairly distributed across groups.

Easterly, Ritzen, and Woolcock (2006), looked at these relationships over a longer period (1960–96) using data from 82 developed and developing countries. They found that more cohesive societies (defined as those with larger shares of income accruing to the middle class and fewer ethnic divisions) always had higher growth rates but that their advantage was even more pronounced after the global recession. An important element in the analysis is the extent to which wealth is shared in society, dubbed the "middle class consensus" (Easterly 2001).

Taken together, these empirical analyses provide strong evidence that capable institutions, especially formal institutions, are empowered by social cohesion in society overall. Improving social cohesion thus has the potential to improve the state–society relationship, translating into more effective institutions and ultimately into sustained development progress. Following on that idea, chapter 3 begins a conversation about the nature of social cohesion and factors that matter for increasing it in fragile situations.

Notes

1. The characteristics of the ideal Weberian bureaucracy are laid out in Weber 1922.
2. Pritchett and Woolcock 2004 define the Weberian ideal in this way.
3. Seabrook 2002 adduces the example of his work on Russia. Weber demonstrated that liberalism failed in that society because of a lack of social and institutional support for its ideas. His analysis of the implosion of tsarist Russia included organizations and norms that contributed to the lack of legitimacy, which crippled the Russian state-society complex.
4. For example, see Leary 2000, which defines citizenship as a "bundle of [mutual] rights."
5. Other scholars have also concurred with this view; for example, see Alavi 1979.

6. The "fragile natural state" is characterized by a continuous threat of violence. The basic natural state is also an arrangement among elites but has durable and stable organizational structure.

7. See World Bank 2011b for a discussion of *milicias* in Fortaleza, Brazil, and martial arts groups in Dili, Timor-Leste; see also Harriott 2003 on Jamaica.

8. For example, see Wallerstein 1964.

9. A vast empirical literature that shows that informal institutions provide state functions. Selected references include the following: O'Donnell 1996; Van Cott 2000; Levitsky 2001; Brinks 2003; Borocz 2000; Collins 2002; Dia 1996; and Sandbrook and Oelbaum 1999.

10. Kiser and Schneider 1995 made that case by studying Prussian tax system that was in place in the seventeenth century. Kiser and Cai 2000 make the same case by studying the bureaucracy in China during the Qin dynasty.

11. Many different disciplines have analyzed how behavior is affected by factors rooted in the society, such as culture. For works that analyze how societal dynamics affect collective behavior, see the following: Weber 1905/2002, a study of the effect of religion on the development of capitalism; Greif, 1994; 2005, explaining the impact of culture on trade activity; Guiso, Sapienza, and Zingales 2003, analyzing the effect of religious beliefs on collective decision making; and Gorski 1993, which argues that the efficiency of the Prussian tax system, recognized as the most efficient tax system in Europe during seventeenth century, can be attributed to the ideological mobilization of the bureaucrats.

12. For example, see Evans 1989 and Robinson 2001 for the characteristics of a predatory state and how the activity of the predatory state affects development and social outcomes.

References

Acemoglu, Daron, and James A. Robinson. 2006. "The Role of Institutions in Growth and Development." In *Leadership and Growth: Commission on Growth and Development,* ed. David Brady and Michael Spence. Washington, DC: World Bank.

Alavi, Hamza. 1979. "The State in Post-colonial Societies." In *Politics and the State in the Third World*, ed. Harry Goulbourne. London: Macmillan.

Andersen, Benedict. 1996. *Imagined Communities: Reflections on the Origin and Spread of Nationalism.* London: Verso.

Aron, Janine. 2000. "Growth and Institutions: A Review of the Evidence." *World Bank Research Observer* 15 (1): 99–135.

Ayubi, Nazih. 1995. *Over-stating the Arab State: Politics and Society in the Middle East.* London and New York: I. B. Taurus and Co. Ltd.

Azarya, V. 1988. "Reordering State–Society Relations: Incorporation and Disengagement." In *The Precarious Balance: State and Society in Africa*, ed. D. Rothchild and N. Chazan, 3–21. Boulder, CO and London: Westview Press.

Bates, Robert H., Avner Greif, Margaret Levi, Jean-Laurent Rosenthal, and Barry Weingast. 1998. *Analytic Narratives*. Princeton, NJ: Princeton University Press.

Berman, Bruce, and John Lonsdale. 1992. *Unhappy Valley: Conflict in Kenya and Africa,* vol. 2. Oxford: James Currey Publishers.

Borocz, Josef. 2000. "Informality Rules." *East European Politics and Societies* 14 (2): 348–80.

Brinks, Daniel. 2003. "Informal Institutions and the Rule of Law: The Judicial Response to State Killings in Buenos Aires and Sao Paulo in the 1990s." *Comparative Politics* 36 (1): 1–19.

Buchanan, James, and Gordon Tullock. 1962. *The Calculus of Consent: Logical Foundations of Constitutional Democracy*. Ann Arbor: University of Michigan Press.

Collins, Kathleen. 2002. "Clans, Pacts and Policies in Central Asia." *Journal of Democracy* 13 (3): 137–52.

Dia, Mamadou. 1996. *Africa's Management in the 1990s and Beyond: Reconciling Indigenous and Transplanted Institutions*. Washington, DC: World Bank.

Diamond, Larry, Juan Linz, and Seymour Martin Lipset, eds. 1988. *Democracy in Developing Countries: Latin America*. Boulder, CO: Lynne Rienner Publishers.

Easterly, William. 2001. "The Middle Class Consensus and Economic Development." *Journal of Economic Growth* 6 (4): 317–35.

Easterly, William, Jozef Ritzen, and Michael Woolcock. 2006. "Social Cohesion, Institutions and Growth." *Economics and Politics* 18 (2): 103–20.

Engberg-Pedersen, Lars, Louise Andersen, Finn Stepputat, and Dietrich Jung. 2008. "Fragile Situations." Background papers, Danish Institute for International Studies, Copenhagen.

Evans, Peter. 1989. "Predatory, Developmental, and Other Apparatuses: A Comparative Political Economy Perspective on the Third World State." *Sociological Forum* 4: 561–87.

———. 1995. *Embedded Autonomy*. Princeton, NJ: Princeton University Press.

Fearon, James. 2010. "Governance and Civil War Onset." Background paper, *World Development Report 2011,* Washington, DC, World Bank.

Gorski, Philip S. 1993. "The Protestant Ethic Revisited: Disciplinary Revolution and State Formation in Holland and Prussia." *American Journal of Sociology* 99 (2): 265–316.

Greenwood, Royston, Roy Suddaby, and C. R. Hinings. 2002. "Theorizing Change: The Role of Professional Associations in the Transformation of Institutionalized Fields." *Academy of Management Journal* 45 (1): 58–80.

Greif, Avner. 1994. "Cultural Beliefs and the Organization of Society: A Historical and Theoretical Reflection on Collectivist and Individualist Societies." *Journal of Political Economy* 102 (5): 912–50.

————. 2005. "Commitment, Coercion, and Markets: The Nature and Dynamics of Institutions Supporting Exchange." In *Handbook of New Institutional Economics*, ed. Claude Menard and Mary Shirley. Dordrecht: Springer.

Guiso, Luigi, Paola Sapienza, and Luigi Zingales. 2003. "People's Opium? Religion and Economic Attitudes." *Journal of Monetary Economics* 50 (1): 225–82.

Habermas, Jurgen. 1998. "The European Nation-State: On the Past and Future of Sovereignty and Citizenship." *Public Culture* 10 (2): 397–416.

Harriott, Anthony, ed. 2003. *Understanding Crime in Jamaica: New Challenges for Public Policy*. Kingston: University of the West Indies Press.

Hibou, Beatrice. 2004. "Conclusion." In *Boundaries and Belonging: States and Societies in the Struggle to Shape Identities and Local Practices*, ed. Joel Migdal. Cambridge: Cambridge University Press.

Hyden, Goran. 1983. "Problems and Prospects of State Coherence." In *State versus Ethnic Claims: African Dilemmas*, ed. Donald Rothchild and Victor Olorunsola, 67–84. Boulder, CO: Westview Press.

Jackson, Robert, and Carl Rosberg. 1982. "Why Africa's Weak States Persist: The Empirical and Juridical in Statehood." *World Politics* 35: 1–24.

Jalal, Ayesha. 1995. *The State of Martial Rule: The Origins of Pakistan's Political Economy of Defense*. Cambridge: Cambridge University Press.

Kiser, Edgar, and Yong Cai. 2000. "Causes of Bureaucratization of the Chinese State: Exploring an Anomalous Case." Paper presented at the Mini-Conference on Rational Choice associated with the American Sociological Association, August, Washington, DC.

Kiser, Edgar, and Joachim Schneider. 1995. "Rational Choice and Cultural Agreements: About the Efficiency of Prussian Tax System: Reply to Gorski." *American Sociological Review* 60 (5): 787–91.

Kohli, Atul. 2004. *State-Directed Development*. New York: Cambridge University Press.

————. 2002. "State, Society, and Development." In *Political Science: The State of the Discipline,* ed. Ira Katznelson and Helen V. Milner. New York and Washington, DC: W. W. Norton and American Political Science Association.

Kymlicka, Will. 2010. "The Rise and Fall of Multiculturalism? New Debates on Inclusion and Accommodation in Diverse Societies." *International Social Science Journal* 61 (199): 97–112.

Leary, Virginia. 2000. "Citizenship, Human Rights and Diversity." In *Citizenship, Diversity and Pluralism: Canadian and Comparative Perspectives*, ed. Alan Cairns et al. Montreal: McGill-Queen's Press.

Levitsky, Steven. 2001. "An 'Organized Disorganization': Informal Organization and the Persistence of Local Party Structures in Argentine Peronism." *Journal of Latin American Studies* 33 (1): 29–66.

Lonsdale, John, and Bruce Berman. 1979. "Coping with the Contradictions: The Development of the Colonial State in Kenya, 1895–1914." *Journal of African History* 20: 487–505.

Migdal, Joel. 1988. *Strong Societies and Weak States: State–Society Relations and State Capabilities in the Third World*. Princeton, NJ: Princeton University Press.

———. 2001. *State in Society: Studying How States and Societies Transform and Constitute Each Other*. New York: Cambridge University Press.

———, ed. 2004. *Boundaries and Belonging: States and Societies in the Struggle to Shape Identities and Local Practices*. New York: Cambridge University Press.

North, Douglas, John Joseph Wallis, and Barry Weingast. 2009. *Violence and Social Orders: A Conceptual Framework for Interpreting Human History*. Cambridge: Cambridge University Press.

O'Donnell, Guillermo. 1996. "Another Institutionalization: Latin America and Elsewhere." Kellogg Institute Working Paper 222, Kellogg Institute for International Studies, Notre Dame, IN.

Ostrom, Elinor. 1990. *Governing the Commons: The Evolution of Institutions for Collective Action*. New York: Cambridge University Press.

Pritchett, Lant, and Michael Woolcock. 2004. "Solution When the Solution Is the Problem: Arraying the Disarray in Development." *World Development* 32 (2): 191–212.

Putnam, Robert. 1993. *Making Democracy Work: Civil Traditions in Modern Italy*. Princeton, NJ: Princeton University Press.

———. 1995. "Bowling Alone: America's Declining Social Capital." *Journal of Democracy* 6 (1): 65–78.

Robinson, James A. 2001. "When Is a State Predatory?" Harvard University, Department of Government, Cambridge, MA.

Rodrik, Dani. 1999. "Where Did All the Growth Go? External Shocks, Social Conflicts, and Growth Collapses." *Journal of Economic Growth* 4 (4): 385–412.

———. 2003. *In Search of Prosperity: Analytic Narratives on Economic Growth*. Princeton, NJ: Princeton University Press.

Sandbrook, Richard, and Jay Oelbaum. 1999. "Reforming the Political Kingdom: Governance and Development in Ghana's Fourth Republic." Critical Perspectives Paper No. 2, Center for Democracy and Development, Manchester, UK.

Seabrook, Leonard. 2002. "Bringing Legitimacy Back in to Neo-Weberian State Theory and International Relations." Working paper no. 2002/6, Department of International Relations, Australian National University, Canberra.

Sellers, Jeffrey. 2010. "State–Society Relations beyond the Weberian State." In *Handbook of Governance*, ed. Mark Bevrir. London: Sage Publications.

Van Cott, Donna Lee. 2000. "A Political Analysis of Legal Pluralism in Bolivia and Columbia." *Journal of Latin American Studies* 32 (1): 207–34.

Varshney, Ashutosh. 2002. *Ethnic Conflict and Civic Life*. Hartford, CT: Yale University Press.

Vu, Tuong. 2010. "Studying the State through State Formation." *World Politics* 62 (1): 148–75.

Wallerstein, Immanuel Maurice. 1964. *Voluntary Associations*. New York: Institute of African Studies, School of International Affairs, Columbia University.

Watts, Nicole. 2004. "Institutionalizing Virtual Kurdistan West: Transnational Networks and Ethnic Contention in International Affairs." In *Boundaries and Belonging: States and Societies in the Struggle to Shape Identities and Local Practices*, ed. Joel Migdal. Cambridge: Cambridge University Press.

Weber, Max. 1922. *Economy and Society.* Berkeley: University of California Press.

———. 1905/2002. "Voluntary Associational Life." *Max Weber Studies* 2 (2): 199–209.

Woolcock, Michael. 2007. "Toward an Economic Sociology of Chronic Poverty: Enhancing the Rigor and Relevance of Social Theory." Chronic Poverty Research Center Working Paper 104, Chronic Poverty Research Center, Manchester, U.K.

World Bank. 2011a. *World Development Report: Conflict, Development and Security.* Washington, DC: World Bank.

———. 2011b. *Poverty and Social Exclusion in India.* Washington, DC: World Bank.

CHAPTER 3

Social Cohesion: A Convergence across Groups

A wealth of literature exists on the benefits of social cohesion for development. Social cohesion is alleged to bring important benefits in terms of higher growth, reduced conflict, stronger institutions, and greater social harmony overall. Politicians and policy makers have made social cohesion a centerpiece of many national policies, and it has an important place on the international policy agenda as well.[1]

Despite the attention it has received in policy and politics, no clear consensus prevails on what constitutes social cohesion. Various authors have described the concept as the "affective bond between citizens" (Chipkin and Ngqulunga 2008: 61) and "the glue that bonds society together, promoting harmony, a sense of community, and a degree of commitment to promoting the common good" (Colletta, Lim, and Kelles-Viitanen 2001).[2] It is generally understood as a property of society, rather than of individuals, and one that can be strengthened through sound social policy (UNRISD 2010).

Those definitions speak to the essence of the concept but offer little guidance in the task of understanding how much cohesion is present in a given context or how much is enough to secure the benefits that social cohesion is supposed to bring. To a certain extent, the concept appears helpful only after the fact; that is, it only becomes evident when society breaks down that there was not enough social cohesion to hold it together.

A key insight from the fieldwork undertaken for the study reported in this book is that a *convergence across groups* in society is essential for reducing fragility. That convergence is a critical element for moving along the continuum away from fragility. Drawing on examples from the five case studies, the following sections describe some of the essential elements of such convergence, as well as some manifestations of the lack of such convergence in the places studied.

It is important to recognize that the notion of social cohesion has some misleading connotations that should be dismissed at the outset. The first is the implication that social cohesion entails cultural homogeneity or intolerance of cultural and social diversity. When used in this way, social cohesion has often been invoked toward very negative—even tragic—ends. Conceptualizations of national unity and "purity" helped provoke the Holocaust and "ethnic cleansing" in various circumstances (Easterly, Ritzen, and Woolcock 2006). The second misleading connotation is the association of social cohesion with a lack of dissent in society. As the following sections will illustrate, socially cohesive societies are not those that lack diversity and dissent, but rather the opposite: socially cohesive societies are able to channel their diversity and dissent (in terms of culture, capacities, ideas, and so on) toward preferred outcomes.

Understanding Convergence across Groups

The in-country phase of the study that this book describes sought to understand the elements of fragility that emanate from societal dynamics and that are reproduced in social interactions. In each of the five countries, research participants were asked to describe how they understood fragility and how they experienced it in their daily lives.[3] Over and over, interviewees and focus group participants overwhelmingly emphasized sentiments of frustration about the seeming inability of groups to come together to work toward common goals. Many groups felt that they had very little in common with other groups beyond living within the same territorial borders and, as a result, were little inclined to work together. The quality of these relationships had a direct influence on how fragile the participants perceived society to be as a whole. Discussion then focused on what the important elements of an effective convergence could be.

"Convergence across groups" means that individuals and groups are connected in such a way that they feel it is better to collaborate than compete, and that they trust in the fundamentals of the overall social norms and networks that govern their behavior. The degree of convergence does not necessarily need to be strong for a society to hold together. It need only be sufficient for groups to coexist. In this way, convergence provides a structure for collective life, which in itself offers a measure of predictability, so that individuals and groups see the benefit in coexisting with a minimum degree of tolerance.

Generally speaking, convergence has a cumulative effect: the greater the overall convergence in a society, the more connected and cohesive society becomes. Indeed, the development process can to some extent be viewed as one of ceaselessly enlarging the scope of convergence in a society, strengthening the framework within which groups can interact. In this way convergence is similar to social capital. The difference is subtle: whereas social capital provides a general stock of relationships and networks across individuals and groups (Coleman 1990; Hardin 1999), convergence provides an *incentive* for groups to coexist peacefully.

Convergence across groups does not mean the assimilation of interests across groups. All groups in the society do not have to see eye-to-eye on all issues, or share the same goals, for convergence to exist. It is sufficient that the groups' motivations be compatible, or at least not in conflict with one another. Societies can find a common interest, even in the presence of conflicting opinions, as long as there is a larger goal (real or imaginary) that makes them understand that it is worthwhile to tolerate other opinions and views. In this sense, convergence can bridge differences among identity groups that are rooted in cultural, ethnic, or other features. Groups need not share the interests and goals of other ethnic or cultural groups; they need only perceive those interests and goals as not threatening their own. Some issues are obviously more important than others, however. If a particular issue becomes especially polarizing, the divergence on the one issue can outweigh the convergence on many other issues. In this way, a society can quickly switch from a dynamic of resilience to a dynamic of fragility, depending on how prominent particular issues become.

Convergence across groups is a necessary condition for collective action but is not enough by itself to guarantee it. Though convergence can exist to different degrees (that is, among a greater or lesser number of groups or on a greater or lesser number of issues), a minimum of convergence has to be present if people are to see the benefit of collective action at all. Yet the fact that such convergence exists does not automatically translate to collective action. Many oppressed groups in a society may share grievances against a corrupt and repressive government, and thus potentially share a desire to change the government, but that does not guarantee that they will act together. In other cases, groups may be unable to coordinate their actions simply because their numbers are too large.

Of course, convergence across groups can also lead to collective activities that do not serve the broader interests of society. This "dark side" of convergence is similar to the notion of "perverse social capital," describing instances when relationships and networks are appropriated by some groups for collective action that narrowly benefits one group, to the detriment of other groups. For example, urban gangs may use strong social ties for criminal ends that benefit the gang members but have negative repercussions for the community as a whole, and that ultimately can break down the social networks of the community (Rubio 1997; Moser and McIlwaine 2004). Convergence is thus a neutral concept in itself. It is only the way in which it is mobilized that gives it positive or negative value.

Convergence is a tremendously context-specific and dynamic concept. It is overall a highly subjective notion, and thus it is difficult to identify and assess in practice. Understanding convergence thus goes further than simply following the maxim that "context matters." It requires rigorous consultation and analysis of the nature of relationships and exchanges, and capacity in a given context. The implications for research and the design of interventions are discussed in detail in chapter 8.

Convergence and Cohesion

Societies that experience convergence across groups have strong incentives to manage internal conflicts and power competitions. The convergence also provides more predictability to individuals in a society, as they can reasonably expect that others will continue to work toward a common goal, or at least will not sabotage the goals of other groups. However, the existence of a convergence of interest is not enough by itself to ensure that society will move along the fragility continuum toward greater cohesiveness. Several factors seem to be important in this regard.

First, the convergence should be long-term. History is full of examples of divided nations that came together for some important event or because of external stresses or opportunities. Some events can create a quite powerful short-term convergence, for example, war against another country, a natural disaster, a political upheaval to overthrow a dictator, or even more mundane events such as a football match or the commemoration of a historic event. A female student participant in a focus group in Port-au-Prince illustrated this point quite well:

> The greatest collective Haitian project was the freedom project, which came to fruition in 1804. However this societal project was not a blueprint for living together. We all agreed to fight for freedom, but we never had an agreement on how to organize our common life afterwards. The Haitian Revolution was a response to the need to put an end to slavery. To this day, we have yet to make a successful transition to an agreed-upon societal project.

Such short-term efforts create a window of opportunity for a convergence to emerge, and they have the potential to pull the population together and create a feeling of common purpose. However, their real impact over the long term depends on how well the convergence can be sustained and strengthened. Many of these events turn out to be too short and too superficial to change societal dynamics fundamentally. Groups that come together for a short while, for an event that does not deeply affect the lives of their members, rarely are able to see a longer-term opportunity. The occurrence can build a sense of confidence and create some connectivity, but the effects are rarely sustained over the long term, unless political leaders and civil society exploit the opportunity very actively.

The case of Aceh is illustrative here. During the conflict, power actors mobilized narrow identities along tribal lines to fuel the violence. The Aceh conflict was rooted at least in part in the production of an Acehnese identity that was not only distinct from Indonesian identity, but fundamentally incompatible with being Indonesian. Although the nationalist ideology of the Free Aceh Movement (GAM) did not at first resonate with most of the population, the application of counterinsurgency tactics against the Acehnese, as the conflict wore on, eventually gave credence to the notion that Aceh was ruled by a hostile, neocolonial government. Eventually, all grievances in Aceh came to be viewed within that identity framework (Aspinall 2007),[4] which created a convergence across groups that served to unify the Acehnese and mobilize many into the GAM. That contributed to a relatively high acceptance of former combatants into their village communities after the conflict ended. The peace agreement that ended the conflict in Aceh embodies some important elements for a long-term convergence across groups (see box 3.1). However, whether the settlement can address the deeper roots of the conflict, particularly the identity divides between Acehnese and broader Indonesian society, remains to be seen.

BOX 3.1

Sustaining a Long-Term Convergence after Violent Conflict: Aceh and the Helsinki Memorandum of Understanding

For three decades, Aceh has been the site of an intermittent but often powerful insurgency aiming to separate Aceh from Indonesia. The violence began in late 1976, when the Free Aceh Movement (GAM) rebellion began with the goal of securing the territory's independence from Indonesia. After the collapse of the Suharto regime in Jakarta, a much more broadly based insurgency developed in 1999–2005. During that war, Aceh experienced profound breakdown in the social contract, with many of its people seeing in Acehnese nationalism a primary political identity that not only lacked ties to the Indonesian state but explicitly rejected identification with the state altogether. Parts of Acehnese society experienced serious horizontal conflict between rival communities, but many rural communities maintained considerable cohesion and resilience, even in the midst of conflict. Indeed, the community-level cohesion was in many cases turned to the purpose of resisting state interference.

The Helsinki Memorandum of Understanding, signed by representatives of GAM and the government of Indonesia in August 2005,[5] contained several important elements that appear promising in supporting a long-term convergence across groups. Many of the formal terms of the agreement—embodied in the Helsinki memorandum and the subsequent Law for the Governing of Aceh (LoGA) passed by Indonesia's national legislature in 2006—are quite forward-looking. They include greater political autonomy for Aceh, greater economic resources for local government, compensation and assistance for conflict victims and former combatants, and an array of measures relating to security, political arrangements,[6] economic development, and the like. Other implicit elements of the settlement can also be observed after more than five years of implementation of the formal agreement. One important element appears to be effective impunity for abuses committed by both the government's military forces and GAM rebels during the conflict years. Certainly neither the government nor the former rebels have stated a desire to establish a formal truth and reconciliation process to investigate past abuses (Aspinall 2008). Another implicit aspect of the settlement is the opening of patronage resources to former GAM fighters and their integration into the clientelistic networks that connect economic and political power throughout regional Indonesia.

However, although the Helsinki Memorandum of Understanding laid out a long-term plan for peace, important risks to sustaining the political settlement remain. First, as suggested by Domingo (2011), are questions of whether the terms of the bargain—formal and informal, local and intergovernmental—are seen as stable and legitimate by the broader society. More important, it remains to be seen whether the terms of the settlement laid out in the memorandum will be able to address the historical roots of the conflict, such as a stark rural-urban divide, alienation from the state, and a hardened, resistant form of Acehnese identity. Those questions are pertinent in light of what might be called a strong "narrative of betrayal" that has arisen from previous cycles of conflict and peace in modern Acehnese history. For many Acehnese, a fundamental feature of the last 60 years has been a repeated pattern of deceit by the central government in Jakarta and (to a lesser extent) repeated betrayals of the Acehnese people by their own leaders.

The Helsinki memorandum and subsequent peace settlement required GAM supporters to set aside their goal of a separate state, give up their arms, and accept that Aceh would remain part of Indonesia. However, the extent to which the settlement brought about deeper transformation of the underlying conflict over identity remains an open question that is very politically sensitive. As the authors of the recent Multi-Stakeholder Review of postconflict programming in Aceh put it, "The most fundamental challenge facing the peace process in Aceh is the transition of all conflict-affected groups from their conflict-era identities, to new roles in a peaceful Acehnese society and polity" (MSR 2009: 129). They also noted that "many ex-combatants are reluctant—or unable—to transform their identities from 'freedom fighter' to 'community member.' They are likely to treat other KRA [Aceh People's Congress] members as their closest friends and prospective business partners" (MSR 2009: 109).

The challenge is not only that individuals remained attached to their conflict-era organizational identities. The deeper question is how (or even whether) they are renegotiating the relationship between their Acehnese and Indonesian identities. In meetings with former supporters of the nationalist movement—ex-combatants or Partai Aceh politicians, for instance—it is very common to hear explanations of how autonomy arrangements should maintain a clear dividing line between "Aceh" and "Indonesia" and of how Indonesia remains an uncomfortable imposition on Aceh, albeit one that cannot be shrugged off (for now). Yet, whereas such responses suggest that the conflict between Acehnese and Indonesian identity is not being overcome or resolved, they leave open the possibility that the conflict may simply be gradually losing salience, as people come to focus on other matters (cf. Brubaker 1998: 280). Thus, GAM fighters-turned-government-officials have increasingly focused on practical matters to do with economic development, improving governance, and attracting investment that do not readily lend themselves to ethno-nationalist appeals. Interestingly, the authors of a recent survey of community perceptions of the peace process found that only one of their informants evoked ideas about Aceh's past history of sovereignty, greatness, and struggle (Grayman et al. 2009: 39), despite the fact that such notions were central to GAM's nationalist ideology and permeated everyday discussion of politics during the conflict years.

In the fieldwork, the team found mixed evidence on this point. Most Acehnese (intellectuals, civil society members, academics, previous GAM members, both in the expert seminar and in the focus groups) tended to speak of Aceh as a distinct part of Indonesia, maintaining their own separate identity but accepting being part of a larger polity. It seemed that how the final structure turns out depends on how the Helsinki Memorandum is implemented, or at least how the Acehnese perceive that it is implemented.

Second, the convergence should be "inclusive enough" to hold over time. It is important to realize that large groups cannot be excluded if the convergence is to be sustained. During the economic and political reforms and rapid development in the Andean countries in Latin America, a strong convergence across social classes and various sociocultural groups, unknown until this century, has been seen. By including a broad range of groups in the reforms, these societies have strengthened institutions, dramatically reduced violence, and supported the emergence of the continent as an important economic power.

When the convergence is not inclusive enough, convergence across a number of groups can coalesce against another group. The group that becomes the scapegoat can be a cultural or religious minority or a migrant or youth group. Many minority groups throughout history have been the focus of active discrimination by other groups for various reasons. They are perceived as having inappropriate behaviors, deemed as unfairly enriching themselves to the detriment of the rest of the society, or seen as unfairly pushing societies to change their beliefs. Such exclusivity negatively affects the ability of the society to converge effectively in the long run.

In other cases, particular groups may react to exclusion by further isolating themselves. Empirical work in the United States demonstrates how strong social ties based on common interests can create a dense network of relationships that isolates a group from the broader society (Wilson 1996). Similarly, ethnic groups such as the Roma often have a strong convergence that binds them together as they maintain their cultural identity but hinders them from integrating into the broader society. The result over the long term is that groups that are not adequately integrated into the broader convergence may hold development back from its full potential.

Third, the convergence has to be based on some level of shared intersubjective meanings. Convergence across groups that is based on shared intersubjective meanings facilitates social cohesion. Intersubjective meanings encompass beliefs of individuals, communities, and societies about themselves, how the world works, and their own agency in confronting change

---

BOX 3.2

Liberia: Convergence to End Violent Conflict

Women in Liberia bore the brunt of the country's brutal, 14-year civil war, enduring rampant physical and sexual violence, displacement, the deaths of family members, and the abduction of their children into armed groups—all in formidable economic conditions. Those experiences formed the basis for a broadly inclusive convergence of women from many different groups in Liberia, which eventually led to a peace agreement.

In 2002, recognizing the commonalities in their experiences, even across deep religious and ethnic divides, a small group of women led by Leymah Gbowee, a social worker, began mobilizing women in mosques and churches around Monrovia to pray for an end to the conflict. A group began to gather in a fish market, praying both Christian and Muslim prayers. The group then escalated their protest by defying the orders of then-President Charles Taylor against public protests and by initiating a "sex strike," which attracted important media attention.

Eventually the movement, Women of Liberia Mass Action for Peace (WLMAP), came to include 3,000 women of many different tribes and religions, including Muslims and Christians. The women established a presence in a soccer field near the road that President Taylor traveled to and from work every day. Drawing on a broad base of support, Gbowee obtained a public audience with Taylor to secure his promise to attend peace talks in Ghana. At those talks, WLMAP staged a sit-in and refused to move until a peace agreement had been signed, even threatening to shame the men in the meeting by removing their clothes if necessary. In 2011, Gbowee won the Nobel Peace Prize for her role in organizing the peace movement across religious and ethnic divides.

and making decisions that affect their own lives (Rao and Walton 2004; Woolcock 2007; Gauri, Woolcock, and Desai 2011. These understandings are motivated by reasons that go beyond interests, incentives, and values. The term "shared intersubjective meanings" pertains to individuals and groups in a society having similar worldviews, similar expectations of their own and others' appropriate behavior, and similar understandings and priorities concerning problems the society faces and the potential and acceptable solutions to those problems. In this sense, a convergence based on shared intersubjective meanings implies that everyone in the society should share the same understanding of what the points of convergence are and how it is to be achieved. It does not mean that all people need to believe the same things and behave in the same way, but that at least a minimum of overlap should exist between various meaning systems, and that people's understandings of the world and the behavior that comes with it must have some elements of compatibility.

BOX 3.3

Yemen: Convergence around a Tradition of Dialogue

An important part of Yemeni identity, rooted in tribal traditions, is a culture of dialogue. The tradition of dialogue is a shared intersubjective meaning in that it provides a point of shared reference and a spirit of dialogue and solidarity. The practice of daily *qat* chewing, in particular, creates a space where ideas can be debated and discussed. This spirit is also present in other "mini-publics," such as those associated with mosque sermons and lessons, newspapers, or television or radio broadcasts, constituting "lively communities of argument, distinct modes of democratic being and acting in which participants often orient their addresses to and receive information as part of a broader public of anonymous citizens" (Warner 2002, qtd. in Wedeen 2008, 3).

This deep tradition of dialogue, as part of a unified national identity, has perhaps been enough to keep the country from falling into full civil war. However, it has not been sufficient to move the society away from fragility. The symbolic national identity, while strong, has not been strong enough to supersede regional loyalties, which remain the most relevant for most Yemenis. Even during times of crisis, the national identity has not been strong enough for people to abandon local identities. As Wedeen (2008) notes, "Yemeni nationalists often espoused and continue to create new, more encompassing identifications without abandoning their local interests, their divergent political allegiances (as royalists, republicans, and socialists) or their sense of place"(47).

Divergence, Bridging Failures, and Bonding Failures

During the fieldwork, the team observed different ways in which groups and individuals were unable to connect with one another in ways that would build convergence. That divergence looked different in different places. The dynamics at play resemble what Rao and Mansuri (2012: 8) refer to as "civil society failures." Those consist of "a situation in which groups, who live in geographic proximity—in rural villages and municipal townships or who draw upon a common pooled resource—are unable to act collectively to reach a feasible and preferable outcome."[7] These failures are generally of two types: "bonding failures," or circumstances in which members of a group cannot connect sufficiently among themselves to effect collective action or manage common resources, and "bridging failures," which are situations where groups can connect to each other but are unable to organize to correct market or government failures that affect their lives.

Anomie

In the Central African Republic, a type of bonding failure seemed to be at play that resembled a state of anomie. The concept of anomie originated with Durkheim, who understood it as a state of normlessless, or deregulation, in which the rules that normally govern social behavior have broken down as a result of some kind of rapid societal change (Durkheim 1893). For example, an economic boom can trigger rapid social change. If the current cultural norms are inadequate to govern behavior, and new cultural norms have not yet evolved to deal with the changes, a mismatch develops between individual desires and aspirations and social norms that would regulate those aspirations. When anomie prevails in a society, people cannot depend on social norms to predict the behavior of others, resulting in confusion and mistrust. Anomie can be self-reinforcing. As the motivation of individuals or groups in a society to coordinate behavior deteriorates, the rules that facilitate coordinated behavior can become obsolete or redundant over time. Without a set of governing norms they can trust to regulate others' behavior, individuals further isolate themselves, which then continues to undermine the potential for any collective action.

In the Central African Republic, people felt that communities were fragmented not so much by state policies as by internal tensions that prevented them from seeing one another as trustworthy. The divisions were reinforced by state policies and the behavior of state officials, but they were not caused by them (Marchal 2010). The internal tensions stemmed from what people saw as a breakdown in social norms and networks that would coordinate social life. Many participants referred to a previous "golden age" in which age, status, family, and authority were respected and provided communities with a sense of social order and predictability. People understood their social place in the community, for better or for worse, as well as the positions of others, and that framework governed their interactions with others. During that time, the state authorities (*chefs*, or community heads) had a recognized place and role in the community (even if their presence as primarily tax collectors was undesired).

The decline in both state authority and customary norms that would govern behavior has been occurring over centuries in the Central African Republic. As a result, a sense of anomie and lawlessness prevails, in which it is virtually impossible to predict or form expectations of others' behavior with reasonable certainty. This sense of anomie undermines the already weak relationship of society with the state. Overall it has led individuals to perceive unmanageable dangers, doubts, and fears in virtually every aspect of ordinary life:

> The past two centuries have been a period of immense upheaval in Central Africa. New solidarities have been created, and new modes of social organization embarked upon, but these transformations have mostly been accompanied by violence and turmoil. This has resulted in the predicament people living in the area currently face, namely the straining of the limited social cohesion that had previously glued together communities under the pressures of poverty, witchcraft and mistrust (World Bank 2011).

This lack of trust and lack of cohesion at the community level have considerably undermined the potential for collective action and strategies of collaboration that are broader than family. Many areas in the Central African Republic are characterized by survival strategies, with very limited collaboration among families, let alone between communities, as well as mistrust, increasing reliance on witchcraft, and a quasi absence of state structure.

Fracture

A second type of divergence observed in the field can be described as "fracture" across social groups. In this case, there seemed to be two or three important groups in society, within which strong social cohesion was present. These groups were also able to undertake collective action toward common goals. Yet they were not able to connect with other groups in society. Thus, this dynamic constitutes a type of bridging failure, in that groups are cohesive within themselves but cannot connect constructively with other groups to undertake broader collective action.

Liberia exemplified this particular dynamic. Although the country has many ethnic groups, deep divisions exist between Americo-Liberians and native Liberians. Some of the key problematic dynamics emerged from the founding of the country. When Americo-Liberians arrived in what is now Liberia, they brought with them expectations about how a country should be governed. They also brought the Christian religion, as well as norms about appropriate, or as they called it, "civilized" behavior. Other new immigrants into the country, such as freed slaves from the Caribbean Islands and Africans intercepted from slave vessels by the U.S. Navy after the abolishment of the slave trade, also quickly adopted the Americo-Liberian way of life and became part of their community. These three groups are today often referred to as the "Congo" people, or "settlers." The division between the settlers and the rest is not ethnic or economic but is based on culture and perceived injustices. The settlers often took in children from native Liberian families and introduced them to formal education. Many of those native Liberian children took settler names and identities and became part of that group.

In the fieldwork, settlers and native Liberians expressed the division between them as a division between cultures. Settlers say that they are stricter with their children and prioritize their education. In one community, individuals described how settlers follow certain customs and rules, such as going to church on Sundays, not washing clothes on Sundays, or not washing clothes upstream from where people bathe. Native Liberians explain that the settlers do not join traditional societies, do not attend community events, and do not "value what they value." Many native Liberians say that they feel a lack of respect by people of settler background because they do not join them in traditional activities: The lack of value put on traditions, they say, shows that settlers see themselves as superior, when in fact, many state, they are guests in a foreign land. These social fractures are a source of fragility in today's Liberia.

Fragmentation

A third manifestation of divergence observed in the field could be called "fragmentation." It differed from fracture in that more, and smaller, groups were at play. Each of the groups enjoyed a certain degree of social cohesion and was able to engage in collective action. Yet the many groups were unable to connect among themselves.

That condition was observed especially in Yemen. For the majority of Yemenis, the notion of one Yemen—as a nation with a long, glorious history, "whose unity, but not its commonality, was interrupted periodically"—is a strong unifying force (Stevenson and Alaug 2008). The idea of a single Yemeni political entity existed long before the emergence of a Yemeni state. The term *Yaman* was used in the *Hadith* (*Traditions of the Prophet*) as a name for the territory south of Mecca, and various local literatures and practices were deemed *Yamani* long before the establishment of the formal state of Yemen (Dresch 2000; Wedeen 2008). The union of North and South Yemen in 1990 was a dream come true for many Yemenis, and the national discourse around it has emphasized "the people's antiquity, their continuous occupation of a territory coincident with unified Yemen, and the sacrifices that 'the people' (or particular heroic figures) have made in the effort to achieve national unity" (Wedeen 2008, 40).

Yet this sense of a common, symbolic national unity is not enough to override narrower loyalties based on clan. The government patronage system in Yemen, which functions by co-opting various clans, religious groups, and regional leaders and then switching alliances when necessary, in a "co-opt, divide, and rule" fashion, encourages the fragmentation of Yemeni identity into more narrow regional and religious identities. Each of the identity groups views itself as different from the rest of country, and many emphasize fundamental incompatibilities between their specific identity and the rest of the country, as was revealed in many of the discussions and focus groups held in Yemen for the study.

In the fieldwork, people spoke of Yemeni society as being fragmented into a large number of narrowly defined identity groups, with significant social fault lines between them. First were divisions between people living in the coastal regions, where resources were still open for appropriation, and people of the highlands who were grabbing those resources. Second were divisions between people from the North, who viewed themselves as the legitimate rulers of the land, and people from the South, who considered themselves to be more educated and more modern. Another divide was evident in the southern region between the people of Abjan and Shewa, and the people of Dalia and Lahj because of old internal conflicts. Aden has its own very specific identity; Taiz and the middle Yemen were also seen as very different than the rest of Yemen. In the North, tensions existed between the Zaydi group and the Suni population. The Hadramawat had a strong specific identity, as well. The divisions could reach down to specific clans or subgroups. Obviously the identities are very old and rooted in specific history and culture. They were, however, exacerbated by the state's divide-and-conquer approach, which approach was particularly harmful because it created a sense of incompatibility between identities and enormous tension and competition between various subgroups.

Some Societal Dynamics Are Especially Counterproductive to Convergence across Groups

Convergence can be affected by many factors, depending on the context. Some societal dynamics are especially prone to derail the potential for convergence and can lead the society down the continuum to fragility. These dynamics undermine social cohesion by creating a climate of insecurity and unpredictability. The result is a vicious cycle, wherein people and groups retreat from productive interactions with other groups, and which can be intensely difficult to exit.

Pervasive Distrust

Convergence depends on a minimal level of trust across groups, such that groups have confidence that other groups will not act to harm them. Trust is understood as the capacity to rely on another person or persons, with the confidence that they will respond reciprocally, or at least not harmfully. Trust is, at least in part, the product of some convergence of interest. According to Hardin (2002), people trust one another because of what he calls "encapsulated" interest, or the confidence that one's interests are in line with the interests of the trusted person, and therefore the trusted person's actions will not jeopardize those interests. That is:

> Your trust turns not directly on your own interests but rather on whether these are encapsulated in the interests of the trusted. You trust someone if you believe it will be in her interest to be trustworthy in the relevant way at the relevant time, and it will be in her interest because she wishes to maintain her relationship with you.

This concept applies at the collective level in the sense that people trust other groups to perform their function, as they have committed to do, because those functions are in line with the overall interests of the group.

As with trust among individuals, trust across groups is directly related to the quality of the relationship and how valuable it is to each group.

Trust is important in a number of ways. It enables cooperative behavior (Gambetta 1988); reduces harmful conflict; decreases transaction

---

BOX 3.4

Haiti: Pervasive Distrust and the Notion of *Marronage/Mawanaj*

In Haiti, the potential for convergence across groups is undermined by pervasive distrust. In the expert interviews conducted during the study, people emphasized that the lack of trust has a long history and is rooted in the particular experiences of slavery and revolution of Haitian society. Haiti's history has been, in the words of one historian, "written in blood" (Heinl and Heinl 1978). The particular form of slavery imposed in Haiti placed large numbers of slaves under the domination of a small number of slave owners, who relied on the arbitrary and brutal use of violence to maintain control. The Haitian Revolution replicated that brutality on both plantation owners and noncombatants. Throughout the two American occupations and the subsequent transition to democracy, the use of violence, including torture and disappearances, by the armed forces became the chief mode of maintaining control. As a result, "Today, the atavistic assertion of personal dominance through the arbitrary exercise of power—whether through physical exactions or other forms of violence—remains an integral part of Haitian societal and political dynamics at many levels, from the family to the State" (INURED 2011: 5).

The distrust that exists among many Haitians today, particularly across social classes, can be seen to some extent as a survival mechanism, developed to help navigate the violent context. Participants in the expert seminar emphasized the Haitian notion of *marronage/mawanaj* to refer to the tactic of maintaining emotional distance from one another. During slavery, *marronage/mawanaj* allowed runaway slaves to sever all ties with family and friends in order to escape to the hills, without allowing themselves to consider what might happen to those they were leaving behind. In today's Haiti, however, according to one female activist interviewed for the study, "it [*marronage/ mawanaj*] has become endemic in our society and how we run from each other, creating the division that prevents us from moving forward." Consequently, individuals have adopted short-term self-interested behavior that, even if it protects individuals temporarily, works against social cohesion in the longer term. These circumstances fuel a vicious cycle in which the lack of trust discourages collective action, and that in turn further undermines trust.

costs; facilitates rapid formulation of ad hoc work groups (Meyerson, Weick, and Kramer, 1996); and promotes effective responses to crisis. In Fukuyama's distinction (1995), high-trust societies have potential for successful long-term cooperative and communal partnerships through civil society, and low-trust societies are characterized by the absence of civil society and the prevalence of in-group relationships.

Pervasive distrust undermines convergence by creating an environment of uncertainty. If there is general distrust in the society, it creates uncertainty about how everyone else will behave. That uncertainty ultimately discourages cooperation and encourages self-interested behavior which, although potentially beneficial to individuals in the short term, is in contradiction with the society's good as a whole in the long term. The expectation that everyone else in the society will follow self-interested behavior leads individuals to choose self-interested, suboptimal behavior, if only in self-defense. The situation results even if everyone in the society may have agreed to cooperate after everyone's intentions are known. This shows that trust has to be pervasive. Even if people have perfectly adequate motives for cooperation, they still need to know about others' motives and to trust one another. Before one acts cooperatively, it is necessary not only to trust others, but also to believe that one is trusted by them.

Chronic Violence

Chronic violence makes it very difficult for a convergence across groups to solidify. The more convergence is present across groups, the greater the potential for groups to work out conflict peacefully. Violence damages social relationships, and the effect is especially harmful if it persists over a long time. Colletta and Cullen (2000) have documented its impact in contexts of prolonged political conflict. Adams (2011) has looked at the impact outside of conflict in Latin America and suggests that violence erodes mobility, social relationships, and governance.

A recent study of chronic urban violence, carried out in poor neighborhoods in Brazil, Haiti, Kenya, South Africa, and Timor Leste, showed that violence prompted people to behave in ways that further broke down social relationships and ultimately made them more vulnerable to victimization. For example, most people reported "doing nothing" to avoid victimization, but many others said they stayed home more, avoided taking jobs or classes that met at hours when they did not feel safe, or relied on extralegal groups for protection (World Bank 2011). Over time, people in high-violence areas become more and more isolated from one another, making it even harder to break out of the cycle of violence.

It has been noted that violence can also be a catalyzing force for social cohesion. A recent cross-country study of women in four conflict-affected countries found that, on average, women who had experienced violent conflict in their communities scored higher on various empowerment measures than women in communities that had not experienced conflict (Petesch 2011).[8] The study concluded that violence had severe detrimental effects on the community but also brought new opportunities for women, as they struggled to recover and rebuild. In some cases the experience of conflict loosened the constraints imposed by strict gender roles. However, the evidence is scant that these effects would be seen where violence remains chronic. The existence of a minimum of security seems to be necessary for survivors to take advantage of any opportunities that arise.

Unintended Effects of Economic and Political Factors on Convergence

It is often assumed that reducing poverty and generating economic growth will heal social divisions. Plenty of examples show that that has indeed happened. Yet no reason exists to expect that the process is inevitable or automatic. In truth, the influence of poverty reduction and economic growth can be positive or negative, depending on how they interact in a particular context.

Economic Growth

It is still generally believed that high levels of economic growth will bring citizens together. It is argued that expectation of collective improvement of living conditions can create strong convergence, especially if people sense that growth gives relatively equal opportunity to all. That can be the case when growth is consistent over a long period and when the benefits are distributed sufficiently equally that people feel they are benefiting from that growth and have a say in its distribution. That is part of the reason for the strong correlation between national GDP and characteristics associated with resilience, such as strong institutions, political stability, and absence of armed conflict.

Yet when growth is inconsistent or unevenly distributed, it can further deteriorate relationships in society. For example, Collier and Heoffler (2004) showed that, in many poor countries, natural resources, and the expected wealth they generate, create more divergence and competition than convergence as groups try to capture them for their own benefit.

Sustained growth over time, together with a redistribution of the growth to various groups, can create a strong convergence across groups. Sustained levels of growth in East Asia over the last 20 years have been important for stability and have created some convergence around improvement of living standards. All of today's developed countries experienced long periods of consistent growth that allowed them to invest in building strong institutional capacity. Sudden spikes of growth will not suffice and may create the opposite effect. In fact, Gurr (1970) shows that rapid economic changes create expectations for transformation in social status that can easily be frustrated, creating more tensions. Unpredictable spikes in growth may only create uncertainty, which promotes a climate in which elites grab what they can when they can, rather than invest in the broader society over the long term.

Poverty Reduction

Similarly, poverty reduction is not a guarantee of convergence. In many cases reducing poverty can foster convergence, as it creates strong buy-in from the most marginalized groups in society. For example, many countries in Asia, such as Indonesia, China, and Malaysia, have seen social cohesion increase with poverty reduction. In other cases, however, poverty reduction—or even the prospect of it—has triggered a backlash against the poor and a reversal of policies when it is seen to threaten the wealth of other groups. For example, some of the harshest opponents of the Civil Rights Movement in the United States were low-income whites, who saw it as threatening their access to jobs and education (Alexander 2010). That is actually a powerful factor in the neglect of indigenous populations and some of the urban poor in a number of quite successful societies, where the government has policies targeting the middle class. Poverty reduction needs to be perceived as benefiting society as a whole if it is to promote convergence. It must include the middle class. It is clear that the recent riots in Egypt and Tunisia would not have brought a change in regime without a very strong mobilization of the middle class.

Political Settlements

Political settlements provide one type of framework for convergence across groups. The term "political settlement" is often loosely used to describe the "social order" based on political compromises between various groups in society that sets the context for institutional and other policies (Khan 2010). Michael Burton and John Higley (1998) define a "political settlement" as "deliberate compromises of core disputes" among prominent groups in a society. Scholars have recognized that political competitions among various societal groups, if mediated through political settlements, can provide political stability and facilitate and foster the adoption of open and inclusive societies (Burton and Higley 1998).

Convergence from political settlements is not a given, however. In particular, if the likely outcome of the convergence of interest is expected to change the political dynamics for major groups in the political settlement, any of those groups can disrupt the process of convergence of interest and affect the ability of the society to achieve that convergence. Elites and political power brokers can exploit identities and create tensions between groups. They can also create smaller groups and reinforce cohesion among them to the detriment of the overall society. In that case, it would not only be difficult to sustain the point of common interest and achieve convergence, but any disturbance within the political settlement would also risk creating political instability.

To be considered legitimate, and to last over time, a political settlement must be acceptable to the majority of actors, especially in post-conflict settings and deeply divided societies. The most fundamental condition for achieving a political settlement is that all sides feel that they have more to gain by pursuing a common goal than by imposing their own, unilateral vision through violence (Fritz and Menocal 2007).[9] Stakeholders in a political settlement may be political or economic elites, religious leaders, civil society members, or citizen coalitions, among others. It is also important to note that political settlements take place not only at the national level (many analyses of distribution of power and political settlements are done at the national level), but also at the subnational and local levels (Parks and Cole 2010). Local actors are also constantly competing for dominance in their area of influence and entering into political settlements.

Political settlements must also be flexible enough to adapt to changes in power relationships. No settlement is static. The state and various groups in the society (including elites) continue to negotiate the nature of their relationship over time and readjust their respective expectations as different needs and demands continue to emerge (Fritz and Menocal 2007).

In fragile areas, political settlements have not yet been reached, are evolving, or have been disturbed by endogenous or exogenous factors. In other words, the distribution of power is currently being contested (for example, in Yemen and Liberia), or the institutional structure (especially when imposed by the state) is not compatible with the distribution of power in society (Haiti). The contestation can be triggered by many factors; for example, external factors may change the bargaining power of various groups (economic development increases the bargaining power of the middle class). Previously excluded groups or the groups that perceived injustices in the past may suddenly become vocal and demand change.

The existing political settlement—whether it has been formalized in a political agreement or remains an informal negotiation—provides the backdrop for all development interventions. The most persistent types of development failure occur when institutions fail because of an inappropriate match between internal political settlements and the institutions and interventions through which states attempts to accelerate development and poverty reduction. The effectiveness of institutional capacities depends directly on their compatibility with the underlying distribution of power (Khan 2002). Policy makers therefore need to be concerned with how particular interventions would work in the context-specific organization of political power and should not take for granted that the existence of a political settlement will ensure a stable environment for interventions.

Going Forward: Building Social Cohesion in Fragile Situations

This chapter has presented the concept of a convergence across groups as the essence of social cohesion. It has highlighted the characteristics of such convergence and discussed some structural factors and societal dynamics that can work against the formation of a convergence across groups.

The next two chapters now focus on two important areas of social interaction in society. The two areas emerged from the fieldwork as important points where social cohesion could be strengthened. Chapter 4 looks at perceptions of injustice across different groups. When a group perceives that they are being treated unfairly compared to other groups, their capacity and incentive to work with those groups, or even to coexist peacefully, are threatened. Justice acts as social glue. The chapter analyzes how injustice is perceived and what kinds of dynamics can instigate perceptions of injustice among groups in a society. Chapter 5 then focuses on the interactions between formal and informal institutions.

Notes

1. See, for example, the Council of Europe Task Force on Social Cohesion (http://www.coe.int/t/dg3/default_en.asp). The European Commission has established fostering social inclusion as a priority for increasing social cohesion and has developed indicators to measure progress.
2. These definitions are cited in King, Samii, and Snilstveit 2010.
3. Specific questions varied across sites but generally were some variation of, How does this society or community 'work'? What are the things that seem to make things function well or to bring people together? and What is it that is not working?
4. These historical narratives set Aceh apart from other provinces in Indonesia that did not erupt in violence and were arguably a driver of the violence (Aspinall 2010).
5. The Indian Ocean tsunami of December 24, 2004, provided an opening for the peace process but added to the burden of social trauma. The economy has begun to improve after the years of conflict and the tsunami.
6. Under the memorandum of understanding, supporters of the former guerrilla movement were able to compete for local government office. They now occupy the governorship, 10 of the 23 district government head posts, and 33 of 69 seats in the provincial parliament.
7. The authors note that these failures can include situations in which the group is unable to undertake any collective action or engages only in action that is inefficient or welfare-reducing for the most vulnerable. The latter would include actions by gangs or other fringe groups who mobilize collective action for their own narrow interests at the expense of the larger group.
8. The study also documented faster rates of poverty reduction in communities that had experienced conflict and that had the highest number of women scoring high on the empowerment measures.
9. Other donors have also emphasized the necessity of working on these issues. According to the OECD Development Assistance Committee (DAC), inclusive and stable political settlements are considered a critical foundation for both state building and peace building, and ongoing fragility and violence are often directly associated with highly exclusionary, predatory, unstable, or entrenched political settlements. The UK Department of Foreign Investment and Development's

2010 Practice Paper "Building Peaceful States and Societies" describes its as aim to "promote inclusive settlements that meet public expectations and address the underlying causes of conflict and fragility."

References

Adams, Tani Marilena. 2011. *Chronic Violence and Its Reproduction: Perverse trends in Social Relations, Citizenship and Democracy in Latin America.* Washington, DC: Woodrow Wilson International Center for Scholars.

Alexander, Michelle. 2010 *The New Jim Crow: Mass Incarceration in the Age of Colorblindness.* New York: New Press.

Aspinall, Edward. 2007. "The Construction of Grievance." *Journal of Conflict Resolution* 51 (6): 950–72.

———. 2008. *Peace without Justice? The Helsinki Peace Process in Aceh.* Geneva: Center for Humanitarian Dialogue.

———. 2010. "Political Economy Analysis: Aceh, Indonesia." Background Paper for *Societal Dynamics and Fragility: Engaging Societies in Responding to Fragile Situations.* Washington, DC: World Bank.

Brubaker, Roger. 1998. "Myths and Misconceptions in the Study of Nationalism." In *The State of the Nation: Ernest Gellner and the Theory of Nationalism*, ed. J. A. Hall. Cambridge: Cambridge University Press.

Burton, M., and J. Higley. 1998. "Political Crises and Elite Settlements." In *Elite, Crises, and the Origin of Regimes*, ed. Mattei Dogan and John Higley. Lanham, MD: Rowman and Littlefield.

Chipkin, I., and B. Ngqulunga. 2008. "Friends and Family: Social Cohesion in South Africa." *Journal of Southern African Studies* 34 (1): 61–76.

Coleman, J. S. 1990. *Foundations of Social Theory.* Cambridge, MA: Belknap Press of Harvard University Press.

Colletta, N. J., and M. L. Cullen. 2000. *The Nexus between Violent Conflict, Social Capital and Social Cohesion: Case Studies from Cambodia and Rwanda.* Washington, DC: World Bank.

Colletta, N. J., T. G. Lim, and A. Kelles-Viitanen. 2001. *Social Cohesion and Conflict Prevention in Asia: Managing Diversity through Development.* Washington, DC: World Bank.

Collier, Paul, and Anke Hoeffler. 2004. "Greed and Grievance in Civil War." *Oxford Economic Papers* 56: 563–95.

Domingo, Pilar. 2011. *Informal Institutions, Social Cohesion and Fragility.* Background paper for *Societal Dynamics and Fragility: Engaging Societies in Responding to Fragile Situations.* Washington, DC: World Bank.

Dresch, Paul. 2000. *A History of Modern Yemen.* Cambridge: Cambridge University Press.

Durkheim, Emile. 1893. *On the Division of Labor in the Society.*

Easterly, William, Jozef Ritzen, and Michael Woolcock. 2006. "Social Cohesion, Institutions and Growth." *Economics and Politics* 18 (2): 103–20.

Fritz, Verena, and Alina Rocha Menocal. 2007. "An Analytical and Conceptual Paper on Processes, Embedded Tensions and Lessons for International Engagement." DFID Effective and Fragile State Teams, UK Department of Foreign Investment and Development, London.

Fukuyama, Francis. 1995. *Trust: The Social Virtues and the Creation of Prosperity.* New York: Free Press.

Gambetta, D. 1988. Can We Trust Trust? In *Trust: Making and Breaking Cooperative Relations*, ed. D. Gambetta, 213–37. New York: Blackwell.

Gauri, Varun, Michael Woolcock, and Deval Desai. 2011. "Inter-subjective Meaning and Collective Action in 'Fragile' Societies: Theory, Evidence and Policy Implications." Background paper for *Societal Dynamics and Fragility: Engaging Societies in Responding to Fragile Situations.* Washington, DC: World Bank.

Grayman, Jesse, et al. 2009. "Community Perceptions of the Peace Process: Annex to the MSR 2009."

Gurr, Ted. 1970. *Why Men Rebel.* Princeton, NJ: Princeton University Press.

Hardin, Russell. 1999. "Social Capital." In *Competition and Cooperation: Conversations with Nobelists about Economic and Political Science,* ed. James Alt and Margaret Levi, 170–89. New York: Russell Sage Foundation.

Hardin, R. 2002. *Trust and Trustworthiness.* New York: Sage.

Heinl, Robert and Nancy Heinl. 1978. *Written in blood: The story of the Haitian people,* 1492–1971. Houghton Mifflin.

INURED (Interuniversity Institute for Research and Development). 2011. "Societal Dynamics and Fragility in Today's Haiti." Background paper for *Societal Dynamics and Fragility: Engaging Societies in Responding to Fragile Situations.* Washington, DC: World Bank.

Khan, Mushtaq H. 2002. "State Failure in Developing Countries and Strategies of Institutional Reform." Draft of paper for World Bank ABCDE Conference, Oslo 24–26 June 2002.

Khan, Mushtaq. 2010. "Political Settlements and the Governance of Growth Enhancing Institutions." DFID Research Paper Series on Governance for Growth, School of Oriental and African Studies, University of London, London.

King, Elizabeth, Cyrus Samii, and Birte Snilstveit. 2010. *Interventions to Promote Social Cohesion in Sub-Saharan Africa.* 3ie Systematic Review 002. Washington, DC: International Initiative for Impact Evaluation.

Mansuri, Ghazada, and Vijaendra Rao. 2011. "Participatory Development Reconsidered." *Development Outreach* 13, no. 1, April.

Marchal, Roland. 2010. "Central African Republic: A Political Economy Analysis." Background paper for *Societal Dynamics and Fragility: Engaging Societies in Responding to Fragile Situations.* Washington, DC: World Bank.

Meyerson, D., K. E. Weick, and R. M. Kramer. 1996. "Swift Trust and Temporary Groups." In *Trust in Organizations: Frontiers of Theory and Research*, 166–95. Thousand Oaks, CA: Sage Publications.

MSR. 2009. "Multi-Stakeholder Review of Post-Conflict Programming in Aceh: Identifying the Foundations for Sustainable Peace and Development in Aceh."

Moser, Caroline, and Cathy McIlwaine. 2004. *Encounters with Violence in Latin America: Urban Poor Perceptions from Colombia and Guatemala*. New York: Routledge.

Parks, Thomas, and William Cole. 2010. "Political Settlements: Implications for International Development Policy and Practice." Occasional paper, Asia Foundation, San Francisco.

Petesch, Patti. 2011. *Women's Empowerment Arising from Violent Conflict and Recovery*. Washington, DC: U.S. Agency for International Development. May 20.

Rao, Vijayendra, and Michael Walton. 2004. *Culture and Public Action*. Palo Alto, CA: Stanford University Press.

Rubio, Mauricio. 1997. "Perverse Social Capital—Some Evidence from Colombia." *Journal of Economic Issues* 31 (3): 805–16.

Stevenson, Thomas B., and Abdul Karim Alaug. 2008. "Sports Diplomacy and Emergent Nationalism: Football Links between the Two Yemens, 1970–1990." *Anthropology of the Middle East* 3 (2): 1–19.

UNRISD (United Nations Research Institute for Social Development). 2010. *Defining and Measuring Social Cohesion*. London: UNRISD.

Wedeen, Lisa. 2008. *Peripheral Visions: Publics, Power, and Performance in Yemen*. Chicago: University of Chicago Press.

Wilson, W. J., 1996. When Work Disappears: The World of the New Urban Poor. Alfred A. Knopf, New York.

Woolcock, Michael. 2007. "Toward an Economic Sociology of Chronic Poverty: Enhancing the Rigor and Relevance of Social Theory." CPRC Working Paper, 104.

World Bank. 2011. *Poverty and Social Exclusion in India*. Washington, DC: World Bank.

———. 2011. *Understanding Access to Justice and Conflict Resolution at the Local Level in the Central African Republic*. Social Cohesion and Violence Prevention Team. Available online at: http://siteresources.worldbank.org/EXTCPR/Resources/CAR_Access_to_Justice_report.pdf

CHAPTER 4

Perceptions of Injustice and Social Cohesion

Over the course of the fieldwork, the team worked to understand the real sources of the divisions in the societies under study. What exactly was keeping people from connecting with one another in constructive ways? Time and again, the answer had to do with a sense that certain groups were being treated unfairly relative to others and that the perception of unfairness deepened the divides between them.

The previous chapter discussed a key component of building social cohesion in fragile situations—the building of a convergence across groups in society. This chapter now turns in more detail to some characteristics of intergroup relationships that matter for generating that convergence and for social cohesion overall. The central premise of this chapter is that the perception by some groups that they are treated unjustly, compared to other groups, can lead to a breakdown in social cohesion in society.

The success or failure of development interventions is heavily influenced by perceptions of injustice. A project or policy outcome is one thing; whether people perceive that they have been treated fairly compared to other groups, or that the process has been fair, can be quite another. A project outcome may result in equal distribution of benefits according to objective measures but may still be perceived as unfair by some groups. That is at least in part due to the fact that different groups use different criteria to assess whether an outcome is fair. When interventions do not sufficiently consider the ways that groups perceive fairness in a given environment, social cohesion can suffer. To demonstrate this point, the third section of this chapter discusses various ways of defining fairness and high-lights how incompatibilities in those approaches can cause tension across groups. Overall, as this chapter will illustrate, perceptions of justice across groups can be even more divisive than more objective measures of relative equality.[1]

The salient question for policy, addressed in this chapter, is: under what conditions are perceptions of injustice more likely to affect social cohesion or, worse, provoke conflict and violence? Beginning in the fourth section, the chapter discusses four contextual factors that emerged from the fieldwork as particularly important in exacerbating perceptions of injustice across groups. They are (1) the rigidity of group identity boundaries, (2) the potential for power groups to manipulate boundaries between groups, (3) historical legacies of social divisions, and (4) the perpetuation of trauma. Relevant examples from the fieldwork illustrate these points.

Perceptions of Injustice, Measurable Inequalities, and Intergroup Tensions

A wealth of literature has been devoted to understanding why tensions form across groups in society. Some of the work initially pointed to inequality, particularly income inequality, as a main driver of social tension and conflict (see Lichbach 1989 for a review of inequality and civil war). That connection has largely been dismissed in more recent empirical work using large samples (Collier and Hoeffler 2004; Fearon and Laitin 2003).

When the social aspects of inequality are included, however, the picture changes. As Stewart (2000) has noted, wars are conflicts between groups, not "a matter of individuals randomly committing violence against each other" (3). A number of empirical studies have shown group-based inequalities to be much more powerful mobilizing factors in social tensions and violent conflict than measures of income inequality. Inequalities across groups appear more instrumental because they often coincide with deeper ethnic or social divisions in a society (Gurr 2000; Hauge 2003; Stewart 2000, 2002; Cederman, Weidmann, and Gleditsch 2011). The influence of these "horizontal inequalities" in provoking various forms of conflict have been documented in a range of contexts, ranging from severe criminality in Brazil to civil war in Uganda and Sri Lanka (Stewart 2000). Ostby (2004) explored the relationship using a large dataset and found that societies with large horizontal inequalities—defined as disparities in education, health, and occupational opportunities across groups—had a higher risk of conflict than societies with fewer horizontal inequalities.

This growing body of work strongly suggests that horizontal inequalities become problematic when they attach to deep-rooted group identities because they can enhance grievances by some groups against others that are perceived to be relatively better off (Stewart 2000). There are many examples around the globe of contexts where income inequality among individuals is extreme, yet there is little systematic resistance to the status quo. In other cases, grievances stem from noneconomic concerns. Groups can feel injustice in political or social terms, even when economic disparities are not large. For example, people perceive the situation as unjust if they are denied citizenship rights, participation in decision making, or economic opportunities, or if they do not feel their personal dignity is respected by others (Sampson 1983).

The work for the study indicated that it is how people *perceive* the inequalities they experience—as unjust treatment of their group, or not, and how hard it is to effect change—that seems to affect whether the situation will be disruptive for society. The sense that one's group has been mistreated can motivate an individual to act even when that individual would not otherwise have done so. That is, the perceived unfair treatment of one's group may motivate an individual to participate in collective action out of solidarity, even if that person does not suffer injustice directly. As an example, a member of a marginalized group, such as the Roma in Europe, may work hard to advance socially and may even avoid identifying explicitly with her ethnicity out of fear of being stigmatized. But if she continually sees other members of her group suffering exclusion and discrimination, she may be moved to act on behalf the group, even if she is individually doing well. These perceptions can be damaging to social cohesion precisely because they are so disruptive for society.

Different Criteria for Assessing Fairness

In any context, people have certain ideas about what a "fair" outcome comprises. The criteria for assessing a fair outcome are different for different people and groups. All groups have accepted ideas as to what is just and fair. It is possible that what is considered just in one group, for one person, at one time, may be considered unjust by another person, or even by the same person in another context. As Nader (1975) stated after a review of conceptions of justice in a number of different contexts, "Ethnocentrism in all cultures probably reigns supreme in the area of justice" (153).

People use various principles when appraising a situation as just or unjust or, in the words of Tyler et al. (1997), when making "judgments about justice." Some of these are well illustrated with the help of an example adapted from Sen (2009: 12–15): Three children quarrel over a flute. One says that the flute belongs to her because she is the only one who knows how to play it; therefore, she will get the most utility out of keeping the flute and also make the most substantial contribution to society by playing it. The second child argues that he deserves the flute because he has no other toy; therefore, on the basis of need the flute should be given to him. The third child argues that the flute belongs to her, since she is the one who made it. This example highlights three different principles. The first child makes a claim to the flute on the basis of utility. The second child claims to deserve the flute on the basis of the need principle, that is, if certain groups have legitimate unmet needs for a good then they are being unfairly deprived. The third child justifies her claim to the flute on the basis of the principle of contribution or proportionality, that is, people should be rewarded according to how much they contribute. Although different observers would make different decisions about who deserves the flute, it is clear that none of the claims to justice can be easily dismissed.

A fourth principle is that of justice as an entitlement because of factors related to identity and history. In the example above, a fourth child would say that the flute belongs to him because his family is a family of flute players and this flute has been handed down through generations in his family or ethnic group. That is the argument that some indigenous communities use when contending that they have special rights related to land because they have lived there for generations.[2]

These principles are not mutually exclusive, nor do they always remain constant across individuals over time or across various situations. The same individual can use different principles when appraising situations in different contexts. Different individuals in a society may also have different conceptions of justice. Relevant perceptions of justice are discussed in a separate section.

Justice as Fairness of Process

Justice can also be understood in terms of the methods, mechanisms, and processes used to determine an outcome, rather than the outcome itself

(Lind and Tyler 1988). This notion of justice is called "procedural justice" or, in Rawls's words, "justice as fairness" (Rawls 1971). The democratic process is built on the principle of justice as fairness of process. As long as the elections are perceived as being carried out fairly, all parties accept the results, even if they would have preferred a different outcome. The notions of "rule of law" and "due process" also attempt to create procedural justice. The ability to make use of these systems is generally termed "political rights"—the rights possessed by a person or group by virtue of law. Indeed, many researchers have found that political rights are much more important than actual inequalities in shaping perceptions of injustice (Langer and Mikami 2011).

During the fieldwork in Yemen it was observed that citizens, especially youth, harbor feelings of injustice against the state because they perceive traditional processes of allocating employment as unfair. Young men and women expressed frustration that their destinies are too often determined by their tribal affiliation and the payments their families are able to make. They felt that their individual skills and achievements did not seem to matter. For example, participants at the seminar complained that the ruling regime differentiated "between people of the country by giving jobs based on party or clan affiliation," and leadership positions were given to sons of privileged elite groups. Similarly, respondents at a focus group in the southern part of Aden explained that "to get jobs, one needs someone to speak for him, particularly from Sana'a."

Similar sentiments have formed around the distribution of land in Yemen. The participants at the experts' seminar in Sana'a explained how "lands in southern governorates and Hodaidah have been expropriated and given to important government officials in the name of 'fake' investments." That was echoed at a meeting with the students of Yemen Center for Human Rights Studies, in Aden, when they mentioned how the state obtains lands "in the name of investments" and redistributes them "to VIPs freely without any charge." This sense of marginalization in the South has reinforced the southern identity against the North and the state.

Justice as Respect

A second principle for assessing justice is respectful treatment. Some researchers have argued that the most commonly reported experiences of everyday injustice involve some form of disrespectful treatment (Lupfer et al. 2000; Messick et al. 1985). In those interactions, the feeling of injustice arises because every individual feels entitled to a certain degree of respect from other individuals. The need for respect runs very deep, and reactions to disrespectful treatment can be extreme. The self-immolation of Mohammed Bouazizi because he felt that he was treated unjustly by Tunisian authorities, which triggered social protest across the Arab world, is an example. Many theorists of violence and conflict place feelings of humiliation and disrespect at the core of violent behavior (Gilligan 2001). The sense of disrespect can come from treatment by other individuals or from structures that place individuals or groups in subordinate positions. Thus on the macro level such considerations affect the propensity of the society to plunge into violence and its ability to deal with conflict (Hogan and Emler 1981; Tyler et al. 1997; Vidmar 2000).[3]

The idea that respect is a component of justice is rooted in classical Libertarian philosophy. Locke, for example, emphasized in the 17th century that individuals are born with "natural" rights that are inalienable, that is, no individual can take those rights from another, not even the individual himself. The rights include the rights to life, liberty, and property, and also the right to respectful treatment. More recently, Sen (2009) has argued in even more forceful terms that dignity and respect are essential components of justice by making access to dignity and respect a component of the basic freedoms that every individual is entitled to enjoy. Today consensus prevails among scholars that every system of law should recognize that respect and dignity are important components of just treatment, as exemplified by Pritchard's statement in his seminal article (1972: 281–82):

> Those who try to formulate substantive principles of justice should reserve a prominent place for human dignity. If this is not done the distinctively moral aspects of justice will be absent; and the claims of justice will be at best legalistic and at worst arbitrary.

Conceptions of what it means to be respected vary even among individuals. It is essentially a question of what people feel they are entitled to in others' behavior toward them. It is often difficult, even for those involved, to specify precisely what constitutes respectful treatment in a given situation. Many justice researchers have concluded that people do not operate under explicit agreements of entitlement when interacting with others. Rather, they have an implicit understanding of what is and is not acceptable in a relationship (Miller 2001) that is greatly influenced by social norms and context. It is also easy to see that if two people interacting have different conceptions of the appropriate norms of interaction, confusion can give rise to conflict. In those situations, a person can feel that they have been treated with disrespect without the other person having so intended.

The ability and willingness of an individual to respond according to the established social rules affects whether the receiver perceives an interaction as respectful or disrespectful. That is to say, if someone is able to understand the context and the antecedents of the current situation and be sensitive to that understanding in their response, it is less likely that another would feel that they are not respected. This aspect of the behavior is called "social interpersonal sensitivity" (Greenberg 1994).

Justice as Inclusion and Voice

An additional principle of justice is the degree to which groups or individuals feel that they have an opportunity to have a say in the process and the final outcome (Folger 1977; Tyler et al. 1997). In other words, if individuals feel that they have participated in the process through which an outcome was brought about, their perception of disrespect is reduced irrespective of whether the outcome is favorable to them. Such opportunities for voice and participation can be provided not only by the formal structure, such as state institutions, but also through informal structures.

In Yemen, for example, daily sessions of *qat* chewing provide an informal forum that creates a perception of participation in decision making. Every afternoon, male Yemenis get together and chew *qat*.[4] The gatherings defy social categories; there is no fixed hierarchy of seating at a chew based on status. Instead seating depends on a variety of factors, including the formality of occasion, the number present, the wishes of the host, and the order of arrival (Varisco 1986). The daily chew serves as an important forum for socializing with one's friends and neighbors, conducting business informally, and discussing current events, as well as dispute mediation and religious instruction. Wedeen (2008) has suggested that in the absence of formal democratic institutions of decision making, *qat* chewing gatherings act as substitute forums for consultation with popular opinion and have helped to mitigate to some extent tribesmen's perceptions of injustice in reference to their tribal leaders.[5]

Inclusion also relates to the extent to which people receive explanations for actions that have consequences for them (Bies and Shapiro 1987; Bobocel et al. 1998; Shapiro, Buttner, and Barry 1994). When individuals are given adequate explanations about actions affecting them, they are more likely to feel respected in an interaction and to feel that the process has been fair. Conversely, the absence of causal explanation for an unfavorable outcome undermines the feelings of interactional fairness (Bies and Moag 1986). Bies and Shapiro (1987) argue that court proceedings and the process of reaching a verdict provide a causal explanation of the final decision, which contributes to the acceptance of the decision as fair by both parties.

Along with the presence or absence of explanation, the perceived adequacy of the explanation is also important in appraising the situation as just or unjust. An essential element of the adequacy of explanation is the credibility and reputation of the actor offering it. For example, if in the past the state has acted in predatory fashion, it is less likely that citizens can accept explanations it provides as truthful. The history of the interactions of citizens with the state, therefore, has a great influence on the overall perception of (in)justice in a society.

Some seminar participants in Haiti spoke to the importance of inclusion and the adequacy of explanations in influencing perceptions of injustice and disrespect. A strong perception of injustice prevails in Haiti against the Haitian government. It was observed that Haitians generally experience the absence of avenues for establishing accountability at the higher levels of state and in the society at large as a lack of respect:

> These are the sources of our divisions: a people that is uneducated; a state that remains uninvolved and does not safeguard the interests of the people; political leaders who violate the constitution they took an oath to respect, who engage in dirty dealings with the international community in order to stay in power, and function as a clan. (a male, private sector and human rights activist)

Participants in the seminar stressed that the perception of injustice between elites and other groups has been reinforced over time by the lack of leadership and accountability on the part not only of the political leadership, but also of the economic elites. The sense of being excluded is reinforced by a perception that both decision makers and state officials are unconcerned about the interests and rights of their fellow citizens.

Contextual Factors Exacerbate Perceptions of Injustice across Groups

The previous discussion has highlighted how different groups use various criteria to assess fairness. Those criteria greatly affect how communities will receive a development intervention, and they thus have important consequences for the success or failure of operations. When these perceptions are understood in context, they can be addressed in ways that promote greater collaboration and cohesion across groups. Chapter 8 takes up the matter of discerning how communities assess justice and fairness. Here the discussion turns to contextual factors that emerged as exacerbating perceptions of injustice across groups and that therefore carry important risks for social cohesion.

Rigid Boundaries across Groups

Experience in various countries suggests that rigid boundaries around group membership exacerbate the perceptions of injustice that attach to inequalities across those groups. In "ranked societies," where groups are hierarchically ordered (Horowitz 1985), the consequences are even worse. In some situations, individuals who are part of a disadvantaged group are not able to change groups at all, or at least not without great difficulty. If members of marginalized groups are not able to move to a different group associated with a more advantageous social or economic position, they can feel that their options for change are quite narrow, such that the option of conflict becomes relatively more attractive (Stewart 2000).

Varshney (2011) has argued that group-based economic and social inequalities are enshrined in certain social orders, making those orders more prone to fragility. Specifically, social orders where ethnicity (or other attributes) and economic status of a group coincide have greater chances of conflict and greater difficulties in converging on a common interest. Varshney calls this kind of social order a "vertical structure." Examples in which such structures have been actively enforced are racial slavery in the United States, the apartheid system of South Africa, and India's caste system. In other cases, the relegation of certain groups to a subordinate social and economic status is not systematic, but more subtle, as in the case of the Roma in eastern and central Europe.

Rigid boundaries around group identity can also contribute to the internalization of injustice and stigma. Groups that have suffered discrimination and deprivation over time may come to accept the injustice as inevitable and unchangeable. It often takes an external trigger event to provoke a rethinking of this kind of systematic discrimination. For example, the Indian caste system was internalized for centuries by most of society. Social cohesion was strong among lower castes, even as they were marginalized from the broader society. Increased contact with other cultures, however, has sparked some questioning of the caste system, which has threatened social cohesion between different classes.

Rigid boundaries create greater social cohesion within the groups themselves, as group members unite against other groups. Stronger cohesion within the group means that individuals within the group identify with each other strongly, do not compete with members of the same group (for example, for an employment position), and are willing to make bigger personal sacrifices for their own group (Ellemers, Wilke, and Van Knippenberg 1993). Because they cannot move to other groups to advance socially, individuals may be more likely to work for the advancement of the group as a means of achieving prosperity and respect (Ellemers, Wilke, and Van Knippenberg 1993). That can take nonviolent paths, as in the Indian independence movement or the U.S. Civil Rights Movement, or it can include more violent means.

The markers that differentiate groups, which become the impetus for perceptions of injustice by identifying an out-group, evolve over time. The process of identification by which individuals categorize themselves into groups is strongly influenced by interaction among individuals (Barth 1966; 1969) and historical processes (Rothbart and Taylor 1992). Therefore, it is not only the "natural" markers, such as ethnicity, religion, and race, that create groups, but also interactions among individuals and social categories, so that that collective forms emerge and become the basis of action (Jenkins 1992) or of perceptions of group-based injustice. These categorizations become reinforced over time and can make the boundaries around group membership more rigid. The process is illustrated by the case of Haiti (see box 4.1).

Manipulation of Perceptions of Injustice by Power Groups

Group boundaries may be rigid in many cases, but they are not static. They can become more porous, allowing the group to expand to include a wider circle of members or even integrate with other groups. Alternatively, they can become more rigid, dividing the group from nonmembers. The dynamism of group identity boundaries implies that both the process of group formation and the markers that divide the group from others can be manipulated. The manipulation usually touches on some feeling of injustice toward other groups or toward the state. History is thick with accounts of power elites drawing on intergroup tensions to foment resentment against particular groups, usually in an effort to gain or hold onto political power (see box 4.2).[6]

BOX 4.1

Haiti: Hardening of Group Boundaries over Time

In Haiti, marked divisions between groups remain an important obstacle to building a convergence of interests in society. The divisions have their roots in the post-independence period (PE Analysis 2010). The most obvious division in Haitian society today is between blacks and mulattos, the lighter-skinned progeny of white plantation owners in colonized Haiti and their slaves. This division is, in the words of one of Haiti's ablest thinkers, Alcius Charmant, "the supreme evil of our Republic and virus that ravages it, and the road to its ruin" (quoted in Jenkins 2002).

The mulattos from the colonial period were part of the elite—a notch above the blacks—economically well-off and better educated compared to the blacks, as the plantation owners usually educated their progeny and often signed over land titles to them. Therefore, in spite of institutional discrimination against them, many mulattos became wealthy landowners, establishing themselves as a viable class. After independence, mulattos established themselves as well-off, urban-based traders in export commodities, while blacks became self-reliant horticulturalists who took up residence in mountains (Fick 1990).

Over time, the distinctions originally based on phenotype became firmly enshrined in the Haitian economic and social order. In today's Haiti, the elite class is separated from the poor majority by language, culture, religion, and economic status. Creole remains the dominant language among the majority, while French is viewed as the language of the Haitian elite. With out-migration, English is also gaining prominence among the diaspora. Similarly, the division based on religion also runs along the line of class and color. Voodoo—an amalgam of the animist cults of West Africa infused with Catholic ritual—is the dominant system of belief in Haiti. The elite, however, proclaim their adherence to Christianity (Jenkins 2002).

Haiti has become divided into a lighter-skinned, urban, economically well-off, educated, French-speaking, dominantly Christian class, and a black, rural, poor, Creole-speaking class who predominantly believe in voodoo. These divisions between the haves and the have-nots have been reinforced by external intervention (specifically the American occupation's favoring of the lighter-skinned elite in Haitian politics) and by Haitian political actors, who have either mobilized popular resentment among the majority black population or served to preserve power among the lighter-skinned elite.

Source: INURED 2011.

Manipulation of Group Boundaries in Liberia

Liberia presents a clear example of manipulation of group boundaries that reinforced perceptions of group-based injustices. Liberia has 17 major ethnic groups, most of which migrated from different areas of Africa at different times. Most have distinctive languages and cultures. Parts of the population continue to interact with one another more on an ethnic than on a national basis, particularly in Liberia's border areas. These strong links have made the boundaries of Liberia porous and citizenship within Liberia fluid.

Ethnic identities were greatly reinforced when Samuel Doe took power in 1980. Doe built ethnic alliances for strategic reasons, seeking to seize power and consolidate it. He then used the power of the presidency to build ethnic constituencies through patronage. He promoted his own tribe, the Krahn, in the government and the military and distributed resources to its members. Doe also sought and gained the support of the Mandingo ethnic group by stating that the Mandingo tribe is a Liberian tribe. That has largely been interpreted as Doe "granting" citizenship to the Mandingo (who already had rights to citizenship) and created feelings of injustice among other Liberian tribes, many of whom did not think the Mandingo should have Liberian citizenship.

Until Doe declared the Mandingo a Liberian tribe, the Mandingo had access to citizenship through the constitution, which says that all those of "negro descent" born in Liberia are Liberians. However, many Liberians consulted for the study considered the Mandingo tribe a Guinean tribe, and therefore Mandingo people would be foreigners. By saying that the Mandingo were Liberians, Doe strengthened their claim to citizenship. The Mandingo are often wealthier than other Liberians, and they see land as property (whereas others see it as inheritance). With their right to citizenship recognized, many Mandingo registered the property they used. Other Liberians saw that as an abuse: they thought of the Mandingo as guests who had no right to property; they do not recognize the deeds or titles issued by the state. The situation led many Liberians to feel that their hospitality had been abused by the Mandingo, and to Mandingo feeling that their rights were being abused by other Liberians. In the research the team ran into land disputes of this type (Mandingo with papers, native Liberian without and claiming to own the land) in two counties. In both places, the Mandingo were described as traitors, and other community members stated that they did not want to live with the Mandingo.

(continued next page)

BOX 4.2 *(continued)*

Doe did not only give preference to the Krahn. During his government, certain (and some would say most) ethnic groups did not feel safe. It seems to have started during a coup attempt by a former commanding general of the Armed Forces of Liberia, Thomas Quiwonkpa. Quiwonkpa was Gio, from Nimba County. The Gio and the Mano are allies, and Nimba County is next to Grand Gedeh County, the home of the Krahn. After the coup, Doe removed (and often killed) the Gio and Mano in his government, and even went as far as sending the armed forces (mostly Krahn at that point) to Nimba to kill supporters of Quiwonkpa. That created a deep division between the Krahn and the Gio and Mano that was evident in the makeup of the armed groups during the civil crisis. Charles Taylor, specifically, received significant support from the Gio and Mano when he first started the National Patriotic Front of Liberia.

When groups started to form against Doe, they also attacked the Krahn as a tribe. However, a Krahn chief told us that the Krahn were not really a unified tribe until then. The Krahn were approximately a dozen separate tribes that were weakly linked by language and some traditions. (In some cases the dialects are not mutually comprehensible.) However, when the Krahn were attacked as if they were a single group, they united and became a more unified tribe.

In some cases, groups can become locked in a vicious cycle wherein group identity markers are manipulated by power groups to fuel conflict, which itself further cements the group boundaries and makes it harder to emerge from conflict. The more political actors mobilize these identities to divide their group from other groups, the more in-group social cohesion is built, but that cohesion serves to divide society even more against itself.

As intergroup tensions rise, any action that is perceived as an infringement on group identity tends to add to group members' sense of injustice. Such infringements add fuel to the fire for political actors hoping to capitalize on the hardening of group boundaries. A threat to language associated with a specific community or group, for example, is an important trigger of feelings of injustice (Giles, Bourhis, and Taylor 1977). Threats to the religious beliefs of a group can also generate feelings of injustice. Declared intentions to destroy a cultural group are the most extreme form of infringement. In the narratives of victims and survivors, such things are expressed as an integral part of the violation of their rights and their emotional experience. The case of Aceh illustrates this point (see box 4.3).

BOX 4.3

Aceh: Infringements on Group Identity Fueled Conflict

The Free Aceh Movement (GAM) rebellion began in 1976, aiming to secure the territory's independence from Indonesia. The Helsinki Memorandum of Understanding (MoU), signed by representatives of GAM and the government of Indonesia in August 2005, brought an end to the GAM's separatist rebellion. Under the MoU, extensive autonomy was granted to Aceh, and supporters of the former guerrilla movement were able to compete for local government office.

A vast literature on the Aceh conflict agrees that the swell of support for the Free Aceh Movement that drove the conflict came from the feelings of injustice on the part of the Acehnese against the Indonesian government, primarily relating to economic discrimination. As the conflict progressed, the methods employed by the state to curb unrest in the area reinforced those feelings of injustice, creating a strong perception "among many Acehnese that they have repeatedly been treated unjustly, betrayed and deceived by the Indonesian state" (Aspinall 2010, 17). Violence committed by security forces against movement supporters further reinforced the movement's cohesion. The feelings of injustice interplayed with unique Acehnese identity. The prior history of conflict in Aceh, the stock of historical myths, and hardened identities that that history provided reinforced perceptions of injustices, which in turn reinforced the identities themselves.

The feelings of antagonism against the state were evident during the fieldwork that was conducted for the study. A female ex-combatant in a focus group in Piddie—an area that experienced massive violence during the conflict—expressed her feeling of injustice, which led her to participate in the conflict, as follows: "The issue of injustice was an important cause of tensions between Aceh and Jakarta. Jakarta [the government] did not keep most of its promises, which triggered the disappointment among Acehenese." During an interview, a leader of the Free Aceh Movement also described issue of injustice and reiterated that injustice toward the Acehnese by the Indonesian government was one of the main drivers of conflict. He also stated that the Helsinki MoU and the subsequent peace settlement have acknowledged these injustices and are therefore a first step toward peaceful coexistence.

Historical Legacies in Intergroup and State–Society Relationships

Events in the past have deep impact on a country's present and future. They shape the nature of institutions, the way people think about world and their agency in it, and the behaviors and relationships between groups. In addition, historical events and their interpretation shape norms and attitudes in a society, as well as the ways that behaviors are interpreted.

History affects both the way groups in society relate to one another and the way that groups relate to the state. Social interactions remain under the influence of conditions that are themselves legacies of events and actions in history. The events or actions may be salient and remembered, and may be a conscious part of the collective identity of a group, but not necessarily.

Colonization, for example, is an important and significant event that has shaped the relationships between groups of citizens in many societies. Mamdani (1996) has studied the legacies of colonialism in Uganda and South Africa and argues that they are similar to those in other parts of Africa. He claims that colonial rule reinforced the rural–urban divide and ethnic differentiation, and sometimes even created new groups, establishing relationships among groups that continue to prevail even today. Colonial rule was based on a division between a citizenship-based government, in which only "the colons" and small minorities of urbanized Africans had civil rights, and the government of the great majority of the predominantly rural population, who were constituted as "subjects" forming communities through localized institutions of autocracy and fused powers. Urban Africans would be controlled through "direct despotism," while in the countryside an indirect despotism of native commissioners and chiefs would prevail. The two modes of despotism created a divide between rural and urban classes, and decentralized despotism exacerbated ethnic divides.

Colonization often leaves behind a division between those who adopted the culture or education of the colonizers and those who retained more traditional cultures. Many southern Yemenites, for example, believe that they have inherited a governance culture from the British that has become part of their identity and is very different from the governance culture of the North. Many of these "urban Adenites" were sidelined by the post-independence Socialist Party because of their positive relations with the British authorities. The Socialist regime also excluded members of the Awaliq tribes from government and army positions (Manea 2010, 6). That has created both a gulf between the groups and a strong sense that certain groups unjustly benefit more than others in the political system.

Similar societal divides are evident in Liberia and Haiti today. Americo-Liberians and those educated in Americo-Liberian towns and villages have a very different culture from more traditional Liberians. The Americo-Liberian culture is often cast as "civilized" culture by Americo-Liberians, and even by native Liberians, and comprises a belief in Christianity, certain processes for taking care of the home, membership in specific organizations, and assignment of value to formal education. In Haiti, the elite class adopted the social and cultural attributes of the colonizers, while the poorer majority did not. That distinction underlies today's division of Haitian society into the haves and the have-nots (INURED 2011).

These historical legacies also shape the relationship between society and the state. For example, histories of violence or oppression often make state violence and oppression acceptable behaviors in a society. The Central African Republic is an example in which history has shaped a deep distrust of the state by citizens. For many years, as far back as the precolonial era of the slave hunters, the legacy left by the state includes bad memories of its violent incursions, its raids on men and products, and its repressive actions, collective punishments, and retaliatory actions. Massive evidence attests that state-building in the country over the last two centuries is a history of oppression, coercion, mass killings, and dispossession. Consequently, the lay population has been very ambivalent about the state and authority. Over time, avoidance has been the best strategy to cope with state encroachments and abuses.

Similarly in Haiti, the historical legacy of slavery, followed by a violent revolution and then by occupation by foreign forces, continues to shape the state–society relationship today. Slavery was a particularly traumatic, long-lasting institution that has had widespread effects into the future. In Haiti the impact of that legacy is marked, especially when one looks at how the coercion used by slave owners to control slaves has developed into the assertion of personal dominance through the arbitrary exercise of power (INURED 2011, 5). Patterns of arbitrary brutality and the making of "examples" as a way to obtain and maintain control can be found throughout Haiti's history. During Duvalier's regime (1957–71), a nationwide paramilitary force extirpated all actual and perceived political opposition through physical elimination of "enemies of the state," including not only those opposing the regime but their families as well (INURED 2011: 7). The Armed Forces of Haiti (FAd'H) led a three-year vendetta (1991–94) against the supporters of the first democratically elected president of Haiti, Jean Bertrand Aristide, leaving more than 300,000 persons displaced, thousands in political asylum, and tens of thousands traumatized, disabled, or dead (Goodman 2004 in INURED 2011, 11). Youth gangs also emerged from this history of violence, taking on the role of "death squads" such as the ones used against the supporters of Aristide (INURED 2011: 28).

Unresolved Trauma

The experience of trauma by groups, if left unaddressed, is a powerful vehicle for deepening perceptions of injustice across groups. The concept of trauma refers to "a response to an extraordinary event that overwhelms an individual's coping resources, making it difficult for him or her to function effectively in society" (Pouligny 2010: 7). Although trauma is understood as a set of symptoms felt at the individual level, one can also speak of collective trauma, in the sense of a series of impacts and the responses that traumatic events provoke in groups.[7] Although trauma can be caused by various kinds of events, most is known about trauma provoked by violence. Trauma on the collective level overwhelms the ability of a group, community, or society to adjust to shocks and continue with its core function.[8] Conversely, a resilient society or community is one that can respond to shocks by adapting in such a way that it continues to function effectively. The emphasis is on the capacity to perform, and not on maintaining stability, as stability may not even be the most desirable outcome in evolutionary terms (Adger 2000).

Trauma deepens divisions in society in several ways. First, it affects trust by transforming the relationships in both the public sphere (between groups, between society and the state, and within communities) and the private sphere (within families, between generations). When violence permeates daily life, as it does in wartime or where chronic violence has taken hold, people often respond by isolating themselves from others; they stay home at night, invest in security for their homes, avoid community organizing efforts, and take other measures that undermine trust (World Bank 2010; Pouligny 2002). Trauma can also contribute to the increase of harmful behavioral patterns, such as rape, domestic violence, and the general normalization of violence, as people reenact the traumatic events (van der Kolk and McFarlane 2006). Collective action becomes harder to facilitate where trauma has taken hold (Coletta and Cullen 2000).

Trauma can transform identities, hardening the distinctions groups draw between "us" and "them." The way traumatic events are remembered has enormous consequences for group identities. The memories deeply affect representations of the collective self, including questions about what characteristics define the group and distinguish it from out-groups. Narratives can be constructed around traumatic events that paint them as attacks against group identity, mobilizing a deep sense of injustice against the enemy group. These "chosen traumas" are depicted as blows to the group's identity and self-esteem and glorified in the retelling across generations (Volkan 1989, 2006). Over time, chosen traumas may come to determine everything from the way a group dresses, to the way they speak to each other and other groups. Chosen traumas may be used to justify revenge against other groups to restore the group's honor or dignity. In the immediate aftermath of violence, competing narratives about the trauma often arise that attempt to give meaning to the traumatic event. In some cases, master narratives of violence are entwined in nation-building processes and become central to national identity. Israel and Armenia are two examples. Such processes serve to reinforce group cohesion, but they also create deep divisions with those who are excluded from the narrative. Trauma can thus be a source both of cohesion and of fragility.

Certain structural factors exacerbate the impact of trauma. They include direct exposure to violence. The more individuals were directly exposed, the stronger the impact on the collective level. The duration of the violence or other traumatic event also matters, as does the intensity of the violence and the specific forms it takes. Sexual violence or mutilations have been established as generating stronger traumatic effects than other forms of violence (Asher, Banks, and Fritz 2008).

The persistence of insecurity is particularly strong in reinforcing trauma. Ongoing violence and insecurity exacerbate the feeling of lack of control over one's situation and environment, creating additional stresses (Basoglu et al. 2005) and reinforcing the sensation that one has no "breathing space in which to unpack one's issues" (Wessells 2008, 7). As chronic violence takes root and changes social behaviors, it can lead to erosion of trust, loss of mobility, and other conditions that make it harder for individuals and communities to heal, as has happened in many postconflict situations that now are plagued by high levels of common crime and violence (World Bank 2011). Internally displaced people living in refugee camps often continue to face violence in their communities, which can hinder healing and engender more traumas. In one study of 26 countries by the Internal Displacement Monitoring Center, the people moved to areas where they continued to face violent attacks, many of them targeted specifically at their settlements (IDMC 2008).

The loss of livelihood can reinforce trauma, particularly for displaced populations. Traumatized groups often feel a sense of deep loss, both material and immaterial. Displaced populations experience the loss of their homes and being forced into a new environment, which many times is hostile. In most cases displacement implies impoverishment, as people lose access to their assets, find themselves with occupational skills that do not fit their new environment, or are shut out of the local economy. These difficulties are compounded by the daily challenges of trying to fit into a new place, often suffering hunger, living in an uncertain economic climate, and the social stresses of not being able to fulfill their roles as parents (Poulingy 2010). The dependence on external aid is often experienced as an "injury to the spirit" (Pouligny 2010: 25). These issues are taken up again in chapter 8 in the discussion of operational implications.

This chapter has argued for closer inspection of the perceptions that groups hold about what is fair or not in society because those perceptions are often more influential in intergroup relationships than measurable outcomes such as income inequality. When groups feel that they have been treated unfairly by another group or by the state, that sense of injustice can seriously compromise social cohesion, hinder collective action, and create the potential for conflict. Alternatively, when people's perceptions of fairness and justice are well understood and acknowledged, they can be tempered to facilitate greater collaboration and mobility across groups.

Certain contextual factors strongly influence perceptions of injustice across groups and thus threaten social cohesion. First, the rigidity of group boundaries can reinforce such perceptions, even as it increases social cohesion within the group. That is, if individuals cannot easily move from a disadvantaged to a more privileged group, their perceptions of unjust treatment relative to the other group are reinforced. Perceptions of injustice are also influenced by the manipulation of group boundaries by power actors. History is full of examples of leaders who have mobilized group identity markers (ethnicity, religion, race) to unify a group against other groups. This mobilization further entrenches perceptions of injustice relative to other groups and can be particularly disruptive for broader society. Historical legacies influence perceptions of injustice by shaping the way groups interact with one another and with the state. The legacies of colonization and slavery are examples of how history sets down patterns of interaction that can continue to divide societies long after the historical event has passed. Finally, the experience of trauma, particularly from violent events, can solidify perceptions of injustice in ways that further isolate groups from one another.

Chapter 5 now moves to another critical element of social cohesion—the interaction between institutions in society.

Notes

1. It is recognized that policy makers need to draw a balance between actual inequalities and perceptions of injustice. Paying attention to perceptions of injustice does not disregard the importance of actual inequalities; it merely indicates that, in addition to actual inequalities, perceptions of injustice are also extremely important in building social cohesion. The problem becomes even more complex with the observation that perceptions of injustice do not always correlate with actual inequalities. For example, see Langer and Mikami 2011.
2. It is important to distinguish in this example that identity groups would not be claiming just any land, but the specific land occupied by their group.
3. Research has termed this kind of justice "interactional justice" (Bies and Moag 1986; Cropanzo and Greenberg 1997; Skarlicki and Folger 1997).
4. Varisco (1986) has likened *qat* chewing in North Yemen to wine in France and beer in England. "The Yemeni discriminates varieties of *qat* similar to the way in which the French discuss wine. The average Yemeni enjoys the fellowship of chewing with his friends the way that the English enjoy a beer in the local pub" (8).
5. These sessions do not typically involve women. The example is used to convey that informal forums can be used to provide opportunities for participation.
6. Many scholars have attributed violence among various groups (most notably ethnic groups) to elite machination and politicking (for example, see Tambiah 1986; 1996).
7. Many authors object to the application of the concept of trauma to refer to large groups. See for example Barselou (2005) on the need to avoid psycho-pathologizing the process of social reconstruction. Others find fault with the tendency to apply lessons from individual trauma to the collective level, on the grounds that "what is required psychologically for an individual to recover from trauma and be reconciled with the past (or with the perpetrator) need bear no resemblance to what might be required for a society to do so" (Hatay 2005). See Pouligny 2010, 10, for a discussion.
8. The relationship between individual and collective trauma is not well understood, but several hypotheses exist. As summarized in Pouligny 2010, individual trauma may affect the communities and societies via (1) the existence of a large group of individuals displaying trauma symptoms in the group; (2) affecting the way victims of trauma think of themselves

and the group; (3) the perpetrator–victim cycle of violence and trauma; and (4) intergenerational effects.

References

Adger, W. Neil. 2000. "Social and Ecological Resilience: Are They Related?" *Progress in Human Geography* 24 (3): 347–64.

Asher, Jana, David L. Banks, and Scheuren Fritz, eds. 2008. *Statistical Methods for Human Rights*. New York: Springer.

Aspinall, Edward. 2010. "Political Economy Analysis: Aceh, Indonesia." Background paper for *Societal Dynamics and Fragility: Engaging Societies in Responding to Fragile Situations*. Washington, DC: World Bank.

Barsalou, Judy. 2005. "Trauma and Transitional Justice in Divided Societies" Special Report 135, April. Washington, DC: U.S. Institute of Peace.

Barth, Fredrik. 1966. *Models of social organization*. Royal Anthropological Institute.

Barth, Fredrik, ed. 1969. *Ethnic Groups and Boundaries: The Social Organization of Cultural Difference*. London: Allen and Unwin.

Basoglu, M., M. Livanou, C. Crnobaric, T. Franciskovic, E. Suljic, D. Duric, and M. Vranesic. 2005. "Psychiatric and Cognitive Effects of War in Former Yugoslavia: Association of Lack of Redress for Trauma and Posttraumatic Stress Reactions." *Journal of American Medical Association* 294 (5): 580–90.

Bies, R. J., and J. S. Moag. 1986. "Interactional Justice: Communication Criteria of Fairness." In *Research on Negotiation in Organizations*, ed. R. J. Lewicki, B. H. Sheppard, and M. Bazerman. Greenwich, CT: JAI Press.

Bies, R. J., and D. L. Shapiro. 1987. "Interactional Fairness Judgments: The Influence of Causal Accounts." *Social Justice Research* 1: 199–218.

Bobocel, D. R., S. E. Agar, J. P. Meyer, and P. G. Irving. 1998. "Managerial Accounts and Fairness Perceptions in Conflict Resolution: Differentiating the Effects of Minimizing Responsibility and Providing Justification." *Basic Applied Social Psychology* 20: 133–43.

Cederman, Lars-Erik, Nils B Weidmann, and Kristian S. Gleditsch. 2011. "Horizontal Inequalities and Ethno-Nationalist Civil War: A Global Comparison." *American Political Science Review* 105 (3): 478–95.

Colletta, N. J., and M. L. Cullen. 2000. *The Nexus between Violent Conflict, Social Capital and Social Cohesion: Case Studies from Cambodia and Rwanda*. Washington, DC: World Bank.

Collier, Paul, and Anke Hoeffler. 2004. "Greed and Grievance in Civil War." *Oxford Economic Papers* 56: 563–95.

Cropanzo, R., and J. Greenberg. 1997. "Progress in Organizational Justice: Tunneling through the Maze." In *International Review of Industrial and*

Organizational Psychology, ed. C. L Cooper and I. T. Robertson. New York: Wiley and Sons.

Ellemers, N., H. Wilke, and A. Van Knippenberg. 1993. "Effects of Legitimacy of Low Group or Individual Status on Individual and Collective Identity Enhancement Strategies." *Journal of Personality and Social Psychology* 64: 766–78.

Fearon, James, and David Laitin. 2003. "Ethnicity, Insurgency and Civil War." *American Political Science Review* 97: 75–90.

Fick, Carolyn E. 1990. *The making of Haiti: The Saint Domingue revolution from below.* University of Tennessee Press, Knoxville.

Folger, R. 1977. "Distributive and Procedural Justice: Combined Impact of Voice and Improvement on Experienced Inequity." *Journal of Personality and Social Psychology* 35:108–19.

Giles, H., R. Y. Bourhis, and D. M. Taylor. 1977. "Toward a Theory of Language in Ethnic Group Relations." In *Language, Ethnicity and Intergroup Relations,* ed. H. Giles. New York: Academic Press.

Gilligan, James. 2001. *Preventing Violence.* New York: Thames and Hudson.

Greenberg, J. 1994. "Using Socially Fair Treatment to Promote Acceptance of a Worksite Smoking Ban." *Journal of Applied Psychology* 79: 288–97.

Gurr, Ted. 2000. *People versus States: Minorities at Risk in the New Century.* Washington, DC: United States Institute of Peace.

Hatay, A. J. 2005. "Peace-Building and Reconciliation in Bosnia Herzegovina, Kosovo and Macedonia 1995–2004." Uppsala University Department of Peace and Conflict Research, Uppsala.

Hauge, Wenche. 2003. "Causes and Dynamics of Conflict Escalation: The Role of Economic Development and Environmental Change—A Comparative Study of Bangladesh, Guatemala, Haiti, Madagascar, Senegal and Tunisia." PhD diss., Faculty of Social Sciences, University of Oslo, Oslo.

Hogan, R., and N. Emler. 1981. "Redistributive Justice." In *The Justice Motive in Social Behavior,* ed. Melvin Lerner, 12–143. New York: Plenum Press.

Horowitz, Donald L. 1985. *Ethnic Groups in Conflict.* Berkeley: University of California Press.

IDMC (Internal Displacement Monitoring Center). 2008. *Global Overview of Trends and Developments in 2008.* Geneva: IDMC.

INURED (Interuniversity Institute for Research and Development). 2011. "Societal Dynamics and Fragility in Today's Haiti." Background paper for *Societal Dynamics and Fragility: Engaging Societies in Responding to Fragile Situations.* Washington, DC: World Bank.

Jenkins, Christopher. 1992. *Rethinking Social Policy: Race, Poverty and the Underclass.* New York: HarperCollins.

Jenkins, Karen. 2002. "Traumatized Societies: Social Cubism and the Predatory State of Haiti." *ILSA Journal of International and Comparative Law* 8: 901.

Langer, Arnim, and Satoru Mikami. 2011. *Relationship between Objective and Subjective Horizontal Inequalities: Evidence from Five African Countries.* Tokyo: JICA.

Lichbach, Mark I. 1989. "An Evaluation of 'Does Economic Inequality Breed Political Conflict?' Studies." World Politics, 41(4): 431–70.

Lind, E. Allan and Tom R. Tyler. (1988). *The Social Psychology of Procedural Justice.* Plenum Press, New York.

Lupfer, M. B., K. P. Weeks, K. A. Doan, and D. A. Houston. 2000. "Folk Conceptions of Fairness and Unfairness." *European Journal of Social Psychology* 30: 299–346.

Mamdani, Mahmood. 1996. *Citizen and Subject: Contemporary Africa and the Legacy of Late Colonialism.* Kampala, Cape Town and London: Fountain Publishers, David Philip Publishers, James Currey Ltd.

Manea, Elham. 2010. "Societal Dynamic and Fragility: Yemen." Background paper for *Societal Dynamics and Fragility: Engaging Societies in Responding to Fragile Situations.* Washington, DC: World Bank.

Messick, D. M., S. Bloom, J. P. Boldizar, and C. D. Samuelson. 1985. "Why We Are Fairer than Others." *Journal of Experimental Social Psychology* 21: 480–500.

Miller, Dale. 2001. "Disrespect and the Experience of Injustice." *Annual Review of Psychology* 52: 527–53.

Nader, Laura. 1975. "Forums for Justice: A Cross Cultural Perspective." *Journal of Social Issues* 31 (3): 151–70.

Ostby, Gudrun. 2004. *Do Horizontal Inequalities Matter for Civil Conflict?* Oslo, Norway: Center for the Study of Civil War, International Peace Research Institute (PRIO).

Pouligny, Beatrice. 2002. "Building Peace in Situations of Post-Mass Crimes." *International Peacekeeping* 9 (2): 201–20.

———. 2010. "Resistance, Trauma and Violence." Background paper for *Societal Dynamics and Fragility: Engaging Societies in Responding to Fragile Situations.* Washington, DC: World Bank.

Pritchard, Michael. 1972. "Human Dignity and Justice." *Ethics* 82: 299–313.

Rawls, John. 1971. *A Theory of Justice.* Cambridge, MA: Belknap Press of Harvard University Press.

Rothbart, M., and M. Taylor. 1992. "Category Labels and Social Reality: Do We View Social Categories as Natural Kinds?" In *Language, Interaction and Social Cognition*, ed. G. Semin and K. Fiedler, 11–36. London: Sage.

Sampson, Robert. 1983. "Structural Density and Criminal Victimization." *Criminology* 21 (2): 276–93.

Sen, Amartya. 2009. *The Idea of Justice.* Cambridge, MA: Belknap Press of Harvard University Press.

Shapiro, D. L., E. H. Buttner, and B. Barry. 1994. "Explanations for Rejection Decisions: What Factors Enhance Their Perceived Adequacy and Moderate

Their Enhancement of Justice Perceptions." *Organizational Behavior and Human Decision Processes* 58: 346–68.

Skarlicki, D. P., and R. Folger. 1997. "Retaliation in the Workplace: The Roles of Distributive, Personal and Interactional Justice." *Journal of Applied Psychology* 82: 434–43.

Stewart, Frances. 2000. "Crisis Prevention: Tackling Horizontal Inequalities." *Oxford Development Studies* 28 (3): 242–62.

———. 2002. "Horizontal Inequalities: A Neglected Dimensions of Development." QEH Working Paper Series. University of Oxford, U.K.

Tambiah, Stanley. 1986. *Sri Lanka: Ethnic Fratricide and the Dismantling of Democracy*. Chicago: University of Chicago Press.

———. 1996. *Leveling Crowds: Ethno-nationalist Conflicts and Collective Violence in South Asia*. Berkeley: University of California Press.

Tyler, T. R., R. J. Boeckmann, H. J. Smith, and Y. J. Huo. 1997. *Social Justice in a Diverse Society*. Boulder, CO: Westview.

van der Kolk, Bessel A. and Alexander C. McFarlane. 2006. *Traumatic Stress: The Effects of Overwhelming Experience on Mind, Body, and Society*. The Guilford Press; 1 edition, November 1, 2006.

Varisco, D. M. 1986. "On the Meaning of Chewing: The Significance of *Qat* (catha edulis) in the Yemen Arab Republic." *International Journal of Middle East Studies* 18: 1–13.

Varshney, Ashutosh. 2011. "Identities, Social Justice and Citizenship." Background paper for *Societal Dynamics and Fragility: Engaging Societies in Responding to Fragile Situations*. Washington, DC: World Bank.

Vidmar, Neil. 2000. "Retribution and Revenge." In *Handbook of Justice Research*, ed. Joseph Sanders and Lee Hamilton. New York: Kluwer Academic.

Volkan, Vamik. 1989. "Cyprus: Ethnic Conflicts and Tensions." *International Journal of Group Tensions* 19 (4): 297–316.

———. 2006. "What Some Monuments Tell Us about Mourning and Forgiveness" In *Taking Wrongs Seriously: Apologies and Reconciliation*, ed. Elazar Barkan and Alexander Karn. Stanford, CA: Stanford University Press.

Wedeen, Lisa. 2008. *Peripheral Visions: Publics, Power, and Performance in Yemen*. Chicago: University of Chicago Press.

Wessells, Mike. 2008. "Trauma, Peace-Building and Development: An African Region Perspective." Paper presented at the Trauma, Development and Peace-Building Conference, Delhi, India, September 9–11.

World Bank. 2010. *Violence in the City: Understanding and Supporting Community Responses to Urban Violence*. Washington, DC: World Bank.

———. 2011. *2011 World Development Report: Conflict, Security and Development*. Washington, DC: World Bank.

Social Cohesion and Interactions between Institutions

Through the fieldwork, the study sought to understand the relationship between institutions and fragility. That focus stemmed from the fact that so much of the existing literature on fragility deals with the importance of institutions, and so much of policy in fragile situations is oriented toward building more effective institutions. During the focus groups and interviews with people in the five sites, the team tried to unpack the notion of effective institutions from the perspective of people living in fragile situations.

The findings on that topic were somewhat surprising. From observations and in conversations with research participants, in addition to the quality, strength, and effectiveness of different types of institutions, the *quality of interactions* between different types of institutions seemed to matter. Of course, the effectiveness of individual institutions and the interaction among them are related; one might reasonably assume that an institution that is able to interact constructively with other institutions is itself relatively efficient. But this relationship is not a given. In many cases, people felt that particular institutions were good at performing their specific functions but were unable to interact effectively with other institutions. Overall, it was emphasized that unconstructive interactions between types of institutions—which can take a variety of forms—tend to harm social cohesion by reinforcing divisions between groups.

To illustrate these dynamics, this chapter focuses on one category of institutional interactions that emerged as especially problematic in the five case studies: those between formal, state institutions and customary institutions.[1] At first glance, the formal, state rules for different activities may seem completely disconnected from the way people actually do things in practice. Over time, communities develop their own ways of doing everything from starting a business and resolving conflict, to getting married or burying a loved one. They may interact little, or not at all, with the state system in these matters; in fact, they may be unaware of the formal rules established to govern those interactions. In other cases, the state may co-opt customary institutions, or try to manipulate them, loosening their accountability to the communities they serve. In still other cases, customary and state institutions may operate in conflict, ultimately undermining each other and reinforcing societal divisions. The consequence of these unconstructive interactions is that the activities of different institutions are not synchronized with one another and may even work against one another. That is, the cumulative effect of unproductive interactions can be a more fragmented society.

The following sections discuss some particular interactions observed in the fieldwork and their relationships with fragility in the five study countries. The first section begins with an example of constructive interactions observed in Aceh that were perceived to have a positive impact on cohesion. That is followed by descriptions of some problems associated with unconstructive interactions observed in different sites, and how they seem to be affecting social cohesion. The final section turns to the role of civil society institutions and suggests that they can help improve the quality of interactions between customary and state institutions when they are sufficiently enabled to do so.

Constructive Interactions between Customary and State Institutions, and Social Cohesion

Customary institutions embody the cultural and social norms governing everyday life. They regulate how people interact to solve problems, to start or run a small business, or even to get married and raise families. The norms may bear little resemblance to the formal rules present "on the books" to govern those interactions. In many cases people may not even be fully aware of the formal procedures or laws that exist.

The mismatch between formal, state rules and procedures and the way people actually get things done in their everyday lives often results in a strong preference for customary institutions over state ones. In some cases, customary institutions can generate more culturally sensitive outcomes

BOX 5.1

Categories of Institutions

Institutions are generally characterized as either formal or informal.[a] Formal institutions emanate from the state and include constitutions, statutes, laws, and other government regulations, as well as agencies and organizations, whereas informal institutions generally refer to nonstate institutions, including codes of behavior, which originate from and are enforced and managed by the society.[b] Because the characterization of institutions as formal or informal is not necessarily consonant with the way people experience or perceive them, in practice the differentiation between informal and formal institutions is not really helpful.

The fieldwork done for the study reported in this book suggested that three broad categories of institutions are important for societal dynamics: traditional and customary institutions, state institutions, and civil society institutions. All three types of institutions can facilitate convergence across groups, but they differ in the specific functions they serve and the groups that access them.

Customary institutions embody the community's prevailing perceptions about the world and transmit the community's values from one generation to another through imitation, oral tradition, and informal teaching. The legitimacy of these institutions is rooted in inheritance or other historical mechanisms of leadership selection (Domingo 2010).

State institutions, which also include institutions officially recognized by the state, have an influence over people's lives and day-to-day functions. State institutions take the form of constitutions, statutes, common law, and the organizations associated with enforcement of those rules, such as police, the military, and the courts. The state also extends into the market sphere by providing many of the institutions that regulate markets.

Civil society institutions are formed when groups of citizens organize outside the government to further a particular public interest. "Civil society" refers to the arena of uncoerced collective action around shared interests, purposes, and values. In theory, its institutional forms are distinct from those of the state, family, and market, though in practice the boundaries between state, civil society, family, and market are often complex, blurred, and negotiated. Civil society is populated by organizations such as registered charities, development nongovernmental organizations, community groups, women's organizations, faith-based organizations, professional associations, trade unions, self-help groups, social movements, business associations, coalitions, and advocacy groups.

(continued next page)

BOX 5.1 *(continued)*

The *private sector* occupies an intermediate space between the state or public sector, civil society, and the realm of informal enterprises. Though in some cases it is considered part of civil society, its function is distinct in that it is focused more narrowly on developing the business environment and private or family economic interests.

Notes

a. In addition to formal and informal, categorization of institutions includes local-central, state or nonstate, and traditional-modern.

b. For example, Milgrom, North, and Weingast (1990) use this categorization.

---

than state institutions because they are rooted in social norms. This preference is often especially strong in the arena of conflict resolution. In many customary legal systems, conflicts are addressed through a long consultative process, in which respected or influential members of the society participate, and which aims both to reach a solution that is accepted by both parties and to preserve the relationship between them. Consequently, the primary enforcement mechanism of the decisions made by the formal courts is also socially based. Social pressure—such as the possibility of being ostracized and other social sanctions—is important in ensuring that the parties accept and honor the decision in the case. In Central African Republic, a number of people interviewed mentioned that putting someone in jail was doing nothing to repair the damage caused by the behavior of the perpetrator. Similarly, Isser, Lubkemann, and N'Tow (2009) found in their extensive survey in Liberia that people prefer to use customary forums because those institutions are more attentive to the underlying issues driving the conflict, and not only the conflict event itself, and thus are more effective in promoting reconciliation.

In some cases, customary institutions have managed to govern quite effectively in the absence of state presence. Practitioners and scholars of fragile situations have often pointed out that there is never a complete institutional void; even where the state is virtually inexistent, customary institutions step in to fulfill basic functions (Pouligny 2010). In some particular cases, governance by customary institutions has been quite exemplary. The example of Somaliland is often cited as a case in which, in the context of total state collapse, social institutions were able to fill the institutional void. Elders and other social leaders effectively drew important connections across different ethnic groups, enforced norms against violent behavior, and contributed to successful, peaceful elections in 2002. The case was all the more notable given that the rest of Somalia was experiencing open warfare, as were some of its neighbors.

In Aceh, the study documented the perception that formal and customary institutions have integrated their functions so as to interact constructively most of the time. These constructive interactions hold great potential to reinforce convergence across groups. Customary institutions (*adat*) in Aceh play an important role in coordinating the social life of communities.

In the post-Suharto era, a series of laws were passed that granted special autonomy to Aceh. In this context, *adat* institutions were revived and recognized by the state. Under the new law, the *imum mukim* (a traditional leader of a supra-village-level institution consisting of a number of villages) controls the land and resources within his own territory, including forest, land, rivers, lakes, mountains, and wetlands. An inventory of a *mukim*'s material wealth is regulated and endorsed by the *bupati* (the head of district) or *walikota* (the city mayor) through agreement and consultation with the people in the *mukim* and the *keuchik* (head of each village in the *mukim*) (Syarif 2005). In addition to these leaders are village-level leaders who administer their own communities. *Panglima laot,* or "sea commanders," administer the use of resources in coastal areas; *panglima uten*, or "forest chairmen," administer the use of land in forest areas; and *kujruen blang*, or "rice field chairmen," regulate the use of rice fields. These traditional leaders issue regulations on such matters as opening up new land for use, cutting the trees, livestock breeding, determination of when to irrigate, division of irrigation water, and others. They also resolve disputes among farmers in forests and rice fields.

With the formalization of these customary *adat* institutions, their leaders are paid a stipend by the state and also receive equipment (for example, a motorbike) to allow them to fulfill their responsibilities effectively. They are still chosen by their communities through elections, but they are no longer appointed for life. (In some places visited for the study, however, most of the leaders remain in their positions for a lifetime when the community does not feel the need to replace them). Access to land and control over land and forest within *adat* territories are still subject to national government regulations. Administrative secretaries, who are part of the civil service, are also attached to each village head.

In addition to *adat*'s roles in the regulation of wealth, the role of *adat* institutions in dispute resolution has also been formalized. The law provides that formal law enforcement authority should give the opportunity to the *keuchic* and *imum mukim* to settle disputes at the village and *mukim* level respectively. Some more severe cases like murder are directly referred to the state authorities. The law also provides that if within a month local authorities cannot resolve a dispute, the case should be referred to formal mechanisms. In almost all the villages visited for the fieldwork in Aceh, most disputes and conflicts are handled by the traditional authorities. The law also provides that the *adat* decision issued to the parties in dispute can be given consideration by legal enforcement authorities in resolving cases, if the cases are referred to them. Usually the formal authority requires a written statement from the *imum mukim* that the case could not be resolved in the community. In addition to adjudication, *adat* institutions can also impose sanctions on the guilty party. The sanctions include advice, warnings, requiring a public apology followed by a forgiveness ceremony, compensation, isolation from members of the village community, eviction from the village, revocation of *adat* titles, and others, in line with local customs.

The integration of customary and formal institutions has not been achieved uniformly in all areas. For example, in Saree the institution of *palima laot* (sea commander) has been formalized; in Sukamulia village (*Aceh Besar*) the institution of *panglima uten* (forest chairman) has not been formalized yet. That provided an opportunity to observe the implications of formalization by comparing the cases of Saree and Sukamulia.

In the case of Saree, the field study illustrated many of the assertions made regarding the positive effects of formalizing customary institutions. Citizens and local leaders alike recognized that formalization of the customary institution of *palima laot* led to an increase in the flow of resources to citizens. For example, fishermen in a Saree focus group stated that "when fishermen need assistance in the form of a ship to go down to the sea, they, through the sea commander, ask for assistance from the Ministry of Fisheries." In Sukamulia village, where the institution of forest chairman has not yet been formalized, greater access to resources from the state was the most eagerly anticipated effect of formalization.

The second positive benefit was associated with the broadening of customary institutions' jurisdictions. Both citizens and local leaders suggested that formalization has led to the widening of the sea commander's jurisdiction, with a positive effect on community life. For example, the sea commander can now resolve disputes in which the parties belong to other villages or even other *mukims* (the number of such disputes has increased with the use of motor boats rather than traditional boats) with the help of state authorities. A sea commander of Saree reported that "if the violators [of *adat* law] resist and disobey us, then the local government structure and its vertical elements will come down to protect and back us up." In contrast, the office of forest chairman, which has not been formalized in Sukamulia village, is unable to deal with illegal loggers (who, the focus group participants reported, did not belong to the community). The leaders and the users of these institutions hoped that formalization of the institution of forest chairman would strengthen the capacity to deal effectively with the loggers.

Problems Associated with Unconstructive Interactions Observed in the Field

Aceh provides an important example of how interactions can be constructive and contribute to social cohesion, although that did not come without trade-offs (see below). Elsewhere the study documented more unconstructive interactions, which were judged to have negative impact on social cohesion.

Confusion and Forum Shopping

One set of problems with interactions between institutions observed in the fieldwork stemmed from situations in which customary and state institutions were operating in competition with one another. That can happen in contexts where formal rules are not systematically enforced, with the result that citizens ignore or try to violate them. In an even more destructive scenario, informal institutions structure incentives in ways that are incompatible with the formal rules: to follow one rule, individuals must violate another (Helmke and Levitsky 2004). Particularistic informal institutions such as clientelism, patrimonialism, clan politics, and nepotism are among the most familiar examples, where informal norms are applied within the state structure with potentially harmful consequences for society.

The team observed two main problems with this kind of situation: First, the competition between customary and state institutions creates confusion among participants in the system. This dynamic can further sideline already-marginalized groups. For example, minority groups who do not share the dominant culture may not believe that formal institutions are legitimate and thus may prefer to use their customary institutions. If they are obligated to use formal institutions, they may hardly understand the principles behind their operation, and that puts them at a disadvantage.

The second issue arises in circumstances where citizens have access to both traditional and state institutions. Then the parties can engage in forum shopping, choosing the one that is most likely to rule in their favor. As one example, two parties may wish to resolve a dispute between them, but disagree on which institution to use, even if both have equal access to both institutions. Such a disagreement can be based on different meaning systems, different cultural backgrounds, or different economic and political interests. If each party chooses a separate institution to resolve the conflict, the result can be two separate and competing rulings, leaving the parties no closer to resolution of the dispute. One party can decide "ex-post" to take the case to the other forum if the decision is not in his favor.

These dynamics are exemplified by Liberia, where the dual existence of customary and statutory law has created confusion about land ownership and left some landowners at a disadvantage compared to others who have better access to both systems, as described below.

At the time of Liberia's founding, two different systems of laws were recognized in the constitution—statutory law that was to govern "civilized" Americo-Liberians and missionaries, and customary laws to govern "natives," non-Christian, indigenous Africans. The natives could not access statutory law, and conversely, village chiefs could not adjudicate a dispute to which an Americo-Liberian was a party. Although the constitution, statutory laws, and common law of the formal legal system now apply to all Liberians, the customary Rules and Regulations Governing the Hinterland still refer to the adjudication of cases for "civilized people" and "natives" (International Crisis Group 2006: 7). The dual nature of the legal system is recognized in current statutory law.

The competing existence of these two forms of law has resulted in a great deal of legal ambiguity about the role of the customary legal system and its place in Liberia's overall justice sector (Isser, Lubkemann, and N'Tow 2009: 13). Forum shopping is a common issue. One study documented how "cases may jump from the customary chain into the formal one and vice versa at nearly any point, due to the assertion of authority by a member of one or the other chain, or by choice of one of the litigants" (Isser, Lubkemann, and N'Tow 2009: 23).

The fieldwork documented similar dynamics. People in the communities recognize that there are two types of laws. However, many Liberians do not understand formal statutory law. Seminar participants stressed that the parallel existence of customary and formal institutions allows the powerful to choose the system that best serves their interest for a given issue, whereas others have fewer alternatives. The system can thus further marginalize groups that do not know how to use it to their own benefit.

These problems are especially evident in the area of land tenure. There are at least three different laws that deal with land tenure and land ownership: The constitution, the Hinterland Law, and the Public Law. However, these laws do not speak to one another. The Liberian constitution articulates the division between customary law and statutory law generally, but then refers specifically only to "property" in the formal, private property sense, when in practice property is articulated very differently in customary law. The Public Law also only mentions the generic term "property," without articulating what it means under customary tenure.

Liberian customary land tenure is based on three fundamental concepts.[2] The first concept is that customary group connection to specific land areas in Liberia is based on the idea of early and later arrivals. The distinction between groups (including their descendants) who arrived first in certain areas of the country and in the chronology of the founding of particular settlements, versus those who arrived later, is a primary customary land concept that serves as a foundation for customary legal arbitration in relation to land. Such descent laws are used to exclude outsiders or restrict in certain ways their rights to land. First-comers in this context are believed to have almost ultimate legitimacy in a customary sense to rights to land. In many cases this concept provides the basis for those in the first-comer group to make laws affecting the transfer of land, inclusion and exclusion of others, and what rights various segments of local inhabitants have and do not have, such as the right to build houses, farm, plant trees, and bury the dead. The second postulate that sets customary belief apart from formal institutions is that land cannot be subdivided or inherited privately and that lineage lands belong to the dead, living, and unborn. Under this arrangement, land rights are vested in communities and are prohibited from sale. The community may be families, a tribe, a clan, or villages (Unruh 2009).

Statutory law does not recognize these principles. For example, the ownership of land by a group or clan is not recognized by the state just because that group had settled on it. The provisions in statutory law claimed that land that was owned by "native" Liberians according to customary institutions actually belonged to the state, when land had clearly been occupied and used for a long time under customary law. Therefore, the land was "public" or "nonprivate." According to the statutory law, therefore, the land could be sold by the state for various purposes. In essence, therefore, whoever buys this land from the state does not recognize the ownership of the group who had lived on it for generations and had considered that the land belonged to them. Conversely, the group or clan that has occupied the land through generations does not recognize the ownership of whoever bought the land from the state, as they understand land to be inalienable.

The conflicts inherent in the two systems have created deep and volatile animosity between people who prefer or refer to different systems of law. The parallel existence of different forms of law also creates ambiguity, which in turn allows opportunism, manipulation, and expropriation through conversion of "nonprivate" holdings into private holdings, reinforcing the sense of injustice among Liberians who adhere to customary law.

Forum shopping was also observed in Yemen, where the confusion caused by the competing systems has been manipulated by elites. The 1990 constitution frames the formal justice system of unified Yemen and designates *Sharia* as a principal source of legislation. Customary law and its application are subordinated to *Sharia* in codifications such as the Civil Code of the Yemen Arab Republic, which states that customary law is only deemed lawful when consistent with Islamic *Sharia* (as determined by the judge). Further restrictions added in latest civil code define what constitutes "lawful custom"—a custom that is "general and long-established, and does not conflict with the public order and public morality." In addition, certain customary laws, such as *hudud* (Quranic crimes) and *lian* (sworn allegation of adultery by a spouse), among others, have been expressly excluded by the statutory law. There is evidence that the customary system does indeed continue to handle those cases, however, and that tribal laws still seem to be dominant in most areas of Yemen (see, for example, Manea 2010).

Customary law in Yemen is often referred to in Arabic by the term *urf*, which is both a code of conduct and a legal code. There are different kinds of customary laws, such as market customs, but the most prominent in the Yemeni context is the tribal custom.[3] Tribal customs regulate "public responsibility," such as protection of persons, honor, and crime, and also define the code of conduct and legal rules for personal matters such as marriage, divorce, and inheritance. In tribal or rural areas, tribal members are usually bound by tradition to refer to the customary law, rather than formal law. In the fieldwork, participants emphasized that it is often considered shameful for people to go to formal courts for resolution of conflicts rather than relying on customary institutions. The fact that formal courts were hard to access and entailed more complicated processes reinforced this tendency.

The confusion and uncertainty around the application of tribal law, *Sharia*, and formal law have been manipulated by the elite, especially those connected to the government through the extended patronage network established by the previous government. The elite have been able to take advantage of the gap between the two legal systems to appropriate land, property, and assets. This manipulation has been more intense where customary institutions are weaker vis-à-vis formal institutions, such as the coastal regions. In the fieldwork, this issue appeared as a major source of discontent and perceptions of injustice.

Loss of Accountability

Another problem associated with unconstructive interactions between institutions that was observed in the field was loss of accountability of customary leaders, stemming from changing relationships with formal institutions. The most prominent example of this dynamic was observed in Yemen, where customary leaders had been co-opted by the state through local governance reform.

In Yemen, the tribe forms the basic unit of society; it regulates the lives of its members through customary laws. Tribal leaders derive their legitimacy by ensuring the enforcement of these customs using various social sanctions. They also mediate among members of their tribes and ensure enforcement of their decisions. One's tribal affiliation strongly determines one's opportunities, from access to education to formal employment. The Yemeni state, since independence, has progressively sought to assert its authority over the tribal structure by co-opting tribal leaders into the formal structure.

In North Yemen (Yemen Arab Republic), the tribes and their leaders had effectively penetrated the state through their representation in the bureaucracy, army, and legislative bodies. In the early 1960s, tribes were formally incorporated in the state structure. That institutionalization converted the political connotation customarily associated with the term "sheikh"—which referred to a religious leader or an honorary notable—into a political entity. It also created what Elie (2009) calls "tribal libertarianism," in which tribal leaders forged political allegiances with the state as it suited them through private agreements. While tribal leaders provided political support to the weak regime in the center, the central regime distributed rents to the political leaders. This practice persists as of the time of this writing.

In the South (former People's Democratic Republic of Yemen), although the colonization by the British tended to minimize the role of tribes in urban areas (particularly the port town of Aden), the tribe remained the primary unit of social structure elsewhere. After unification in 1990, the incorporation of tribal leaders into formal institutions was reinforced through the introduction of the "sheikh system," which in practice was the "whole-sale transfer of the tribal social structure in North Yemen" to the unified state (Elie 2009). In 2000, the government of Yemen enacted a comprehensive reform of its governance system aimed at decentralizing the administrative apparatus and delegating authority and power to locally elected representatives. This system formally preserved the rule of the sheikh, as most local-level positions are now held by tribal leaders.

Following the local governance reforms, sheikhs have become easy targets for co-optation, which gives the opportunity to the weak Yemeni state to push its agenda outside Sana'a without carrying state-building efforts in the rural areas (Philips 2008). In return for political support, tribal leaders get a number of perks and privileges. The Department of Tribal Affairs regularly provides stipends to tribal sheikhs throughout the country either in cash or in kind. They also get preferential access to development goods and are able to secure employment for many of their constituents, sometimes as "ghost employees" (salaries paid to nonworking employees) in the public sector.

This co-optation into the state's patronage system has changed the relationship of tribesmen with their sheikhs. Traditionally a tribal sheikh has often needed the support of and consensus from tribal members to assume his leadership. He was often regarded as a man among equals, and his function as a sheikh entailed this devotion to the tribe and its needs. This is clearly expressed in the tribal proverb, "The master of the people is their servant." With co-optation, tribal sheikhs are no longer exclusively dependent on their tribes for their influence and often live in the capital, Sana'a, away from their own constituency. Since the tribal system has been institutionalized, instead of being representatives of their tribes to the state, tribal sheikhs of Yemen have become representatives of the state to their tribes (Fattah 2011).

The co-optation of tribal leaders has also facilitated corruption, allowing some tribal sheikhs to benefit personally at the expense of the tribe, and has left the tribe without mechanisms to hold them accountable. By some accounts, tribal leaders have also started to abuse their power. News reports have often alluded to the existence of tribal prisons run by sheikhs, who use them to intimidate and terrorize their own tribesmen (Manea 2010). In the fieldwork, participants emphasized that these dynamics, along with the inadequacy of the state's provision of services, have increased the feeling of exclusion among some groups. They also spoke of abuses of power by the sheikhs, claiming that "the state granted security enforcements to sheikhs in the tribal areas, which gave them more power in their areas and weakened the state existence" (field seminar in Sana'a).

Customary Institutions' Loss of Discretion in Decision Making

A separate problem observed in the field had to do with the loss of discretion on the part of customary institutions as a result of their interaction with state institutions. Partly this stems from the loss of knowledge and context that occurs when customary laws are codified into formal law. For example, customary dispute resolution institutions often prioritize preserving the relationship between disputing parties over other goals, such as compensation. The institutions necessarily rely on solid knowledge of the relationships in the community to come to decisions that maintain harmony. Formalization often implies the codification of customary mechanisms into standardized procedures, and as a result, traditional decision makers lose discretion in making decisions. Consequently, the decision is not as effective or efficient as it would have been if the rules were fluid. In other words, codifying the rules may not be able to provide justice as perceived and demanded by the community members in a specific context.

The loss of discretion was observed in Aceh. The formalization of customary institutions meant loss of discretion in making decisions because of the codification of laws. As discussed above, one of the main attributes of customary institutions is that their decisions are context-specific. Codification and application of universal laws may not result in the most efficient decision for every context.[4] Participants in focus groups in Aceh expressed their preference by arguing that *adat* law can take the social and cultural context into account in making decisions and is therefore preferred by communities over formal institutions and laws. A participant in a seminar in Aceh expressed this in the following way: "The world is occupied by diversity; the *adat* communities are able to take advantage of this diversity while formal institutions cannot since they have to apply equal treatment to each person." In a focus group, one participant expressed the need for discretion in applying laws in the following way: "Someone should be sanctioned depending on how much he can afford. If he is sanctioned, he will be sanctioned based on what the village head thinks will not burden him" (focus group, Bebasan). They argued that codification of *adat* laws will not be able to deliver justice in a way that the community wants.

Moreover, many focus group participants expressed the view that the full meaning of customary law and local customs could not be translated into written form. Important context and meaning are inevitably lost in the codification process. "Every action we do is arranged in the custom;

there is too much to be written" (village secretary, Bener Meriah, focus group). People understand the meanings and logic behind the rules, which are passed down through generations and, participants insisted, cannot be taught in a formal way. Therefore, when traditional laws are codified, they said, a lot of this information is lost. Every decision is not based on the people's perception of justice. When people do not receive justice as they understand it, it further alienates the conflicting parties, breeds conflict, creates perceptions of injustice, and contributes to fragility in the society.

Collapse of Both State and Customary Institutions

An additional and more extreme problem observed in the field occurred as a consequence of weakness of both state and customary institutions. In this case, the weakness of both types of institutions does not allow for constructive interactions between them, leaving the population without solid measures for resolving conflict, accessing services, and meeting other basic needs. These dynamics were observed in both the Central African Republic and Haiti.

In Central African Republic, both the state and the customary institutions are weak, leaving large gaps in service delivery, conflict resolution, and mechanisms for collective action. The state has a long history of predation, reaching back to the 17th and 18th centuries and the slave-trading kingdoms that were situated in the area and nearby regions. The slave trade resulted in massive migrations from the surrounding areas. The period of slave trade was then followed by a particularly oppressive colonial order. The French, far from their bases in West Africa, implemented a model of private concessions. Those concessions had practically full power over the territory and the population that inhabited it, with minimal supervision from colonial authorities. The obsession was to extract quick profit from the natural resources at the lowest possible cost. Because of the distance to the ports, portage was enforced in a very violent way.

The impact of this system on the population was horrendous. In the 1920s, concession companies started to introduce new crops, such as cotton and coffee cultivation, but because the change was introduced at the same time as the poll tax, it had the effect of making farmers quasi slaves on their own land, as most of their revenues were appropriated by the state in the form of the poll tax. Following independence, the new state, needing to control a large, relatively underpopulated territory with very limited resources, continued with a predatory approach to development, following many practices inherited from colonial times.

For much of its history, the main state presence in Central African Republic has been in the form of armed men representing central authority at the local level—rendering justice, resolving disputes, and being paid and fed in exchange. The population learned how to handle that presence over time, whether by escaping or through a variety of arrangements with authority that looked like anything but a social contract.

The history of escapism and brutality also tremendously eroded the customary institutions that were already extremely weak in the 19th century. Today's customary institutions tend to be a mix of remnants of the ancestral structures, maintenance of the colonial system of chieftaincy established in the early 20th century, and a number of coping mechanisms that have been elaborated by the local population over the years. Over time, the power and knowledge of many traditional leaders, even village healers, have been lost (Marchal 2010).

In these circumstances the interaction between the customary systems and the state is extremely weak. The state has made some attempt to expand its reach by formalizing the local chieftaincy system, but in practice the system works in a very imperfect fashion. In some way both the state and the customary systems are too weak, especially in rural areas, to interact efficiently, leaving many local problems unresolved.

One manifestation of the weakness of both customary and state systems in resolving local problems in a constructive manner is the increasing use of witchcraft. In the Central African Republic, "witchcraft" refers to the manipulation by malicious individuals of powers inherent in persons, spiritual entities, and substances to cause harm to others.[5] In an environment of exposure to unmanageable dangers, doubts, and fears in virtually every aspect of ordinary life, witchcraft provides a framework of moral agency that can make sense of seemingly random coincidences in space and time (Evans-Pritchard 1937). In undeserved misfortune—suffering that cannot be satisfactorily construed as justified punishment or as self-inflicted—the invocation of witchcraft provides ways of understanding by blaming the malice of another person as the source of suffering. Ashford (1998) calls this struggle "spiritual insecurity"—the condition of anger, doubt, and fear arising from exposure to the action of unseen forces bent on causing harm.

Witchcraft is not a new phenomenon in Central African Republic, but its recent resurgence has been quite dramatic. Extreme poverty and very weak basic services delivery have resulted in the erosion and collapse of social networks (trust, connections, traditional and customary institutions, and civil society connections across groups) (MacGaffey and Bazenguissa-Ganga 2000; Meagher 2004). Fisiy (1998: 158) also stresses, in analyzing the resurgence of witchcraft in Cameroon, that to understand the underlying factors fueling the practice of witchcraft, "it is tempting to situate the answer in the context of the persistence of economic crisis and worldwide globalizing tendencies [which] . . . has led to the collapse of community-based safety nets. Where life changes have become uncertain . . . alternative interpretations of the human condition have flourished . . . . It is in this context of uncertainty that one should look for explanations for the remarkable resurgence of witchcraft accounts all over Africa."

It seemed in the fieldwork that this resurgence of witchcraft—itself a product of a deep institutional void—was overwhelming the capacity of customary institutions to deal with its negative effects. In the past, witchcraft had been used, but informal systems were in place to handle allegations of witchcraft and resolve the underlying conflicts. People complained that now the traditional chiefs had disappeared and were replaced by people with much less legitimacy and ability to resolve the problems of the community. There was a sense that the traditional healers, the *nganga*, were no longer able to effectively address witchcraft and other social problems because they had lost their knowledge. This lack of social regulation of witchcraft allows people to prey on each other and made some groups particularly vulnerable, especially women and children. People wanted to see some checks and balances on the practice but did not agree on how or by whom rules should be made and enforced.

In Haiti, interactions between weak customary and weak state institutions are similarly problematic, but in different ways. As in the Central African Republic, the people of Haiti have over time developed a strong distrust and skepticism toward the state. Generally speaking, "average citizens from all walks of life are more likely to seek to protect themselves from such [state] institutions, rather than to approach them either as putative service providers or good-faith arbiters in everyday affairs" (INURED 2011: 19). The idea that the state is something one must guard against comes from the historical role of the state as an outsider and as an extractive presence.

Avoidance of the state by many Haitians is rooted in the legacy of a predatory state presence. In the past the contact of many Haitians with the state was limited to the presence of the military as an instrument of control and surveillance and government tax collectors. Both were understandably unpopular. Those functionaries have since been replaced by local elected representatives, and there is a perception that things have improved as a result. However, even with those improvements, the average Haitian perceives little benefit in terms of resource distribution, as the proceeds from decentralization are quite small or may be siphoned off for uses other than the intended ones. In addition, a sense prevails that new political processes intended to increase popular participation have instead simply replicated the top-down approaches of the past. The small presence of the national police in many rural areas is sometimes perceived as evidence of the limited and strained interactions with state institutions (INURED 2011).

These dynamics play out in a context of social organization that is ill-suited to support convergence across groups. In Haiti, the concept of community—in the sense of a group of people, usually living in close proximity and with some shared access to resources, or with a shared identity—did not develop in most of the country. Nor is there a history of indigenous organization based on solidarity and communality. Instead, "Haiti's kinship system is bilateral and, for all intents and purposes, quite 'shallow,' not lending itself to kinship-based group formation . . . even over time" (INURED 2011: 20). Relationships of patronage are most common, such as those between sharecroppers and landowners, or rural children and wealthier "godparents" in urban areas. These types of relationships are beneficial to both parties but do not accommodate the formation of broader relationships across groups.

Indeed, this social structure often works against the building of convergence by emphasizing competition and individualism. Access to patrons generates intense competition and conflict. The same applies to access to "external" resources brought in by the state or nongovernmental organizations (NGOs) in the form of microcredit, employment, or other opportunities. The insertion of development projects into this vertical structure has been problematic in many cases because leaders quickly appropriate the resources for distribution through bilateral channels, often provoking the collapse of the common enterprise and the erosion of trust among the collaborators.

Some forms of horizontal cooperation and organization have arisen in Haiti, most of them promoted and fostered during the 1970s by local agriculture and peasant organizations. These were later supported by some international organizations, with some success (White and Smucker 1997) in the form of small groups (called *gwoupman*) involved in agricultural cooperatives, revolving credit funds, and other collective activities. These structures remain the exception, but they represent a potential source of cohesion to counterbalance the negative effects of the existing social organization.

Based on observations of various forms of interaction between state and customary institutions, a fundamental question arises—What are the factors, institutional, social, and political, that give rise to one form of interaction over the other, and what is the process through which a constructive interaction can emerge? In other words, what has led to a constructive interaction in Aceh but an unconstructive one in Liberia? Although this question is a natural next step for research, it is beyond the scope of the present study.

The Role of Civil Society in Improving Interactions between Customary and State Institutions

Civil society institutions potentially have an important role to play in fragile situations by improving the quality of interactions between customary and state institutions.[6] They occupy a middle ground between the two systems. They can bring people together around interests, purposes, and values, creating links among individuals and groups across social and cultural cleavages. These links, or "bridging", networks can act as agents of peace in times of conflict or can be instrumental in preventing conflict (Varshney 2010). Civil society institutions can also help individuals develop a sense of identity that transcends ethnic, religious, or other social boundaries (Wollenbaek and Selle 2002; Rebosio 2010). In Yemen, for example, many recently formed youth organizations, some heavily financed by the private sector, connect youth to one another for social support and help in searching for jobs, dealing with financial problems, and organizing community activities. Participation in the practices of these associations also has the potential to instill in its members habits of cooperation, solidarity, and public spiritedness (Newton 1999). It can also help individuals develop skills in organizing, mobilizing, and problem solving (Godfrey and Sheehy 2000; Rebosio 2010).

Also in Yemen, the National Water Resources Authority (NWRA) co-funds the activities of local water users associations and helps enforce rules on water use. It appeared in the fieldwork that the coupling of modern technology (brought by the NWRA) with traditional decision-making structures was an effective way to manage these resources fairly. Members of a water users association in Kalyba village, in Taiz, told the research team that since the establishment of the association in 2008, 30 to 40 illegal wells had been closed, of which 22 had been buried. Similarly it was noted that the local police often act on information from the water users association to prevent illegal drilling.

A different example of civil society playing this mediating role was observed in Central African Republic. There, with the support of international NGOs and the United Nations Development Program, civil society is helping to improve interactions between customary and formal justice institutions by establishing houses of justice. They help the population access justice and resolve conflicts by mediating between customary and formal justice systems and by helping people have fair and informed access to state justice and mediation systems. The houses of justice are open to anyone, but some target vulnerable groups such as poor women or minorities. They provide advice, information, mediation services, and legal assistance. Some international NGOs (including the Danish Refugee Council) have a program of outreach to avoid the worst cases of violence linked to witch hunts. The houses of justice are particularly effective at resolving conflict, and they seem to be quite popular. They represent an interesting example of civil society helping people who must deal with customary and state systems, ensuring that they can have the most beneficial support from one or the other.

Some faith-based institutions often play an important role in mobilizing collective action. They are among the most grassroots-based civil organizations. In Haiti, both *vodoun* and the Catholic Church have traditionally been very active in connecting people across various identity groups. *Vodoun*, in particular, represents an important source of cohesion because of its recognized role as a "key social and cultural achievement of Haiti's traditional majority culture," with the potential to build relationships across different groups in society (see text box) (INURED 2011: 25). However, not all faith-based organizations are successful in promoting cohesion because their reach or interests may be limited. In Yemen the mosque and the local *imam* play an important role, and Islamic charities are a crucial source of social support. They also are fundamental in providing a normative framework that the population demands. A similar dynamic is occurring with Christian sects in Central African Republic. However those religious groups, in contrast to more established religious organizations like the Catholic Church, are relatively localized and have less ability to foster connections across communities. Their contribution to social cohesion may be limited, particularly if they are intolerant of other religions or unable to integrate into the larger community. In particular, the "pentecostalization" of some streams of Christianity has been damaging to relationships across groups because it requires members to renounce all other sources of spiritual sustenance and shun friends or family members who do not do the same; it prioritizes personal advancement and achievement over values of solidarity and community (Adams 2011; INURED 2011).

BOX 5.2

Religious Institutions in Haiti: A Source of Cohesion and Connection

Vodoun is the religion of the majority of Haitians. A defining characteristic of *vodoun* is that, in contrast to most religions, it is not based on faith or belief. The spirits that are served in *vodoun*—the *lwa*—are asserted to exist in the world independently of whether one believes in them. The *lwa* are linked to all Haitians at birth and are passed along through bloodlines through the generations. A Haitian can choose to serve the *lwa* or not, but cannot negate their existence by choosing not to believe in them. It is this element of *vodoun* that has made it enormously resilient to the influx of other religions, most notably the Catholic and Protestant churches. Rather than being extinguished by these new beliefs, *vodoun* was able to absorb them and integrate them into the notion of the *lwa*.

Vodoun rituals, which usually take place once a year, are some of the largest collective undertakings in Haitian history, bringing together upwards of five hundred to a thousand people in some cases for periods ranging from several days to several weeks. These rituals convoke a group of common heirs (*eritaj*), who share an *lwa* ancestor. As they have persisted over time, *vodoun* rituals represent an important long-term achievement of collective action and management of a common (spiritual) resource by large numbers of people, spanning many different groups (INURED 2011).

The Catholic Church also has traditionally played an important role in connecting groups across various social divides and in mediating between the state and society more broadly. Its role has not always been positive for all groups. Over the course of Haiti's history, the church has been a force for both good and ill, dating back to colonization. During slavery, the church both endorsed the process of enslavement and ministered to the slaves. In the 20th century, Francois Duvalier obtained approval from the Vatican to nationalize the church hierarchy and thus ensure its service to the state. The dynamics shifted in the early 1980s when the church, following the Liberation Theology movement elsewhere, then helped incite and sustain the popular movement that toppled Jean-Claude Duvalier. The church played various (often controversial) roles in the years that followed, including supporting the election of Aristide, a priest, to the presidency. Today the Catholic Church continues to play a harmonizing role by giving voice to those who have opposed abuses by political powers and promoting values of reconciliation, solidarity, and nonviolence. Some parts of the Protestant church community in Haiti also play a similar role, although their history and reach are much more limited.

Source: INURED 2011.

Civil society organizations face several important challenges in carrying out this connecting function between society and the state. In fragile situations, generally speaking, what civil society organizations can do is limited, often because of capacity issues. Civil society organizations can be important in helping deliver economic and social services, but they sometimes lack legitimacy and are not well established to mediate across groups. For example, in Yemen the government for many years had sponsored water users associations that performed an important job and were relatively well integrated into village life. However, participants in the fieldwork perceived that these associations were not powerful enough to deal with complex governance issues, such as managing scarce underground resources. In addition, several members of government and high-ranking civil servants had created NGOs, which enabled them to influence civil society debates and had attracted funding from donors and the private sector. As a result, civil society was seen as not able or willing to establish connections across groups and was only minimally effective at service delivery.

These capacity challenges are often reinforced when civil society institutions try to meet demands for project implementation. The most efficient civil society organizations in fragile situations are usually the first ones tapped by donors and international organizations to be project implementers. Their staff may receive training from those organizations, and the organizations themselves gain an important source of funding from the arrangements. But whereas donors' reliance on local civil society groups for service delivery undoubtedly improves service delivery in the immediate term, it can have more detrimental effects over the longer term. Local staff who have received training from international organizations may be wooed away to work for those organizations themselves, draining the human capital of the local institution. Perhaps more important, treating civil society organizations as primarily project implementers diverts time and resources away from their broader role of promoting greater state accountability. That can ultimately undermine the work of civil society institutions in creating and advocating strategies for development (Schirch 2011).

Risk also exists that effective civil society organizations, or their leaders, will be co-opted by political interests. In Haiti, participants in the national seminar expressed frustration that many of the traditional leaders (*notabs*) had become "corrupted brokers" when they began to act as intermediaries between communities and the state. That dramatically reduced their legitimacy in the eyes of the communities they were serving. Similarly, in

Yemen, the process of establishing local water users associations under the NWRA had a tendency to fall victim to patronage politics and corruption in some instances. Members of the water users association in Sai'yon told the team that they "get disappointed when drillers bribe the police so that they will ignore the illegal drilling process, which puts the association in direct conflict with the farmers."

In sum, civil society is a very heterogeneous category and will reflect a diversity of views, motivations, and capabilities in a particular context. It cannot be assumed that civil society will want to, or be able to, play a positive role in improving interactions across institutions. Yet the potential is undeniably there. This topic is taken up again in more detail in chapter 8, where recommendations for supporting civil society in ways that increase cohesion are discussed.

Moving Forward: Understanding How Social Cohesion Affects Broader Relationships in Society

The previous chapters have described in detail two key factors that emerged in the fieldwork as particularly important for fragility: the perception of injustice across groups and the quality of interaction between institutions. The present chapter explored the nature of interactions between institutions, arguing that the quality of these interactions has an important relationship with the degree of social cohesion in society. Constructive interactions among institutions can help connect people across groups in society, whereas unconstructive interactions reinforce divisions. These interactions and their effects look very different in different contexts, as the examples show.

The present chapter applies an analytical lens emphasizing societal dynamics to particular relationships in society. The purpose of that is to show how considering societal dynamics opens up for analysis a range of salient issues that a traditional approach to fragility—with a central focus on the state—might miss.

Notes

1. The emphasis on interaction between state and customary institutions does not suggest that that is the only interaction that matters or that it is somehow more important than the interaction between, say, civil society and

state institutions. The limitations of time and scope of the study required choices, and this node of interaction emerged the most prominently in our fieldwork.

2. Much of this discussion is derived from Unruh 2009.

3. The majority of Yemen's rural population—more than 70 percent—self-identify as tribal members.

4. There is of course a downside to allowing discretion in dispute resolution mechanisms. If rules do not apply equally to each person in every situation, discrimination can occur. The need is greater to ensure consultation and consensus on all decisions—instruments that community-based dispute mechanisms tend to rely on heavily.

5. "Witchcraft" also refers to a great many occult and supernatural forces (Ashford 1998).

6. It must also be noted that not all civil society organizations support values or activities that connect across groups. Sometimes they can espouse values and promote practices that discriminate, promote violence, or create divisions within a society (Rebosio 2010). Examples are vigilante groups, ethnic militias, and gangs. These groups can be quite cohesive internally, but their purposes are to protect a set of narrow interests that may go counter to the interests of broader society, isolating them from other groups.

References

Adams, Tani Marilena. 2011. *Chronic Violence and Its Reproduction: Perverse Trends in Social Relations, Citizenship and Democracy in Latin America.* Washington, DC: Woodrow Wilson International Center for Scholars.

Ashford, Adam. 1998. "Reflections on Spiritual Insecurity in Soweto, South Africa." *African Studies Review* 41 (3): 39–67.

Domingo, Pilar. 2010. "Informal Institutions, Social Cohesion and Fragility." Background paper for *Societal Dynamics and Fragility: Engaging Societies in Responding to Fragile Situations.* Washington, DC: World Bank.

Elie, Serge. 2009. "State–Community Relations in Yemen: Soqotras Historical Formation as a Sub-National Polity." *History and Anthropology* 20 (4): 363–93.

Evans-Pritchard, E. 1937. *Witchcraft, Magic and Oracles among the Azande.* Oxford: Clarendon Press.

Fattah, Khaled. 2011. "Yemen: A Social Intifada in a Republic of Sheikhs". Middle East Policy, Vol. XVIII, No. 3, Fall 2011.

Fisiy, Cyprian. 1998. "Containing Occult Practices: Witchcraft Trials in Cameroon." *African Studies Review* 41 (3): 143–63.

Godfrey, S., and T. Sheehy. 2000. *Civil Society Participation in Poverty Reduc-tion Strategy Papers*. London: Department of Foreign Investment and Development.

Healy, K., and G. Meagher. 2004. The Reprofessionalization of Social Work: Col-laborative Approaches for Achieving Professional Recognition. British Journal of Social Work, 34(2), 243–260.

Helmke, Gretchen, and Steven Levitsky. 2004. "Informal Institutions and Com-parative Politics: A Research Agenda." *Perspective on Politics* 2: 725–40.

ICG (International Crisis Group). 2006. "Liberia: Resurrecting the Justice Sys-tem." *Africa Report*. Brussels: International Crisis Group.

INURED (Interuniversity Institute for Research and Development). 2011. "Soci-etal Dynamics and Fragility in Today's Haiti." Background paper for *Societal Dynamics and Fragility: Engaging Societies in Responding to Fragile Situations*. Washington, DC: World Bank.

Isser, Deborah, Steven Lubkemann, and Saah N'Tow. 2009. "Looking for Justice: Liberian Experience with and Perceptions of Local Justice Options." *Peace-works*. Washington, DC: United States Institute of Peace.

MacGaffey, Janet, and Remy Bazenguissa-Ganga. 2000. *Congo-Paris: Trans-national Traders on the Margins of the Law*. Oxford: International African Institute.

Manea, Elham. 2010. "Societal Dynamic and Fragility: Yemen." Background paper for *Societal Dynamics and Fragility: Engaging Societies in Responding to Fragile Situations*. Washington, DC: World Bank.

Marchal, Roland. 2010. "Central African Republic: A Political Economy Analy-sis." Background paper for *Societal Dynamics and Fragility: Engaging Societies in Responding to Fragile Situations*. Washington, DC: World Bank.

Milgrom, Paul R., Douglas North, and Barry Weingast. 1990. "The Role of Insti-tutions in the Revival of Trade: The Law Merchant, Private Judges and the Champagne Fairs." *Economics and Politics* 2 (1): 1–23.

Newton, Kenneth. 1999. "Social and Political Trust in Established Democracies." In *Critical Citizens: Global Support for Democratic Governance,* ed. Pippa Norris, 169–187. Oxford: Oxford University Press.

Phillips, Sarah. 2008. *Yemen's Democracy Experiment in Regional Perspective: Patronage and Pluralized Authoritarianism*. New York: Palgrave Macmillan.

Pouligny, Beatrice. 2010. "Resistance, Trauma and Violence." Background paper for *Societal Dynamics and Fragility: Engaging Societies in Responding to Frag-ile Situations*. Washington, DC: World Bank.

Rebosio, M. 2010. "Civil Society in Fragile Contexts: A Guidance Note." Unpublished.

Schirch, Lisa. 2011. "Beyond Beneficiaries." U.S. Institute of Peace, Interna-tional Network for Economics and Conflict, Washington, DC. http://inec.

usip.org/resource/beyond-beneficiaries-changing-landscape-local-civil-society-development-efforts.

Syarif, Sanusi M. 2005. *Gampong dan Mukim di Aceh: Menuju Rekonstruksi Paska Tsunami.* Bogor: Pustaka Latin.

Unruh, Jon. 2009. "Land Rights in Postwar Liberia: The Volatile Part of the Peace Process." *Land Use Policy* 26: 425–33.

Varshney, Ashutosh. 2010. "Identities, Social Justice and Citizenship." Background paper for *Societal Dynamics and Fragility: Engaging Societies in Responding to Fragile Situations.* Washington, DC: World Bank.

White, T. A., and G. R. Smucker. 1997. "Social Capital and Governance in Haiti: Traditions and Trends." In *Haiti Poverty Assessment,* vol. 2, ed. World Bank. Washington, DC: World Bank.

Wollenbaek, D., and P. Selle. 2002. "Does Participation in Voluntary Association Contribute to Social Capital? The Impact of Intensity, Scope and Type." *Nonprofit and Voluntary Sector Quarterly* 31: 32–61.

CHAPTER 6

Changing Relationships and Social Cohesion

Many fragile contexts are facing dramatic social changes that shake the very structures of society. The globalization of communications media offers new modes of interacting that may directly contradict traditional norms for behavior; enhanced mobility allows people unprecedented access to different cultures and ideas; and advanced technologies seem to speed the pace of human interaction. Exposure to these changes creates stress on any society, affecting the way individuals and groups relate to one another. In fragile situations, their impact may be exacerbated if the social structures governing relationships are too rigid to adapt appropriately.

This chapter deals with three areas of relationships that are particularly affected by rapid social change. First, rapid social shifts have provoked population movements, creating tensions between migrant populations and their hosts. Second, the relationship between youth and their elders is also shifting today, as young people are exposed to new opportunities and ideas and have, in some ways, more options to challenge social traditions. Finally, relationships between men and women are increasingly under stress in a globalizing world, as both sexes take on new roles to meet the demands of a changing economic and social climate.

These relationships are closely interlinked with one another and with other issues presented earlier in the book, but they are discussed separately here. They do not pretend to encompass the full range of relationships that are affected by social changes today. They were selected because they are among the most pressing concerns in the field sites and because they affect most fragile situations, if not all.

The three issues are explored in this chapter through an approach emphasizing societal dynamics. Specifically, each is analyzed in terms of how it interacts with the societal dynamics introduced in the two previous chapters. It is hoped that taking such an approach will highlight important relationships and divisions that are often underexplored in designing and implementing development interventions. These relationships will undoubtedly look different in different contexts, and so the analysis is necessarily general; it is intended mainly to demonstrate the value of applying the lens of societal dynamics.

Population Movements

Migration changes the demographic makeup of a state, region, or community and thus has important implications for the functioning of society.[1] When populations move out of a country and into a host country, or when they return to a home country, they influence the intergroup relations and institutions in their environment. Migrants often significantly change their norms and values, their perceptions of their state and communities, and their expectations for the future. Communities where migrants settle also have to adapt to a different group of individuals, who bring with them different norms, values, and behaviors. Depending on how long these populations stay, they may also expect rights to citizenship, to participation, and to have their culture reflected in local institutions. In cases where migrants are returning to their home country, they may bring back with them outdated or otherwise mistaken concepts of local power dynamics and cultures, creating divides between themselves and populations that did not emigrate.

The reason for the migration of a particular group strongly influences how that group interacts in its new environment. Migration can be driven by the presence or lack of economic opportunities; in other cases it is a forced displacement due to violent conflict or political persecution. Some groups migrate repeatedly, driven by different reasons. A group may have originally emigrated for economic reasons, then find itself a persecuted minority that must flee for political reasons, only to become part of a diaspora that influences events in their home country, to which the group may or may not return. The needs and desires of these groups are quite different, depending on the reason for the migration, and they pose different challenges and opportunities for the host society.

Those who are forcibly displaced face a set of particularly intense problems. Most displaced people are in protracted displacement that has lasted more than five years. Even where people are able to return from displacement, that does not in itself ensure durable economic and social reintegration. Forcibly displaced populations may bring with them trauma from violence, the loss of land or livelihoods, and other challenges. Those, in turn, affect how they will integrate into their new environment, the expectations they have of their host society, and how long they intend to stay there.

In countries suffering from fragility and conflict, an influx or continued presence of large numbers of displaced people can strain institutions, and the areas can become breeding grounds for crime, conflict, and instability.[2] Refugees and internally displaced people may compete with host populations for scarce resources including water, food, housing, and medical services, and for natural resources such as grazing land for livestock or firewood. That can create tensions with host communities, leading to more conflict. In other cases displaced populations can integrate with, or even strengthen, the local economy, but even then, winners and losers are created. These complex dynamics represent important challenges for both host and displaced communities, as well as for the international community.

How the migrant group is received by the host community or country is also an important influence on interactions with native groups. As groups settle and resettle in different parts of the world, diversity increases, creating challenges for host communities and for migrants. Management of diversity is difficult in all circumstances. The extensive literature on migration and integration in the European Union illustrates the challenges there. Even in the United States, a country made up of immigrants, debates surrounding present-day migration create a great deal of controversy and division. "As a result, governments across the world are increasingly engaged in finding ways to manage the diverse societies and groups that form part of the countries they govern" (Marc 2010).

Historically, migrants were expected to assimilate into the dominant culture in their new community. They were expected to follow the norms and values of the new community if they wanted to advance socially and economically. For example, in the United States the first groups of Italian immigrants to arrive largely isolated themselves in ethnic enclaves, keeping their language and culture alive and limiting their economic activities mostly to other immigrants. In turn, broader American society stigmatized the group, which limited their access to jobs and other opportunities. It was only the second generation that began to assimilate culturally and socially and achieved important advancements (Gans 1962). The cost of that advancement was the abandonment of much of their culture.

Today one can point to many examples of migrants beginning to reject the notion that their culture of origin should be a private matter and that they should assimilate to the dominant host culture. In these cases, migrants hold to the customs of their location of origin more rigorously than they would have done at home. (Ratha, Mohapatra, and Scheja 2011: 18). In some cases, that attachment to the culture of origin can cause deep divides with the dominant culture. In fact, research shows that *in the short run*, migration and ethnic diversity can reduce social solidarity and social capital because societies are fragmented into different identity groups (Putnam 2007: 137).

Other migrants find a middle ground, interacting with individuals in the dominant culture while keeping the culture of their origin alive. This creates a positive environment for a multicultural identity to form (Guarnizo, Portes, and Haller 2003; Faist and Gerdes 2008, in Ratha, Mohapatra, and Scheja 2011: 18).

Increased In-migration and Perceptions of Injustice across Groups

Migrants to a new community or country bring with them particular expectations of their hosts. They may expect to find temporary refuge from political persecution or war, economic opportunities, a chance at more stable livelihoods, or other benefits. Some cross-border migration is widely accepted (Adepoju 2005, in Ratha, Mohapatra, and Scheja 2011: 14), but sometimes immigrants, even from neighboring countries, are treated as unwanted foreigners (Crush 2000, in Ratha, Mohapatra and Scheja 2011, 14). Perceptions of injustice and disrespect can arise because of multiple factors, including increased competition for resources, lack of understanding of the reasons for actions, or differing norms and values. The sense of injustice can also reflect real losses for a particular group, including property loss or loss of networks. In addition, the sense of injustice and disrespect can also be due to the idea that the "other" is not doing things "the right way." This problem is particularly important when populations are displaced for long periods.

In the case of international migration, the legal status of new arrivals is often ambiguous, raising questions about citizenship and entitlements. Large-scale immigration can raise questions about a nation's identity if it has many groups that are excluded from citizenship (Ratha, Mohapatra, and Scheja 2011: 3). Countries where there is large-scale immigration may have trouble determining at what point the immigrants may become citizens and acquire the right to participate in society. In some cases displaced populations remain present for generations in a host country without ever acquiring formal, legal status there. The Palestinian refugee camps in Lebanon are but one example. Without formal status it becomes impossible for first- or even second-generation immigrants to assimilate because they may be denied access to jobs, education, or other means of livelihood. If returning home is not an option, they remain in a state of limbo, and that can be a source of instability for society.

In many contexts, citizenship itself becomes a resource and a potential source of exclusion. For many cultures, strong ties exist between land and place and identity. When people who are not "originally" from a place migrate and stay for long periods, the immigrant populations often start to demand citizenship rights. These "immigrants" often have no attachment to other lands or rights to citizenship in other countries. However, they are still seen as foreigners in the country where they live. In this type of situation, citizenship becomes a resource. Those who already have citizenship sometimes think that "granting" citizenship to long-term immigrants makes the territory less theirs, especially if the new citizens do not have to follow norms of, or have common beliefs with, the original population. Granting citizenship to those individuals can then be seen as unfair. When citizenship is denied to groups that have been in a specific place for generations, that population also perceives the situation as unfair. Lack of access to rights that citizens have, including the right to civic and political participation, creates a population that is excluded and feels a sense of injustice.

In the fieldwork carried out for the study, several populations fell into the category of long-term residents of a country without citizenship. This was the case of the Chadians in Central African Republic and the Lebanese in Liberia. For the Lebanese in Liberia, lack of access to citizenship makes it impossible for anyone in their group to own land or to vote in elections. Even though officially the Lebanese could support political parties, in practice that is hotly debated in Liberia, and some in the Lebanese community question whether the support is to their advantage. Some non-Lebanese focus group participants in Liberia, however, pointed to the economic success of the Lebanese population as a sign that they should not have citizenship: They stated that if, in addition to economic power, the Lebanese also have political power, they will have too much power in the country.

The marginalization of immigrant groups can exacerbate perceptions of injustice across groups of native and non-natives. The Akdham people in Yemen are one example. The Akdham arrived in Yemen from Africa and are culturally and ethnically different from the majority of the Yemeni population. The difference has caused them to be marginalized and considered inferior to the average Yemeni. They have the same civic and political rights as others, yet the community remains socially isolated. As a community, they have largely internalized their own marginalization (focus group in Al Akdham, Sa'wan). The situation of the Somali population in Yemen presents a similar problem. The study fieldwork in Yemen found that many people born in Yemen of Somali ancestry claim that they face discrimination because of their origin. Many of these individuals are denied identity cards and other citizenship rights. That makes it difficult for them to fully participate in decision making, both because of language and because they are culturally different from the majority.

In other cases, the discrimination against non-native groups is much more discreet. They may be granted formal citizenship but still be socially or economically excluded. They thus continue a parallel existence, not fully part of broader society but not separable either. The Mandingo ethnic group provides an example of this dynamic and how it fuels perceptions of injustice (see box 6.1).

Perceptions of injustice across groups can be exacerbated when a migrant group is seen as advancing economically over the native population. In places where competition exists for resources, migration into the area may exacerbate tensions or create new ones. This argument is similar to the one made more broadly in chapter 4, which explains how perceptions of injustice can arise when social and economic inequalities are linked to specific identity groups. When groups that migrate are or become particularly economically successful, host communities develop a sense of injustice, and immigrant groups sometimes become the focus of tensions

This is the case with the Chadians in the Central African Republic. Some Chadians are successful business leaders there, whereas others are in the country as part of a rebel movement. Because they come from

BOX 6.1

The Mandingo in Liberia

The mutual feelings of injustice between the Mandingo—an ethnic group which migrated to Liberia—and native Liberians illustrate many implications of migration for perceptions of injustice. Many Liberians have persistently stated that the Mandingo should not be citizens for various reasons. First, the Mandingo are different culturally from other tribes in Liberia. The Mandingo choose not to participate in the activities of the Poro and other cultural organizations that are important components of Liberian cultural and civic life. Mandingo women do not often marry men from other tribes, which many in the study interpreted to mean that "they do not think our sons are good enough for their daughters." The Mandingo are also Muslim, and although other Liberian tribes also follow Islam, the Mandingo seem to follow stricter rules than other tribes. Second, the ethnic group of Mandingo is spread across Africa in Guinea, Ivory Coast, Gambia, Niger, and elsewhere. Many Liberians believe that the Mandingo should be considered Guinean, because that is where Liberians believe the Mandingo originated and where most of them live. Because many Mandingo retain close ties to Guinea, their allegiance to Liberia is often questioned.

Although the differences between the Mandingo and other native Liberian tribes had always existed, the relationship with the Mandingo became significant to politics when Samuel Doe stated in November 1985 that the Mandingo were a Liberian tribe. Doe's statement is thought to have been a political survival strategy, as his support was waning among most Liberians (the manipulation of identities in Liberia is discussed in a separate section). That some Mandingo changed allegiances during the civil crisis was also perceived as a sign that the Mandingo could not be trusted.

Even today, violence often flares between the Mandingo and other Liberian groups. Violence erupted between the Mandingo and Loma tribes in February 2010 and between the Mandingo and other groups of Liberians in October 2004, and is a common result of land conflicts in Nimba County. The disputes regarding land are especially important. Many perceive that Doe "granted" citizenship to the Mandingo (that is not the case, as Mandingo born in Liberia have always had the same legal rights as other native Liberians), making it possible for the Mandingo to own land. Many Mandingo, in fact, have obtained documentation for the land that they use, which other Liberians see as betrayal. According to them, the Mandingo have been allowed to use the land by members and leaders of other tribes, who in no way intended for the Mandingo to own the land.

(*continued next page*)

BOX 6.1 *(continued)*

The Mandingo also feel that they are treated unfairly by other tribes in Liberia. For example, some members of the focus group expressed that feeling by saying that "it was unfair that they would be asked for citizenship papers when people from other tribes wouldn't be." For example, Mandingo in Grand Gedeh believe that Krahn people from Cote d'Ivoire are less likely to have to present identity papers than are Mandingo from Liberia. Many Mandingo and Krahn in Grand Gedeh also said that a Krahn from Cote d'Ivoire could settle in Liberia and be considered Liberian. A Mandingo person, on the other hand, is assumed to be Guinean unless the person can prove otherwise.

---

elsewhere, however, the success of the Chadians is seen as illegitimate by many of the local people. Chadians who come from Salamat, a predominantly Muslim region, are often part of the rebel movement. Many in the Central African Republic see that as evidence that the Chadians are only in country to reinforce the penetration of Islam. Box 6.2 illustrates this further.

In the case of forcibly displaced populations, inequalities between refugees or internally displaced people and host communities can fuel social tension (Betts 2009). In some cases, host populations view refugees as unfairly benefiting from their situation and receiving privileged access to resources unavailable to them. For example, if a humanitarian organization is providing services, refugee or displaced status may qualify people for education, literacy or vocational training, health and sanitation improvements, and basic livelihood that may not be available in the same quantity or quality to everyone else. For that reason, providing services to both host and refugee communities has been effective in some cases, both in increasing access to important services and in reducing perceptions of injustice across groups (Puerto Gomez and Christensen 2010).

Large numbers of refugees or internally displaced persons can have an impact on the ethnic balance of hosting areas, on social conflicts, and on the delivery of social services. The impact may come simply from their presence. If tensions already exist between the refugee and host groups,

Central African Republic: Distrust of Foreigners

The distrust of foreigners in the Central African Republic has various dimensions and various causes. The republic's porous borders make entry very easy for foreigners. Chadian and Cameroonian traders have a long tradition of settlement there. The Chadians are mostly in the distribution sector. Cameroonians have a good share of the transportation and building material imports business. It is the Lebanese business community, however, that today appears quite unilaterally in the popular perception as the key private sector economic power in the country. Lebanese are present in the trade and service sectors and also in transportation and diamond mining. Because of the overwhelming presence of foreign businessmen, very few skilled Central African people hold prominent positions in the business sector. This reality does not escape the view of native Central Africans, and it creates a sense of injustice against all elements foreign. The general feeling in the republic is that foreigners are there to loot, to take away the little that the Central African people have, and destroy their country.

People's feelings of injustice relative to various actors were also observed in the fieldwork carried out for the study. Antagonism was particularly strong against Chadians, who were also perceived as being very involved in Central African Republic politics, both on the side of the government and on the side of rebel movements. People were not shy in showing their hostility, even though many Chadians were present in Bangui and the rest of the Central African Republic before the country fell into quasi civil war after the death of Bokassa.

Hostility against Chadians is sometimes confounded with hostility toward Muslim businessmen. Not all Chadians involved in the conflict were Muslims, but they can be called Zaghawa (a northern Chadian tribe holding power in Chad), Muslims, or Arab people (*bengue*) in a very depreciative manner. They are often described as people who would draw a knife in any argument and be able to fight to death for nothing, whereas Central Africans are peaceful and hospitable. People spoke resentfully about the small businesses in their neighborhoods and never mentioned bigger operators who had more influence on pricing and market supply. "To be blunt, one can say that the basic assumption was that white people are rich and wealthy by nature whatever their nationality is. African Muslims may be hard workers and greedy, but their fortunes would always be compared to the daily universe of the lay Central Africans," according to the field report for the study. "Some dream that Muslim economic operators are expelled so that they can take over their businesses."

Source: Authors, based on report of fieldwork in Central African Republic

they can be exacerbated. For example, in the late 1990s, the presence of Kosovo-Albanian refugees in Macedonia generated tensions between ethnic Albanians and Serbs in Macedonia (Pini 2008). When refugees are from the same cultural and linguistic group as the local population, the potential for peaceful coexistence and interaction among them may be greater (UNHCR 2004). For instance, approximately 25,000 refugees from the Central African Republic were in the Democratic Republic of Congo during the 1990s. Like their Congolese hosts, the refugees belonged to the Yakoma ethnic group, so their integration into the host society was relatively smooth. Similarly, three million Afghan refugees, mostly ethnic Pashtun, resided for more than a decade among fellow Pashtun communities in the North-West Frontier Province (NWFP) of Pakistan. During the entire period, relations between the refugees and the host population were largely peaceful. The same has been the case with the massive influx of Somali refugees into the Dadaab area in Kenya, which is inhabited by people sharing the same culture and language and who are often related by clan or tribal ties to the refugee population (Puerto Gomez and Christensen 2010).

The return of diaspora emigrants is another example of a population movement that can destabilize social relations between groups. Diaspora populations often remain close, at least in their imagination, to their place of origin. Even generations that are born in another country and have never been to the location of their family's origin sometimes retain imaginary ties (Rogge 1994: 39; Allen and Turton 1996: 6; Matsuoka and Sorensen 2005: 164, in Jeffrey and Murrison 2011: 133). In some cases, a significant proportion of those "returning" (such as the children of refugees or migrants) have never lived in the place of origin. Often those returning to the home country assume that they share certain values and norms with those who stayed behind, simply because of their common place of origin. In fact, norms and values of migrant and nonmigrant groups are likely to have changed in different ways because of their interaction with different events, peoples, and contexts.

There is often a strong sense of injustice against diaspora groups on the part of those who stayed in the home country. The return of diaspora groups raises questions about where the returnees belong and whether they should have full citizenship rights in more than one place. This is especially challenging in situations where an end to political or group violence brings elections, since at that time the countries often redetermine who has the rights to vote and hold office.

An example is the return of the diaspora to Liberia. Before and during the Liberian civil war (1996–2003), many Liberians (estimates range from 100,000 to 400,000)[3] left the country. In many cases, they moved to places where other Liberians were already present. Liberian communities abroad were vibrant, politically involved places, where individuals kept alive several traditions and supported family and friends who stayed behind. The return of the diaspora to Liberia has been seen as an extremely positive development for the country, as those individuals have taken back a great deal of knowledge and investment. However, the returnees have not integrated into mainstream Liberian society. Differences in education, exposure to outside values and customs, and standards of living separate the diaspora from the rest. The returnees' belief that they understand the situation in the country is often challenged by those who stayed behind during the civil war, many of whom believe that the diaspora cannot understand the country because they were not there during the violence. Participants in focus groups for this study noted that perceptions of injustice often arise when those in the diaspora obtain highly paid government positions that others believe should go to people who did not leave Liberia.

Internal migration presents a slightly different dynamic but can be equally socially disruptive if it mobilizes perceptions of injustice. Migrants from rural to urban areas leave behind their social networks and cultures, which can be quite different from those they find in the city. The social norms governing behavior are often looser than those they left behind, and coupled with disconnection from their families and social networks, that can be disruptive. In Haiti the urban violence in recent years has been attributed, in part, to massive migration from the countryside. Migrants have swelled the populations of the slums in the capital, where jobs and resources are already scarce. Youth in marginal neighborhoods, where public services are minimal, have been vulnerable to manipulation by powerful actors in Haiti's political system. One study of youth violence in pre-earthquake Port-au-Prince found that many parents and elders felt that the youth had slipped out of control of urban communities, as young people engaged in common crime as well as violent political mobilization. The social controls on behavior that would have restricted such acts were no longer present. These dynamics were exacerbated by the fact that many youths had become the breadwinners for their households through illegal or violent activities, making it difficult for parents, who were dependent on those resources, to hold them accountable (Willman and Marcelin 2010).

Migration, Change, and Institutions

Institutions in a host country or community must adapt, sometimes rather quickly, to the social and economic shifts brought by in-migration. Migrants arrive with distinct needs for resources, including land or housing, and basic services, which can stretch government capacities to provide them. In fragile situations, significant rural-to-urban migration occurs not only for economic reasons but also as involuntary displacement from violent conflict. Urban areas often must accommodate a large number of people who have experienced trauma. Those areas then also become the residence of groups of people who are unable to return home after violence, whether because their home or community is inhabited by others, because they lack the means, or because of actions they committed in their place of origin.

Migration creates challenges for institutions, which not only have to provide services to a larger number of people but also must adapt to the needs and cultures of the incoming populations. Migrants bring particular cultural, social, or religious beliefs and customs that may not be compatible with those of the host country and can create tensions with host populations. If migrants are perceived as competing for jobs, it may provoke significant tension and backlash. Some examples include anti-migrant measures against Zimbabweans in South Africa, Mexicans in the United States, or northern African migrants in Western Europe.

Migration to urban areas can reinforce an urban–rural divide that is difficult for institutions to mediate. It is often the case that people who live in urban areas and rural areas do not share the same norms, values, and belief systems, even if they assume that those systems are shared. The location of government institutions in cities can further reinforce the divide and marginalize those living in rural areas. That has implications for governance because it widens the perceived distance between government and rural constituencies.

Institutions created by or for the majority of a population may not be able to adapt immediately to the social or economic shifts brought on by migration. Because they are likely to be members of minority cultures in their host country or community, migrants are likely to have less access to institutions, or at least to use them less. Dominant cultures in a society often make institutions and systems legally available to all, but access is effectively denied to nondominant cultures because of language or norms that are inherent in the institutions (Fernandes 2000). In a single-culture community, for example, basing the selection of community leadership on an individual's knowledge of the community's culture and rules may be appropriate. With an influx of individuals from other cultures, however, mechanisms for including the new citizens need to be put in place. Again, however, that is unlikely to happen because of the costs of change and because of the vested interests of existing power holders.

In Liberia, for example, local-level traditional institutions are not flexible. Because of their ties to local spiritual beliefs and their hierarchical nature, these institutions lack mechanisms to interact with people who do not share the same background. Moreover, because the belief exists in Liberia that the tribe that inhabited the land first has the right to establish the rules for the area, the consequences of migration are often negative for the newcomers. They have to choose whether to adapt to this new way of governance, changing their ways of participation and interaction. In some cases the newcomers are systematically excluded from decision making because of their origin or because of differences in spiritual beliefs (Montserrado County focus group).

Failures of institutions or processes in one location can transfer a problem to a new location through migration. In Yemen, where blood feuds are a problem for justice institutions in rural areas, migration into urban areas has transferred the problem into cities. Blood feuds between tribes in rural areas are now often being extended to urbanized tribal members, who lack direct protection from their rural kinfolk. Consequently, Sana'a, the capital, has now become a "free zone" for revenge killings (Manea 2010: 20). Sana'a has no institutions that can adequately address these problems.

Generational Relationships

"Youth" is generally understood as the life stage between puberty and adulthood. There is no single definition or agreement on the age boundaries for youth.[4] The most widely used definition is that of the United Nations, which considers the term "youth" as covering people between the ages of 18 and 25. The study reported in this book adopted a broader definition that understands youth as a social construct, and not just a biological process or a life stage. Youth is a time in which people are making transitions from the dependencies of childhood to assume the responsibilities of adulthood. (Flanagan and Syvertsen 2006: 11, in Kurtenbach 2010: 1). "Youth is both a social position [. . .] as well as part of a larger societal and generational process, a state of becoming" (Christiansen, Utas, and Vigh 2006: 11, in Kurtenbach 2010: 2). In many countries "youth" can include anyone who has not yet become part of the decision-making structure, often people in their early thirties. In other countries, youth can include people in early adolescence.

Youth are a crucial group in society not only because they comprise a large and growing proportion of the population (at least 20 percent in most countries), but also because they are absorbing society's values and norms and will be the transmitters of those to future generations. Youth are engaged in a process of *socialization*, through which they acquire the behaviors and beliefs of the society around them (Arnett 1995: 618). On the macro level, socialization involves the imposition of norms and practices by political societies and systems to mold youth as citizens (Sapiro 2004). Altogether, socialization is

> a complex process with a certain conservative bias favoring the inter-nalization of existing forms of social cohesion, norms and rules. At the individual as well as at the collective level it provides elements of societal continuity and path-dependency rooted in historical and cultural experi-ences as well as day-to-day social practice. Nevertheless, socialization is not static but—at least theoretically— is a dynamic process able to adapt and change according to structural as well as to context-specific develop-ments and needs. (Kurtenbach 2010: 2–3)

As it prepares young people for adulthood, socialization produces cer-tain expectations about the transition to adulthood and the entitlements associated with adult status. If those expectations cannot be met, for example, if institutions governing generational relationships are too rigid, deep conflicts between youth and older generations can arise and can be an important source of fragility in society. In many cases, youth will seek alternative routes to adulthood, some of which can be highly disruptive to society. Conversely, a certain flexibility in these institutions can promote greater resilience.

Alternative Routes of Socialization for Youth

The identity of a "youth" is particularly malleable. Youth is a time when people are still determining how they fit into the larger societal structure and experimenting with different identities. The institutions responsible for socialization—usually a group of elders or other respected body—determine the norms and values to be passed on to youth, and they deter-mine who can transition to adulthood. Many times the rites of passage are fairly strongly set and enforced, clearly defining who is and who is not an adult in the community, and therefore who has access to key assets such as land, or who is allowed to participate in community decision making. If these institutions are too rigid, they can leave few options for those who are not allowed to make the transition.

Institutional rigidity can take different forms. Adults may apply strict limits to the type of youth who can successfully go through the process and become full citizens of a community. For example, they may exclude ex-combatants or youth who have otherwise engaged in violence, youth with handicaps, and so on. Alternatively they may create complicated processes for initiation that youth perceive as excessive or not worth their time. Different mechanisms restrict youth passage into adulthood, but they all have the same impact: They create groups of excluded individuals, who either find alternative ways to transition into adulthood or who are stuck in a state of limbo that generates vulnerability and grievances.

Traditional institutions can be strained by global changes that expose youth to new values and norms, raising their expectations for their own futures. Because youth are in a process of identity formation, they are more susceptible than other age groups to influences outside their communities. Exposure to other cultures and ways of life via global technologies, such as social media, as well as urbanization and other experiences, prompts youth to reflect on their own cultures and values in relation to those of others. These new processes can "promote inclusive forms of social cohesion and support processes of individualization, or boost exclusionary identities." (Kurtenbach 2010: 14; see box 6.2).

Frustration with the rigidity of institutions governing the transition to adulthood can prompt youth to seek alternative routes. Some of those can be positive ways for excluded populations to acquire the full citizenship rights normally associated with adulthood. Rebelling against an exclusive system and adopting a new one can in fact be quite positive.

Many other young people make the transition to adulthood through emigration. "The pressure to conform to ancestral collective norms and habits is often cited by young migrants in developing countries as a reason to move to urban centers or abroad" (Marc 2010: 9). In urban areas, where norms tend to be more flexible and there is more anonymity, these young people often have more freedom to determine their own values and ways of living. Young people from rural areas who find a way to make a living and become community leaders in an urban area can find that

---

Global Self-Socialization via the Internet

Where young people have access to new communication technologies, they have access to geographically distant places and cultures. That affects their socialization in different ways: Most of the Internet's content transmits Western cultural norms, values, and consumption patterns, while other cultures are underrepresented. That begins with language, as 80 percent of websites are in English. At the same time, new technologies change or even replace face-to-face contacts with peers and family. That may help to overcome negative effects of mobility; for example, in cases of migration it allows for regular contact with home, but it also makes personal engagement more arbitrary and volatile. With reference to Chinese children sent by their parents to study in the United States, Zhou (2009: 39) describes a change from direct control to remote control. Although parents may be happy to have their adolescents under control via cell phone, that cannot substitute for the processes of negotiation and mediation inside the family (for example, on the time a young person is to be at home at night).

New communication platforms also seem to change the quality of relationships, which are no longer bound to the idea of a community having a certain stability, coherence, common history, embeddedness, and social recognition. Conversely, network sociality derives not from a common narrative but from informational acts. The social bond is created on a project-by-project basis (UN-DESA 2003: 327).

The influence of global communications media reaches out even to the selection of partners. Although Western-dominated media broadcast the ideal of romantic engagement and relationships, that clashes with the reality of many young people; for example, in India most partners are chosen by the family according to criteria beyond the emotional feelings promoted by Bollywood movies (see Verma and Saraswathi 2002: 115–16).

Source: Kurtenbach 2010.BOX 6.3

---

their social status in their home community also changes because of their accomplishments in the city. People who "make it" under other systems can also be drivers of change toward inclusion and innovation in more traditional socialization systems.

In other circumstances, however, migration can simply compound the marginalization of youth when they are not able to integrate into the host community. Many urban gangs comprise second-generation migrant youth from rural areas, who face social exclusion when they migrate to cities. The gang identity tends to form around the shared experience of exclusion. The sentiment of exclusion, together with the rigidity of the institutions that cannot make room for these youth, can contribute to antisocial behavior, most notably violence.

Marriage or parenthood can be another way for youth to achieve the social status of adults. These transitions are very different for men as opposed to women. In Central African Republic, for example, the fieldwork for the study found that young girls trying to be accepted as adults among their society often choose to have children at a young age. Having a child is supposed to be a sign that the person is mature enough to take care of another life and is therefore an adult. Girls as young as 12 decide to have children, so that they can be seen differently in their community. That, however, causes a great deal of fragility, as these young girls and their families are not prepared to take on such responsibilities. Males may also seek to acquire adult status through marriage. However, because males often need to acquire certain material means (land, housing) to provide for a wife before the community will allow them to marry, they may be pushed to postpone marriage (see box 6.3).

Other youth find that the route to adulthood leads through violent territory. For youth in countries that are at war or experiencing chronic violence, the traditional routes to adulthood may be blocked. They are blocked, first, through the impact of violence on the institutions responsible for socialization; the family, kinship networks, and schools. Those institutions are weakened or destroyed by chronic violence, leaving youth either stunted in their transition or pushed to join violent groups as an alternative.

Young people who join such groups are socialized through exposure to violence, when they are forcibly recruited into conflict or gangs or pushed into them by circumstance. The initiation into an armed group often involves extreme brutalization of young recruits or forcing them to perpetrate acts of violence against others. In Sierra Leone, young recruits were sometimes forced by their commanders to kill or rape people in their communities, sometimes even including the recruit's family (Human Rights Watch 2003: 35–42; TRC 2004). Enduring, observing, and committing those acts of violence became a part of the socialization process for combatants of the Revolutionary United Front (RUF) in Sierra Leone (Maclure and Denov 2006; Denov and Gervais 2007). As a result, many young recruits saw their commanders as replacement father figures and the RUF as a replacement family (Maclure and Denov 2006). In this

---

BOX 6.3

Male Postponement of Marriage

According to Mensch, Singh, and Casterlina (2005, 159–61), the explanation for male post-ponement of marriage is related neither to education nor to urbanization, but mostly to economic conditions such as poverty, lack of financial security, and lack of access to land. The Middle East is an interesting case in point (Singerman 2007). There, adulthood and sexuality are traditionally closely linked to marriage. But demographic change, the greater participation of women in the labor force, and education, as well as changing gender norms, delay marriages.

Another important factor for postponing marriage seems to be the financial costs of housing, celebrations, and furniture. This is a problem most of all for unemployed, educated young people trapped in a situation of "wait hood" that puts young people in an adolescent, liminal state in which they are neither children nor adults. In this liminal state, young people remain financially dependent on their families (who in large part finance the cost of marriage) far longer than previous generations, and they must live by the rules and morality of their parents and the dominant values of society, which frown on unchaperoned fraternization and unmarried relationships.

Yet as more and more men and women delay marriage, the institution of marriage is changing, and new marriage substitutes and sexual norms are emerging beyond the mar-gins of society (Singerman 2007, 6). This came up again and again with the youth focus group in Yemen. Marriage was seen by all youth as an essential step toward adulthood, and lack of revenue and employment as major obstacles to being able to afford a mar-riage. Many of the youth organizations and Islamic foundations were supporting young people in financing and organizing marriages and the festivities that accompany them, which are essential to ensure social recognition and status.

Source: Kurtenbach 2010

---

way normal socialization processes were transformed and used when convenient by armed groups (Wood 2008).

Similar socialization processes are common in urban gangs. Studies of the transnational gang MS-13, for example, have documented that male initiates are "beat in" to the gang, and females are "sexed in," via gang rape (Small Arms Survey 2010). These initiations can create such trauma for young people that they have the perverse effect of bonding them even more closely to the gang, which becomes a replacement family for many.

Involvement in violent groups serves various functions for young people, among others the achievement of social status and respect. In Haiti, for example, some urban youth reported feeling able to achieve the status and respect they desire via violent activity because they are not able to obtain them through other means. For others, membership in a violent group offered opportunities for economic gain via looting or crime.

For young women, involvement in violence may promise social status and power that are unavailable to them in peacetime or mainstream society. A growing body of research on the involvement of young women in conflict and urban gangs suggests that overall their motivations are quite similar to those of boys. Girls are probably more likely to be motivated by a need for protection, either from domestic violence or from the threat of violence from other groups. The promise of social mobility is also strong if they can ascend to positions of authority.[5] Although some young women achieve positions of power and break out of traditional roles, at least temporarily (see for example case studies in Coulter, Persson, and Utas 2008; Specht and Attree 2006), most find themselves relegated to subordinate tasks such as cooking meals or serving as messengers, and many are subjected to sexual violence and harassment.[6]

Barriers to Youth's Transition and Perceptions of Injustice

In the fieldwork for the study, tensions were visible between youth and elders about access to power and resources. The perceptions of injustice went both ways. Youth often felt that they were excluded from participation in decision making and from opportunities for community leadership, and as a result their energy and talents were going to waste. They were especially concerned about exclusion from the means to transition to adulthood in the eyes of the community. Older adults, for their part, felt that they were "held hostage," in the words of one Haitian community leader, to the violent behavior of a handful of youth who they felt no longer respected the traditional power structures.

The greatest generational divisions seem to come from the exclusion of youth from access to the means of achieving the social status of adults. In Rwanda, for example, youth have little access to land or to the resources needed to build a house, yet a man who has not built his house is not an adult. Similarly, in many communities in northwest Liberia, it is difficult for a person to become an adult if they have not been initiated into a cultural organization. Young people coming from tribes that are not in the majority in the community, displaced youth, and some former combatants are often not initiated into those societies because elders assume that they do not know or follow community norms.

Youth are often excluded from decision making, although they often make up a large percentage of the population, especially in fragile settings where populations tend to be younger overall. They are often excluded from decision making at the local level, which is the level that most affects them. In Liberia, for example, the official youth age is 18 to 35, and the voting age is 18. In communities, however, those considered youth can rarely participate in community decision making, even though the definition of "youth" includes some who are in their early 30s. Similarly, expert seminar participants in Yemen indicated that the government and political parties there use "the patriarchal system, thus excluding the younger generation from participation in the decision-making process" An example cited in the seminar was the Islamic Party (Al Islah), 70 percent of whose members are categorized as youth, but all of whose party leaders, with one exception, are in their 60s.

In some cases, excluded youth create parallel governance structures, further exacerbating generational divides. In Gbesseh Town, Liberia, youth leaders are very much engaged in Islamic organizations. They espouse a more conservative version of Islam than their elders: The elders see no incompatibility between Islam and traditional organizations and beliefs, but the youth believe that a Muslim cannot be part of traditional organizations and must renounce traditional beliefs. By virtue of their age, young people are excluded from the normal decision-making structure, but in this particular town they have taken upon themselves the reform of traditional governance structures and have created parallel decision-making bodies. Their actions have caused a deep divide between youth and elders in this community.

Lack of access to civic participation often excludes youth from labor markets and limits their access to services. That is especially the case in contexts where those in power also allocate resources and jobs, and it can lead to a great sense of injustice. In southern Yemen, for example, most of the participants in the riots against the government are youth. As a Yemen seminar participant said, "these are the most radical in expressing their feelings because these are the classes which are more subjected to injustice and unemployment." Also in Yemen, young people complain about government jobs being given to the sons of people in power, even if they are ill-qualified. It is perceived that even opportunities to attend college are restricted to those with influence, limiting the possibilities for those without such support networks. Seminar participants stated that during the 1970s, younger qualified people could reach higher places in the government (as ministers or managers). Recently higher places in the government are reserved for sons of sheikhs, commanders, or leaders in the ruling party and former VIPs, regardless of their qualifications or commitment in work. This perception was repeated elsewhere; youth in several contexts complained about the "rules of the game" being rigged, either as in Yemen, concerning position, or as in Liberia, where younger people complain about not being able to acquire land because its distribution and ownership are controlled by elders in the community.

Becoming "included," and thus being allowed to transition to adulthood, often requires demonstrating knowledge and stewardship of community norms and cultural practices. In Foday Town, Liberia, for example, residents of the community who are of minority tribes are often labeled "strangers" (as opposed to those born in the town of the majority tribe, who are labeled "citizens"). "Stranger" youth in Foday Town have to ask for acceptance by the community elders, first to become citizens and then potentially to obtain access to community socialization processes. If the "stranger" youth does not adhere to community norms and values, or if it is not convenient for the "stranger" youth to become a "citizen," the elders do not let the youth gain access to adult status.

Challenges to Gender Relationships

Just as with generational power relationships, rapid social changes often deliver powerful shocks to existing gender power dynamics. In many fragile situations, the structures governing gender norms are too rigid to adapt effectively to rapid social change. In these contexts, the rules that regulate how men and women interact are in flux or are directly challenged, and that can be disruptive for society. In some cases the reason is that the economic role of men as providers is challenged by shifts in the global economy. In others, the challenges come from exposure to other systems of gender norms, as people travel more and are exposed to other cultures through the expansion of global communication technologies.

Gender Roles and Rigid Institutions

Many characteristics of everyday life have historically been considered family affairs, out of the sphere of public life and thus not subject to intervention by those outside the family. However people today spend more time outside the household, or being exposed to influences outside the family, than previous generations. More children are in school and for longer hours each day. The advent of global communication puts people in touch with distant cultures and ideas from around the world. That exposure has challenged the traditional public/private divide and, with it, strict gender roles. These social shifts call into question some established ways of maintaining social cohesion, such as requiring obedience of children, especially girls, subordination of wives to husbands, and other practices.

The family as an institution is central to how flexible society can be in the face of these social shifts. Traditional masculinities and hierarchies are directly challenged by rapid social change. Parents, especially fathers, lose substantial power and control with these changes. The absolute authority of the father, once undisputed, is now questioned as young men and women are able to travel and access other ways of life through technology, without his supervision (Kurtenbach 2010; Nsamenang 2002). The spread of socially conservative forms of traditional religions, from Islam to Christianity, can be seen as a response to these trends. Many of these groups openly dispute the loss of traditional patriarchal hierarchies and advocate for a return to a traditional social order (Kurtenbach 2010).

These challenges to gender roles create important opportunities but also leave men and women vulnerable, in different ways. The growing economic empowerment and independence of women can be a huge achievement for families and societies. In many cases families adapt smoothly to the shifting power dynamics. However, if women's economic and social empowerment is perceived to come at the expense of men's economic and social status, it can provoke a sense of injustice by men against women and potentially fuel a backlash (Bannon and Correia 2006). Francis and Amuyunzu-Nyamongo (2005) documented how global shifts that create more demand for female labor have fractured Kenyan society by disempowering men. The shifts have challenged men's role as provider, leaving many feeling emasculated. In a cross-section survey of urban and rural women in Kerala, India, Panda and Agarwal (2005) found that women whose husbands were employed were significantly less likely to report domestic violence than women with unemployed husbands. Other studies have described how unemployed men may be treated with disrespect or find it difficult to marry and thus be recognized as an adult (Barker and Ricardo 2006).

Some men may react to their perceptions of injustice by acting out violently against women, most often within an intimate relationship. In a recent survey covering six countries, the percentage of men who reported having perpetrated violence against a partner ranged from 25 percent to 40 percent; women reported even higher rates (ICRW 2010).

Women who live outside traditional gender roles can be very vulnerable to violence, and institutions are often ill-equipped to protect them. Female combatants are one obvious example, as described in the previous section. Trafficking of young females is another area of vulnerability. Very often trafficking victims are among the most ambitious and entrepreneurial of their communities, who challenge traditional notions of femininity by seeking opportunities to migrate. Traffickers exploit these characteristics outside the authority of the state, or sometimes with its complicity, with tragic consequences.

The phenomenon of femicide in Central America is the most extreme manifestation of the inability of institutions to adapt to these social shifts. It is difficult to draw broad generalizations given the lack of data (in many cases the murders are not rigorously investigated), but the trend exhibits strong elements of "social cleansing." Victims tend to be young women who have migrated for work and who are living without male companions, thus going against the established gender norms.[7] The motives alleged for these crimes vary, and the nature of the perpetrators varies as well (both state and non-state actors have been involved), but in all cases the victim's gender is a key factor both in the type of violence and in the authorities' response (Amnesty International 2003).

These problems are rooted in negative ideas of what it means to be a man. "Harmful masculinities" that equate being male with negative behaviors such as violence, domination, and other characteristics are often at the base of unhealthy behaviors. Intimate-partner violence has long been theorized as a means for men to recover control over women and, in the case of domestic violence, maintain cohesion inside the family. A recent cross-national study looked at these dynamics empirically and suggested important links between rigid gender attitudes, stresses related to employment, and the use of violence by men against their female partners (ICRW 2010). The loss of male entitlement has also been associated with perpetration of other forms of interpersonal violence, particularly in Latin

America, in what Barker (2005, 10) calls a "crisis of masculinity." That dynamic has been observed in South Africa as well (Marks 2001).

In contexts where gender norms are very rigid, projects that target women's empowerment without involving men run the risk of exacerbating men's perceptions of injustice, leading to perverse effects. Rigid gender power relationships often do not allow for the recognition that women's empowerment need not come at the expense of men's power. When interventions are implemented in this type of context, the risks of alienating men entirely are high. For example, microcredit projects that exclusively deliver funds to women, without involving men in some form, can generate resentment in households and in communities. Inevitably in very rigid structures some male power will be lost, but the potential gains can far exceed the initial costs in both social and economic terms. Projects in a variety of contexts in the developing world have shown that involving men in programs that empower women—from microcredit, to HIV/AIDS prevention, to violence reduction programs—dramatically increases the chances of success (ICRW 2010).

This chapter has discussed some important areas of relationships through an approach emphasizing societal dynamics. Population movements, land issues, problems in acquiring the status of adult, and rapid changes in gender roles strongly reflect societal structures and are affected by societal dynamics in a way that can rapidly lead to high levels of violence and fragility. They are, to use the language of the *World Development Report* on conflict, security, and development, important internal stressors, and depending on how the societal dynamic is playing out in an area, lead to increased fragility or the opposite—increased resilience. Those are the reasons why these areas should be well understood when work is undertaken in fragile situations.

Notes

1. This section discusses "migration" and "population movements" as equivalent terms, including all movements of groups of individuals whether they cross borders or not. Difficulties arise with this approach in that most researchers have focused on a particular type of population movement and not on its impact.
2. An example is the way that the support in Pakistan for Afghan refugee involvement in the resistance against the Communist regime in Afghanistan and its Soviet backers during the 1980s created conditions within Pakistan that radicalized sections of the population. It also led to a proliferation of arms and weakened government authority. Another example is the way that obstacles to returnee reintegration in parts of southern Sudan (e.g., in Jonglei state or parts

of Equatoria) have contributed to conflict and instability, which in turn adds to state fragility (Pantuliano et al. 2008).

3. Estimates range from the 100,000 cited by Dr. Mary Moran, of Colgate University (2005), to more than 400,000, as asserted during the 1995 peace negotiations in Accra, Ghana.

4. There is no consensus on a global definition of "youth." International organizations rely on different age boundaries. For example, *United Nations World Youth Reports* (UN-DESA 2003; 2012) include the cohort aged 15 to 25; the World Health Organization uses ages from 15 to 29 (WHO 2002); the World Bank's *World Development Report* (2007) includes young people between 12 and 24. Others have put forward more sociologically based definitions; for example, White (2006, 257) documents a gender-based distinction of the term in East Africa, with "youth" referring to males between puberty and age 30, but to females between puberty and age 18 or 19. See Kurtenbach 2010 for a detailed discussion.

5. Opportunities for women in today's conflicts differ in this respect from those of prior revolutionary movements that fought for independence or social change in the 1970s and 1980s, as those movements viewed women's rights and equality as an integral part of the overall struggle for independence (Coulter, Persson, and Utas 2008, 15).

6. See, for example, Coulter, Persson, and Utas 2008; and Specht and Attree 2006, concerning female fighters in African wars; see Small Arms Survey 2010, 184–207, on female gang members.

7. Femicide claimed the lives of at least 400 women in Juarez, Mexico, alone between 1993 and 2003, and more than 2,500 Guatemalan women since 2001.

References

Adepoju, Aderanti. 2005. "Review of Research and Data on Human Trafficking in Sub-Saharan Africa." *International Migration* 43 (1–2): 75–98.

Allen, T., and D. Turton. 1996. "Introduction: In Search of Cool Ground." In *In Search of Cool Ground: War, Fight and Homecoming in Northeast Africa*, ed. T. Allen. London/Trenton: Africa World Press.

Amnesty International. 2003. "Intolerable Killings: 10 Years of Abductions and Murders of Women in Ciudad Juárez and Chihuahua," Amnesty International, New York.

Arnett, Jeffrey Jensen. 1995. "Broad and Narrow Socialization: The Family in the Context of a Cultural Theory." *Journal of Marriage and Family* 57 (3): 617–28.

Bannon, Ian, and Maria Correia, eds. 2006. *The Other Half of Gender: Men's Issues in Development*. Washington, DC: World Bank.

Barker, Gary. 2005. *Dying to be Men: Youth, Masculinity and Social Exclusion*. London: Routledge.

Barker, Gary, and C. Ricardo. 2006. "Young Men and the Construction of Mas-culinity in Sub-Saharan Africa: Implications for HIV/AIDS, Conflict and Vio-lence." In *The Other Half of Gender,* ed. Ian Bannon and Maria Correia, 160. Washington, DC: World Bank.

Betts, Alexander. 2009. *Forced Migration and Global Politics.* New York: Wiley and Sons.

Christiansen, Catrine, Mats Utas, and Henrik Vigh, eds. 2006. *Navigating Youth, Generating Adulthood: Social Becoming in an African Context.* Uppsala: Nor-dic Africa Institute.

Coulter, C., M. Persson, and M. Utas. 2008. *Young Female Fighters in African Wars: Conflict and Its Consequences.* Uppsala: Nordic Africa Institute.

Crush, J. 2000. "Migration Past: An Historical Overview of Cross-Border Move-ment in Southern Africa." In *On Borders: Perspectives on International Migra-tion in Southern Africa,* ed. David McDonald. Southern African Migration Project and St Martin's Press.

Denov, M., and C. Gervais. 2007. "Negotiating (In)Security: Agency, Resistance and the Experiences of Girls Formerly Associated with Sierra Leone's Revolutionary United Front." *Signs: Journal of Women in Culture and Society* 32 (4): 857–910.

Faist, Thomas, and Jurgen Gerdes. 2008. *Dual Citizenship in an Age of Mobility.* Washington, DC: Migration Policy Institute.

Fernandes, Walter. 2000. "From Marginalization to Sharing the Project Benefits." In *Risks and Reconstruction: Experiences of Re-settlers and Refugees,* ed. Michael Cernea and Chris McDowell. Washington, DC: World Bank.

Flanagan, C. A., and A. K. Syvertsen. 2006. "Youth as a Social Construct and Social Actor." In *Youth Activism: An International Encyclopedia,* ed. L. Sherrod, C. A. Flanagan, R. Kassimir, and A. K. Syvertsen, 11–19. Westport, CT: Green-wood Publishing.

Francis, Paul, and Mary Amuyunzu-Nyamongo. 2005. *Bitter Harvest: The Social Cost of State Failure in Rural Kenya.* Washington DC: World Bank.

Gans, Herbert J. 1962. *The Urban Villagers: Groups and Class in the Life of Italian-Americans.* New York: Free Press of Glencoe.

Guarnizo, Luis Eduardo, Alejandro Portes, and William Haller. 2003. "Assimilation of Transnationalism: Determinants of Transnational Political Action among Contemporary Migrants." *American Journal of Sociology* 108 (6): 1211–48.

Human Rights Watch. 2003. *We'll Kill you if You Cry: Sexual Violence in the Sierra Leone Conflict.* January 2002, Vol. 15, No. 1 (A).

ICRW (International Center for Research on Women). 2010. *What Men Have to Do with It.* Washington, DC: ICRW.

Jeffrey, L., and J. Murison. 2011. "Guest Editorial: The Temporal, Social, Spatial and Legal Dimensions of Return and Onward Migration." *Population, Space and Place* 17 (2): 131–39.

Kurtenbach, Sabine. 2010. "Youth and Gender and the Societal Dynamics of Fragility." Background paper for *Societal Dynamics and Fragility: Engaging Societies in Responding to Fragile Situations*. Washington, DC: World Bank.

Maclure, R., and M. Denov. 2006. "'I Didn't Want to Die so I Joined Them': Structuration and the Process of Becoming Boy Soldiers in Sierra Leone." *Terrorism and Political Violence* 18 (1): 119–35.

Manea, Elham. 2010. "Societal Dynamic and Fragility: Yemen." Background paper for *Societal Dynamics and Fragility: Engaging Societies in Responding to Fragile Situations*. Washington, DC: World Bank.

Marc, Alexandre. 2010. *Delivering Services in Multicultural Societies*. Washington, DC: World Bank.

Marks, Monique. 2001. *Young Warriors: Youth Politics, Identity and Violence in South Africa*. Johannesburg: Witwatersrand University Press.

Matsuoka, A., and J. Sorenson. 2005. "Ideas of North: The Eritrean Diaspora in Canada." *Eritrean Studies Review* 4: 85–114.

Mensch, Barbara, Sushele Singh, and John B. Casterlina. 2005. "Trends in Timing of First Marriage among Men and Women in the Developing World." In *The Changing Transitions to Adulthood in Developing Countries: Selected Case Studies*, ed. Cynthia Lloyd, Jere Behrman, Nelly Stromquist, and Barney Cohen, 118–71. Washington, DC: National Academic Press.

Moran, M. 2005. "Social Thought and Commentary: Time and Place in the Anthropology of Events: A Diaspora Perspective on the Liberian Transition." *Anthropological Quarterly* 78, no. 2.

Nsamenang, B. 2002. "Adolescence in Sub-Saharan Africa: An Image Constructed from Africa's Triple Inheritance." In *The World's Youth: Adolescence in Eight Regions of the Globe*, ed. B. B. Brown, R. Larson, and T. S. Saraswathi. New York: Cambridge University Press.

Panda, Pradeep, and Bina Agarwal. 2005. "Marital Violence, Human Development and Women's Property Status in India." *World Development* 33 (5): 823–50.

Pantuliano, Sara, Margie Buchanan-Smith, Paul Murphy, and Irina Mosel. 2008. *The Long Road Home: Opportunities and Obstacles to the Reintegration of IDPs and Refugees Returning to Southern Sudan and the Three Areas*. London: Overseas Development Institute.

Pini, Justin. 2008. "Political Violence and the African Refugee Experience." *International Affairs Review, 2008*. http://www.iar-gwu.org/node/19.

Puerto Gomez, Margarita, and Asger Christensen. 2010. "The Impacts of Refugees on Neighboring Countries: A Development Challenge." Background paper for *2011 World Development Report: Conflict, Security and Development*. Washington, DC: World Bank.

Putnam, Robert. 2007. "E Pluribus Unum: Diversity and Community in the Twenty-first Century: The 2006 Johan Skytte Prize Lecture." *Scandinavian Political Studies* 30 (2): 137–74.

Ratha, Dilip, Sanket Mohapatra, and Elina Scheja. 2011. "Impact of Migration on Economic and Social Development: A Review of Evidence and Emerging Issues." Policy Research Working Paper, World Bank. Washington, DC.

Rogge, John. 1994. "Repatriation of Refugees—A Not So Simple 'Optimum' Solution." In *When Refugees Go Home—African Experiences,* ed. Tim Allen and Hubert Morsink, 14–50. James Currey and Africa World Press.

Sapiro, V. 2004. "Not Your Parents' Political Socialization: Introduction for a New Generation." *Annual Review of Political Science* 7: 1–23.

Singerman, Diane 2007. "The Economic Imperatives of Marriage: Emerging Practices and Identities among Youth in the Middle East." Middle East Youth Initiative at the Brookings Institution, Washington, DC. http://www.shababinclusion.org/content/document/detail/559/.

Small Arms Survey. 2010. "Gangs, Groups, and Guns." *Small Arms Survey*. Geneva: Graduate Institute of International and Development Studies.

Specht, Irma, and Larry Attree. 2006. "The Re-integration of Teenage Girls and Young Women." *Intervention* 4 (3): 219–28.

TRC. 2004. *Witness to Truth: Report of the Sierra Leone.* Truth and Reconciliation Commission, Sierra Leone.

UN-DESA (United Nations Department of Economic and Social Affairs). 2003. *World Youth Report.* New York: United Nations.

———. 2012. *World Youth Report.* New York: United Nations.

UNHCR (United Nations High Commissioner for Refugees). 2004. *Economic and Social Impacts of Massive Refugee Populations on Host Developing Countries, as well as Other Countries.* Standing Committee. UNHCR, EC/54/SC/CRP.5.

Verma, Suman, and T. S. Sarswathi. 2002. "Adolescence in India: Street Urchins or Silicon Valley Millionaires." In *The World's Youth: Adolescence in Eight Regions of the Globe,* ed. B. B. Brown, R. Larson, and T. S. Saraswathi, 105–40. Cambridge: Cambridge University Press.

White, Michael A. 2006: Afterword, in: Christiansen, Caterine/Mats Utas/Henrik E. Vigh (eds.): *Navigating Youth, Generating Adulthood. Social Becoming in an African Context.* Uppsala: Nordic Africa Institute, pp. 255–266.

Willman, Alys, and Louis Herns Marcelin. 2010. "If They Could Make Us Disappear, They Would! Youth and Violence in Cite Soleil, Haiti." *Journal of Community Psychology* 38 (4): 515–31.

WHO (World Health Organization). 2002. *World Report on Violence and Health 2002.* Geneva: WHO.

Wood, Elisabeth Jean. 2008. "The Social Processes of Civil War: The Wartime Transformation of Social Networks." *Annual Review of Political Science* 11: 539–61.

World Bank. 2007. *Development and the Next Generation.* 2007 world development report.

———. 2007. *World Development Report.* Washington, DC: World Bank.

Zhou, Min. 2009. *Contemporary Chinese America: Immigration, Ethnicity, and Community Transformation.* Philadelphia: Temple University Press.

CHAPTER 7

From Concept to Practice: Fostering Social Cohesion to Reduce Fragility

The previous chapters have offered a lens emphasizing societal dynamics for understanding the problem of fragility from a society-centered perspective. By placing society at the heart of the analysis, they have shed some light on the ways that societal dynamics—interactions among groups in society—support, or work against, the convergence of interests that is necessary to improve cohesion and increase resilience. The objective of the analysis is not to pretend to establish a comprehensive understanding of societal dynamics or to present new theories about how society influences the state, but rather to provide direction for building social cohesion to increase societal resilience.

This chapter and the next one discuss the operational implications of a society-centered approach. Addressing the societal dimensions of fragility requires a comprehensive approach, and thus the discussion here necessarily covers a broad range of sectoral and technical areas. Clearly many factors and dynamics affect fragility and could be discussed here. Those covered in the following sections were selected because they emerged in the fieldwork as particularly important. This chapter covers the general approach for supporting policy and program development, including how to develop knowledge and information, and chapter 8 provides recommendations on specific programs.

The changes proposed here are very much in line with the reforms recommended in the Aid Architecture put forth in the *2011 World Development Report* (WDR) and aim to complement those and other existing interventions. The WDR highlights the importance of institutional change, underscoring that it is a long process that requires trial and error and careful sequencing of different actions. It stresses that institutional transformation needs to go hand-in-hand with efforts to build better state–society relations (World Bank 2011).

The present chapter provides some overall recommendations for applying an approach emphasizing societal dynamics, perceptions of injustice across groups, and the interaction between institutions. These factors affect the ability to generate a convergence of interests in society by influencing the incentives that encourage groups to converge on those interests, or discourage them from doing so. The recommendations in this chapter are thus geared toward creating stronger incentives for states and societies to engage with one another in positive ways.

Defining a New Approach: Placing Social Cohesion at the Center of Development Strategies

Social cohesion is rarely clearly articulated in an operational way in national strategies or donors' country strategies. Governments and donors tend to use social cohesion more rhetorically than operationally. For the study, the team reviewed World Bank country strategies for 42 fragile and conflict-affected countries. Only 16 of the strategies mentioned that social cohesion was an important issue.

Usually the strategies that discuss cohesion also discuss inclusion, and in most cases the definitions are extremely similar. Cohesion and inclusion are seen as very similar concepts, but in reality they are very different. The strategies usually do not try to define the two concepts, which therefore remain vague and often not operational. In addition, only rarely are milestones in social cohesion explicitly included. The 2008 World Bank Country Partnership for Colombia, for example, mentions social cohesion in broad terms related to risks posed by the presence of illegal armed groups, narco-trafficking, and extreme poverty and inequality but does not include milestones to monitor progress.

There are exceptions, however. The country strategies for Kosovo, Nepal, Rwanda, and Philippines include a specific definition of social cohesion, designate it as a pillar, and set clear milestones to measure progress. The 2009 Interim Strategy Note (ISN) for Nepal, for example, recognizes "social inclusion" as fundamental to progress toward peace and development. The new political system in Nepal sets among its goals the transformation of social relations toward shared citizenship and inclusion of all social groups.

BOX 7.1

Social Cohesion in Kosovo's World Bank Interim Strategy Note, 2009

The 2009 Interim Strategy Note (ISN) for the Republic of Kosovo is the first strategic note to be developed for the country since it achieved independence in 2008. The ISN for Kosovo is one of the few World Bank country strategies that address social cohesion as an important development issue. The strategy recognizes that tackling issues of social cohesion is crucial for long-term sustainable development. "Strengthening Governance, Public Institutions and Social Cohesion" is one of the two pillars of the ISN (the other being "Accelerating Economic Growth"), which focuses on supporting social cohesion along with governance reform and transparent, inclusive, and effective institutions.

This pillar is in line with the government of Kosovo's (GoK) own development priorities, which acknowledge how important it is to support social and ethnic cohesion to ensure long-term, inclusive growth and minimize institutional fragility. Historically, ethnic fragmentation in Kosovo has damaged service delivery and contributed to marginalization and ethnic discrimination. The ISN argues that "the social and historical enforcement of different ethnic categories for vested or political interests in Kosovo presents serious difficulties in the accurate targeting of services such as health, education, water, waste management, etc." To tackle this issue, the GoK is currently unveiling policies to support multiethnic institutions and ethnic cohesion. Proposed measures to enhance cohesion among communities from different ethnic backgrounds include ethnic-inclusive employment and labor policies that focus on skilled jobs, as well as empowerment of and support for youth through increased access to services, quality education, and better-targeted social protection for vulnerable groups.

The ISN devotes particular attention to societal tensions and the fragility of institutions and plans accordingly a number of activities aimed at lessening societal tensions. Under ISN pillar II, "Strengthening Governance, Public Institutions and Social Cohesion," three sets of activities are envisaged:

- Supporting the creation of strong, transparent institutions;
- Fostering interethnic cooperation through two State and Peace Building Fund (SPF) operations: the Social Inclusion and Local Economic Development Project (US$5m) and the Second Kosovo Youth Development Project (US$2m);
- Increasing access to social services.

Focusing on Prevention, Even in Countries that Appear Relatively Cohesive and Have Strong Institutions

Adapting policies to take social cohesion into account requires understanding fragility as a continuum (or spectrum) rather than a static condition. As this book has argued, fragility can be seen as a continuum in which resilience and fragility compete to pull countries or societies toward more cohesion and stability or to push them down the continuum toward societal breakdown, massive violence, and collapse of institutions. That means that it will be ineffective to focus on fragile situations only when state breakdown, conflict, and violence have already occurred. Prevention is essential for an effective approach to reduce fragility and should be applied to countries that might actually be operating well, with seemingly strong institutions, but where societal dynamics might be playing out in a way that increases the risk of their moving toward increased fragility.

Thinking has evolved considerably on how to intervene in conflicts and fragile situations, and the importance of prevention is now fully recognized. The WDR 2011 insists on the importance of prevention. However, many of the classification systems and indicators that donors use still view fragility as a threshold, which limits interventions to countries below the threshold. The World Bank, for instance, defines "fragile states" as countries with a CPIA (Country Policy and Institutional Assessment) of less than 3.2.[1] Those countries are then eligible for special financing instruments that can help them address fragility. Establishing a threshold is important and necessary for allocating funds, but it should not be an indicator of when or where to intervene. Seeing fragility as a continuum changes the picture and shows the importance of intervening in countries with scores above the 3.2 threshold to prevent them from slipping toward state collapse and violent conflict.

The societal dynamics framework is useful not only for low-income countries, but for middle- and high-income countries as well. When designing development policies for most middle-income countries, a solid understanding of societal dynamics is necessary to identify the incentives that can create more cohesion. Even the richest countries have elements of fragility they know they must monitor. For example, the gap that continues to exist between African Americans and the rest of the U.S. population is an element of fragility in that country. Tensions surrounding the integration and assimilation of Muslim immigrants have fueled resentment between groups in many European countries. The isolation of youth in decaying towns in Russia, Ukraine, and other former Soviet countries is also a source of antisocial, self-destructive behaviors. These are fragile points in the countries' societal dynamics that can ultimately undermine social and economic development. Of course, in these examples countries have institutions that can help mediate and manage fragile situations before they start to undermine institutions and create uncontrollable violence.

Some very healthy and fast-growing countries might experience serious fragility at the subnational level. Some countries with strong institutions and relatively cohesive societies have subregions under serious stress. Actually, in many countries that have enjoyed real progress in institutional development, democratization, and growth, development has been undermined by localized conflict. In Mexico, drug trafficking has created enormous stress in the U.S. border region; Indonesia has various autonomy or independence movements at its fringe; and India suffers from violence related to the exclusion of some ethnic groups, while violence in slums around large urban areas has impeded growth. Brazil and Colombia are two countries that have taken clear actions to address the pockets of fragility via comprehensive policies to improve security, including important programs that support social inclusion and cohesion.

An important barrier to a greater emphasis on cohesion is that donors and development organizations tend to be reluctant to discuss issues perceived as political, which are often at the heart of social cohesion policies. However, by that avoidance they tend to ignore the political economy realities and dynamics that are central to policy making in fragile situations. Donors and development agencies can introduce a vision of social cohesion into dialogues with governments, one that transcends short-term power struggles and is essential for sustaining economic and social development. Failing to conduct a debate on social cohesion weakens the engagement of donors and development agencies, even on issues related to growth and poverty reduction, because it leaves no room to discuss some of the central considerations for the success of those policies.

Prioritizing Social Cohesion through a Flexible Programming Approach

Engaging societal dynamics requires much more flexibility than standard development programs often allow. The dynamics in fragile situations can be prone to sudden shifts that are difficult, if not impossible, to predict or plan for. Often multiple institutions are active and competing for influence, and social relations may be in flux.

A more flexible approach entails, above all, a more learn-by-doing attitude in project design and less-rigid sequencing that can accommodate change as it really happens in societies. This issue is very well illustrated by Barron, Diprose, and Woolcock (2011: 261) in their description of the experience of the Kecamatan Development Program (KDP) in Indonesia:

> A consistent lesson of social and political theory for development policy is that institutional change is rarely a linear process. As in evolutionary biology and intellectual paradigm shifts, institutional change is more accurately characterized by punctuated equilibriums—long periods of stasis that give way relatively suddenly (triggered by exogenous forces or the accumulation of endogenous pressures) to a new alignment of prevailing interests and ideas.

It is very difficult to understand societal dynamics in all their complexity at the start of an intervention. They are better engaged through constant feedback loops that can inform project implementation as the project develops. A tight planning process is not advisable, as it is impossible to predict exactly how groups will react to incentives and support. In fragile situations, it is usually not effective to follow a strict project cycle by assessing conditions, designing interventions, implementing the interventions, evaluating the impact, and repeating, because so much is unknown. As with many social interventions, success does not come in clear sequences; learning must occur constantly. Modifying actions cannot wait years and come about only after long and complex evaluations. That does not mean that impact evaluations should not be attempted but that they must be carried out differently than in situations where formal institutions mediate societal dynamics predictably and effectively (see text box).

These insights have important implications for the replicability of projects. The approach described above also has important implications for the idea, quite generalized among development practitioners, of encouraging projects and policies to be replicable across regions, countries, and continents. However, there is often a trade-off between replicability and flexibility in adapting to context. This is well articulated in the 2011 WDR discussion on best fit versus best practices (World Bank 2011). As mentioned in the previous section, context and history matter a great deal, as do norms and values. Also important is the way interventions are processed through the prism of intersubjectivity.

That is not to say that learning from successful projects is not important; indeed there has been great success in transferring experiences. The National Solidarity Program (NSP), which is widely recognized as the most

---

BOX 7.2

Action Research in Korogocho Slum in Nairobi to Understand Societal Dynamics around Violence

A Kenyan NGO, the National Institute for Health and Development (NIHD), is implementing a small action research program in a Nairobi slum. The program is financed by a World Bank program on violence prevention. Two researchers, young graduates who were born in the slum and live in the area, have been recruited to support small activities with the community to reduce violence. At the same time, they spend a large part of their time discussing issues with community members and having one-on-one discussions with youth in difficult situations. They use various methods to elicit participants' views, such as participatory mapping and focus groups, in addition to observing the behaviors of various local stakeholders. Once a week, they report their findings at the headquarters of the organization and discuss them with a social scientist, who provides advice on the way they collect data, the sampling, and issues to probe, but also on ways to ensure their personal security and manage trust with the community. This method provides invaluable data on the way the community handles issues of violence and helps answer questions about why some neighborhoods are better able to manage violence than others.

---

successful local-level program in Afghanistan, and the Yemen Social Development Fund, which provides basic community infrastructure, are seen as genuinely helping the poor,[2] and both were based on successful experiences in other places. The NSP was much influenced by the KDP, a very large community-driven development (CDD) program in Indonesia, and the Yemen Social Development Fund is based on similar experiences in Moldova and Armenia. However, all these projects have massively adapted the approach during implementation. A recent study of KDP (Barron, Diprose, and Woolcock 2007) shows that what seems to be most important in replication are the methods and approach used to identify how best to support resilience in a society, rather than the specific instruments employed. At the same time, some specific instruments can be replicated, such as including local facilitators to help communities produce project proposals. The balance between adaptability and replicability is one that has to be weighed carefully in each development context.

Development agencies and other external actors also bring their own values and worldviews, which interact with local dynamics, to their work. Donor organizations and development agencies are not value-neutral. To the contrary: they respond to political and other agendas defined by their boards or by the political systems of the countries in which they operate. Even the most technocratic organizations are guided by a set of values that are implicit in the design and implementation of programs.

That influence is felt in many areas: in an organization's requirements for financing programs, the way they work in the field and the people they employ, and the set of values embedded in the programs they finance. Most of the largest donor groups are Western and espouse an ideology in which the individual is of primary importance and individual rights are the foundation of development. As a result, they sometimes clash with societies that hold a more collective vision of the world, in which the community takes precedence over the individual. The sense that aid is equivalent to a "cultural invasion" can be particularly strong in some cultures. In such a case, development interventions can inadvertently increase fragility.

Creating Space to Support Voice and Mediation between Various Understandings of World and Society

Institutions, especially well-functioning state institutions, have an important function in mediating across different groups in society. The term "mediation" is used here to refer to the practice of helping groups with different values and understandings of the world, and which operate according to different intersubjective meaning systems, to be able to interact and undertake common projects. That role includes conflict resolution but is not limited to it. Mediation is creating a cultural space where various groups can exchange peacefully and where people can start to incorporate the views of others in their own understanding. Mazzarella (2004: 346) gives the following definition: "Mediation is a name that we might give to the processes by which a given social dispensation produces and reproduces itself in and through a particular set of media."

Mediation can therefore be understood as spaces, mechanisms, or more broadly, institutions that allow groups to address their differences peacefully and build convergence. It will undoubtedly look different in different contexts because it involves bridging different intersubjective meanings and different values and views of the world, as well as political interests and power competitions. In that sense, one could argue that a well-functioning democratic system is essentially a well-functioning mediation process, allowing for peaceful and constructive competition between different views on society and governance. As opposed to a more minimalist definition, based on contested elections, this definition of democracy better captures its substantive conceptions, allowing for "degree-oriented notions of democracy that better describe the dynamics of lived political experience in many cases" (Wedeen 2008: 107).

The process of mediation should support and facilitate the processes of social change, as any society today is confronted with rapid changes, even ones in the most remote areas. That process of change plays out in particular through issues of changes in gender roles, relationships between youth and other generations, the growing influence of conservative religious movements, and other trends. These social shifts inevitably create conflict because they alter the balances of power in society. Institutions need to respond by creating spaces for various groups to participate, especially women, youth, lower castes, and other, often marginalized groups. The goal is to work toward empowering these groups, rather than advocating a top-down change in power relationships, by opening spaces for dialogue outside of traditional institutions.

Every society has institutions that allow people to express their views, under different rules and in different manners. Sometimes it is best to build on these spaces because they are adapted to the particular context. They can be highly controlled or very open, or they can be segregated according to age, gender, caste, or ethnicity. For instance, Wedeen (2008) argues that the "mini-publics" created by *qat* chewing sessions in Yemen are a central institution for expressing voices and for mediating competition for power, different ideas, and the like (see box 7.3).

Building on the existing spaces where mediation occurs is key. For example, in many places, markets for selling food and other goods are extremely important space for mediation. They are typically where different groups meet. Various studies have examined the mediation between herders and farmers in Sahelian Africa and how the disruption of that process can undermine the resilience of those communities and increase tensions among groups. For instance, Lovejoy and Baier (1975) demonstrated how colonization disrupted the once-peaceful corporation/trade between the nomadic Tuareg and the sedentary Hausa people in the regions of northern Nigeria and Niger, undermining the local specialization patterns and the ability

---

BOX 7.3

Qat Chewing in Yemen

The majority of Yemenis chew the leaves of the *qat* plant *(Catha edulis)*—a mild stimulant—on a daily basis during afternoon social gatherings. According to some estimates, as many as 72 percent of males and 35 percent of females habitually chew *qat* in Yemen (World Bank 2009). High demand has also made *qat* the number-one cash-crop in Yemen, crowding out food crops and other vegetation from arable lands. A 2007 World Bank study found that *qat* production accounted for 6 percent of Yemen's GDP and one-third of the country's agricultural production. However, the water-intensive nature of the plant has raised concerns about irreversible depletion of groundwater levels. Concerns have also been raised about the impact of *qat* chewing on health and poverty. "*Qat* is consumed by men, women and children; its use is extremely time consuming; it drains the family budget; has adverse health effects; negatively affects work performance and thus contributes to poverty" (World Bank 2007: i).

However, in her book *Peripheral Visions*, Lisa Wedeen (2008) argues that everyday practices of political contestation, like the discussions at *qat* chewing, can create democratic publics where ideas are exchanged and contested. In addition, she argues that discussions at some of the *qat* chews can escalate all the way up to decision makers directly influencing policy. Therefore, she argues, the gatherings can also play an important mediation role between groups in society. She adds that this role can be even more enhanced in fragile states like Yemen, where state capacity to generate national loyalty is weak.

---

of communities to deal with droughts. Similarly, Davidheiser and Luna (2008) highlight how changes in production systems and the adoption of Western-style land tenure regimes have disrupted the symbiotic relationship between the Fulbe pastoralists and farmers in West Africa, leading to intercommunal conflict. These examples demonstrate the importance of mediation in promoting resilience and intergroup cooperation, emphasizing the need for governments and development agencies to consider these mediation processes and the potential impact on them of proposed interventions.

In some cases, it may be necessary to build new, neutral spaces for mediation to occur. Development policies should actively seek to include spaces for voice and mediation to deal with the main differences. Mediation mechanisms will change based on the type of situation. Creativity is important, and policy makers need to identify the spaces and the mechanisms to ensure that mediation reaches its ultimate outcome of a peaceful society. Some development interventions specifically seek to create a mediation space for marginalized groups. For instance, the *Association Des Femmes Juristes in Central Africain République* tries to provide a mediation space to facilitate better access to justice for women in the Central African Republic (see box 7.4).

Some very practical operational approaches are available that can support mediation. These can include creating spaces for dialogue and mediation as permanent features of local and central government structures in the form of consultative councils; permanent mechanisms for citizen consultation; or support for activities that involve various sociocultural groups in discussing public policy concerns. One-time consultations around specific projects do not allow real mediation to take place, as it requires long-term engagement between partners as a basis to establish the necessary trust.

Another way to foster mediation is to support the involvement of civil society organizations in a mediating role between various groups in society. Mediators can be NGOs, local leaders, or staff of local government agencies. They must be people or organizations that are cognizant of various intersubjective meaning systems at play and can help bridge from one to the other (such mediators are used in Afghanistan National Solidarity Program). These mediators can be indispensable in helping project managers

---

BOX 7.4

The *Association des Femmes Juristes in Central Africain République*

The *Association des Femmes Juristes* is a group of women with training in law who try to ensure that poor and often illiterate women in the Central African Republic have a fair trial. They help mediate between various systems of justice, provide access to the formal system if possible, and if not, ensure that women have a fair trial through local mechanisms. By mediating between the modern state system of justice and local mechanisms for conflict resolution, this NGO seeks to help women have better access to resolution of disagreements. In effect, the NGO creates a space for women, as individuals or as groups, to voice their concerns and helps them navigate various systems of conflict resolution to obtain the fairest treatment possible.

engage internal societal dynamics and can ensure that some subgroups that might not have voice have a way to express themselves.

The mediation spaces are most effective if they are open to a wide variety of groups, especially vulnerable groups, such as youth and women. In some cases different spaces will need to be provided for different groups, at least at the beginning. In some cases women will not speak up in an assembly where men are present, for instance. Finally, it is also important to ensure that traditional and other local systems for consultation and discussion are not "crowded out" by the new processes.

Improving Analytical Methods and Tools to Better Assess Societal Dynamics and the Context in Which They Operate

To be operational, the concept of social cohesion needs to be defined in each specific historical and social context. Relatively little can be said about what constitutes good social cohesion policy in the abstract, without relating it to a specific context. Governments and donors too often use the concept of social cohesion in their strategies without anchoring it to a country's reality. As a result, social cohesion often comes across as a vague, poorly articulated concept and fails to become associated with clear programs and policies. Without a specific understanding of what social cohesion means in the context of each country, it is impossible to establish benchmarks that can assess whether policies and programs have achieved their goals.

Asking the Right Questions: Defining Social Cohesion in Context

The study of societal dynamics is essentially the study of how a given society works. This implies asking questions about how groups define fairness and justice, how identity forms for different groups, where the divisions are, how those divisions developed, where the sources of resilience and cohesion are, and so on. Researching these dynamics does not require an entirely new set of research tools. Rather it challenges the researcher to apply a particular lens to the analysis of data. The questions that will be asked of the data will differ from those asked in other types of analysis.

An analytical approach emphasizing societal dynamics focuses on group dynamics, rather than on individuals. A very important difference between this and some of the classical analyses of economic and social development is that an analysis of societal dynamics attempts to capture group dynamics. "Group dynamics" refers to behavior influenced by the larger group, where individuals are interconnected through shared identities. Economic and social analyses tend to focus on individual behaviors and household behaviors but rarely on sociocultural group behaviors. A group-based analysis starts with an understanding of the different groups that are present in a society or area of intervention, their roles and interests. From this, efforts will need to be made to gather information from all the different groups. It will be important to speak not only with group leaders, but with other members of the groups as well, to obtain varying perspectives from within the group. Questions could focus on how the group is identified, what makes it different from other groups, what "works" and does not work in terms of group dynamics and collective action, and how the group relates to other groups and the state.

Such an analytical approach will also emphasize the sources of cohesion and fragility in society, as different groups perceive them. For example, during the fieldwork for the study, focus group facilitators opened conversations by asking questions such as, What holds this community together? What is currently "working" in this community? What is dividing people? Where are the main conflicts here, and between whom? Where are the sources of resilience and cohesion, and how are they currently being mobilized? These kinds of questions allow the researcher to understand the specific experiences of people in what are often divided societies, through their own words and experiences. This perspective can be very informative in discerning how to implement programs that can address the divisions.

It is also important to understand how people perceive different outcomes, rather than only the outcomes themselves. Such an analysis might begin by assessing the measurable inequalities across groups in a society, but it will not stop there. The perceptions that accompany those inequalities need to be given equal importance, if not more. How do people understand these differences and how do they feel about them? Are they rooted in history, and how? What factors have exacerbated these perceptions, and what factors seem to have reduced them in the past? However, assessing perceptions requires care. Perceptions can change quickly and are not always a predictor of how people will behave. Assessing perceptions through opinion polls, for instance, is often superficial and fails to reveal the deeper views people have on an issue. Assessing perception well requires interviews in depth and focus group discussions. It needs careful interpretation based on context and history.

Looking at group dynamics also means understanding how groups define fairness and justice. What criteria are used to assess a situation as fair, and by whom? What makes the criteria important to different groups over other criteria? It can also help to explore specific events or incidents when perceptions of injustice have been created, to understand what drives these perceptions and the type of incidents that incite them. It is also useful to assess what type of processes or actions would be considered fair in addressing those perceptions.

Defining social cohesion in context means taking a problem-oriented approach to program and policy design. Rather than looking first at how to implement, for example, a set of policy reforms or a specific program, donors and governments would do well to ask how people are connecting, or not, to achieve different goals, resolve disputes, and so on. In other words, putting social cohesion at the center means defining, first, the types of convergence that are present, and among whom.

Last but not least, it is crucial for a focus on societal dynamics to view these dynamics in historical context. Researchers must constantly ask about the origins of current divisions and the factors that have helped to perpetuate them. Similarly, they can work to understand the factors that have allowed certain groups to coexist peacefully. By placing the present in a historical context, it is possible to explore how specific trajectories involving actors, events, and experiences unfold. Studying the past along with the present explains how and why the past affects the present in different ways, at different junctures, and how an understanding of the past can be used to move forward constructively.

Choosing the Right Tools: Challenges to Measuring Social Cohesion and Fragility

Taking a society-centered approach will ultimately be more challenging than more standard social or political analysis in fragile situations because the dynamics under study are inherently sensitive and difficult to measure. Conducting research in fragile situations presents clear challenges to collecting data and understanding what the data mean in context. Existing data collected by official sources are often weak and unreliable. Weakened infrastructure, security concerns, or other issues may make it difficult to access some areas and conduct research. No less important are issues of trust, as communities or societies that are deeply divided may be reluctant to share information with researchers.

The study of societal dynamics has much to learn from previous attempts to measure social cohesion in particular. Those studies, mainly in the field of economics, have attempted to establish some kind of relationship (causal or not) between some proxy for social cohesion and particular economic indicators (see Easterly, Ritzen, and Woolcock 2007; UNRISD 2010 for a review). Various indices have been developed, comprising a variety of indicators. Most include measures of inequality, usually in terms of the Gini coefficient, poverty rates, or income inequality. Others add in measures of inclusion, often defined in terms of access to different services, such as education (literacy rates, school enrollment) or health care (mortality, life expectancy), or access to employment. Some even include access to technology. Some of the studies have found important relationships between these proxy indicators for social cohesion and institutional performance, as well as economic outcomes that one has reason to value (income equality, for example) (UNRISD 2010).

Other studies have attempted to unpack the concept into its constituent elements. For example, Kearns and Forrest (2000) identified five components of social capital: (a) common values and civic culture; (b) social order and social control; (c) social solidarity and reduction in wealth inequality; (d) social networks and social capital; and (e) territorial belonging and identity. It often requires specialized surveys to get at questions of trust, feelings of belonging, values, participation, and so on. Early such attempts include the work of Easterly, Ritzen, and Woolcock (2006), who used indicators of ethnic diversity and data from the World Values Survey. Others have focused on a single country where census data and opinion surveys are available. For example, Rajulton, Ravanera, and Beaujot (2007) drew on data from a national survey of volunteering and participation to develop an index of six indicators that cover the economic, political, and social realms. The need for such specialized data collection creates obvious challenges in terms of comparability across societies and countries, and doing it is practically impossible in many fragile settings where data are scarce. One particularly promising initiative in this regard is the Indices of Social Development project, being developed by the International Institute of Social Studies, which includes a dimension on intergroup cohesion (see box 7.5).

Indices of Social Development

The International Institute for Social Studies has developed a set of indices bringing together 200 indicators from 25 data sources in 193 countries. The current data set covers 1990 to 2010. The indicators are clustered around five dimensions of social development:

- Civic activism, measuring use of media and protest behavior
- Clubs and associations, defined as membership in local voluntary associations
- Intergroup cohesion, which measures ethnic and sectarian tensions and discrimination
- Interpersonal safety and trust, focusing on perceptions and incidences of crime and personal transgressions
- Gender equality, reflecting gender discrimination in home, work, and public life.

The inclusion of dimensions on cohesion and trust offers potential for understanding those dynamics and monitoring them in various countries. The use of data from internationally comparable sources allows for comparability across countries and for tracking trends over time. Because the coverage includes countries at various stages of development, the indices also allow understanding of societal dynamics in countries that are not deemed fragile but that may have pockets of fragility.

Given the challenges in measurement, it is no surprise that establishing relationships, let alone causal relationships, associated with social cohesion has been difficult. As Durlauf and Fafchamps (2004: 61–62) note, the concept of social cohesion has seen

> the development of a number of interesting data sets as well as the development of a number of provocative hypotheses, [but] much of the empirical literature is at best suggestive and at worst easy to discount. So while one can point to no end of studies in which a variable that is asserted to proxy for social capital has some effect on individuals or groups, it is very difficult to treat the finding as establishing a causal role for social capital.

Social cohesion is probably best viewed not as a single quality that can be measured and affected directly by policy, but instead as a set of attributes that interact in complex ways and in different combinations. Given that complexity and dynamism, purely quantitative methods will be insufficient for a full understanding of the extent of these dynamics—the value of some indexes notwithstanding. The ideal approach will combine quantitative tools with rigorous political and social analysis, using some of the tools described below.

Combining Social and Political Analysis

A society-centered approach sits at the intersection of political and social analysis. Political economy analysis is increasingly being seen as a very relevant analytical tool in fragile environments to capture the interactions between political and economic processes—especially the distribution of power and wealth between different groups—and their impact on fragile (and nonfragile) situations. In fragile environments, however, societal dynamics are complex and multilayered, which necessitates going beyond political economy analysis. Societal dynamics can be better understood at the intersection between social and political analysis. Each brings important elements to the understanding of societal dynamics from different angles. Ideally, both types of analysis should be carried out together, so as to inform one another.

Political analysis provides an understanding of power issues. Political analysis examines how power structures and state institutions affect societies; how historical relations between stakeholders contribute to societal tensions; and how external influences impinge on internal political developments. It explores the interface between formal institutions and informal ones and explains how their interactions affect relations between the state and communities. It locates current political dynamics into a historical perspective, making it possible to understand why stakeholders are likely to act the way they do, how past hatred and negative perceptions affect current relationships. Finally, it looks at how external forces, such as regional political developments (conflicts, coups, refugees, economic crises), and the diaspora affect societies internally.

Social analysis also has a strong part to play in elucidating the nature of the relationships between and within groups, the divisions among them, and so on. At the heart of social analysis lies the objective to investigate the way that social and cultural processes shape society. Social analysis can help explore how notions of ethnic identities, vis-à-vis citizenship, and vertical and horizontal inequalities affect societies; how stakeholders, especially marginalized ones, influence social processes; how opposing values, cultures, and perceptions damage societies; and lastly, how war-induced trauma, violence, and resilience alter the character of a society. More specifically, social analysis investigates the interaction between identities based on ethnicity, religion, region, and tribe, and citizenship in a polity. It examines how vertical and horizontal inequalities influence each other, especially if horizontal inequalities lead to mobilization of relatively deprived groups. Social analysis probes the interaction between society and its most vulnerable stakeholders, such as women and youth.

It is clear that political analysis and social analysis are not watertight categories; they deal with matters that are strongly interconnected. To illustrate, political elites use their status to acquire economic power, and economic status is used to acquire political power. Identities are activated to highlight the us-versus-them syndrome, exacerbate divisions, and include certain groups while excluding others. Identity becomes the basis for specific groups to access power at the cost of others. In a similar vein, those in political power use their status to reward supporters from a similar identity-based group (be it ethnic, tribal, religious, or regional). Political and social analyses are important to deepen understanding of these nexuses and how they unfold. State–society relations need to be viewed with both a political and a social lens to capture how political institutions influence communities and are influenced by them. Finally, in a society, group cultures and values that are at odds with each other can affect the functioning of the state. Both political and social analyses are needed to shed light on their interactions, which are often based on deep-seated historical resentments. These are just a few examples, but they demonstrate why these analyses ought not to be carried out independently of each other, since social and political issues affect, and are affected by, each other.

Data Collection and Analytical Tools

Some research tools may be particularly useful for getting at the layers of dynamics that are at play in a particular society. In some cases participatory methods may be useful in bringing people to articulate their own perceptions and place them in historical context. Depending on the cultural context, people may prefer to speak in groups or as individuals, and that needs to be assessed in each environment. In some cases the composition of interview or focus groups will need to reflect divisions in society (for example, by gender, or age, or ethnicity), whereas in others it may be more useful or possible for groups to mix. Regardless of the specific tools used, it will be important to combine different methods and triangulate them in the analysis to capture all the dynamics at play in a given context.

Using a mix of quantitative and qualitative methods is often an effective way to understand the general trends in a place, as well as the processes and meanings behind them. In fragile contexts, it may not be easy to elucidate the dynamics at play or the meanings that different groups assign to them—underscoring the need to gather data from different sources and, if possible, at different times. For example, as detailed in box 7.6, the KDP program in Indonesia combined ethnographic investigation, informant surveys, and newspaper evidence. The triangulation of data from the

---

BOX 7.6

Kecamatan Development Program: Conflict Analysis Using Mixed Methods

The KDP in Indonesia is one of the world's largest social development projects. Its aims are to provide small-scale development assistance to poor rural communities and also create a bottom-up democratic movement, in a fragile environment, that allows villages to participate in local conflict resolution. KDP requires villages to submit proposals for funding to a community forum, comprising a committee of their peers, which decides which proposals will receive funding. Proposals are selected through open discussion and transparent decision making. The important question is whether these forums enable villagers to acquire skills of local conflict mediation and whether the forums complement existing local conflict resolution institutions. The question cannot be examined with solely quantitative or solely qualitative methods. It requires the use of innovative mixed methods.

In KDP, the team began by selecting project locations. It was decided that the work would be done in two provinces that were very different (demographically and economically), in regions within those provinces that demonstrated different levels of capacity for conflict resolution, and in villages within those regions that were comparable except that some participated in KDP and others did not. Thus quantitative methods were used to select sites for qualitative investigation, and results from qualitative work fed into quantitative surveys:

a. *Ethnographic Investigation*. Researchers conducted qualitative fieldwork in 41 villages over nine months to develop 68 cases that explored the evolution of local conflicts. They used the process-tracing method to identify the factors that transform tensions

(continued next page)

BOX 7.6 *(continued)*

into different outcomes. Under KDP, research was conducted on key themes so that the data could enrich the cases and be used for cross-village comparisons. In general, researchers used four qualitative techniques—in-depth informant interviews, focus group discussions, informal interviews, and participant observations—to collect data on cases and on the key themes.

b. *Quantitative Methods.* Quantitative techniques were used to capture observable variables. This complemented qualitative analysis, increasing the reliability of results. Key informant surveys, involving participant observation, were carried out to gather comparable responses to questions dealing with perceptions. These surveys covered both KDP and non-KDP villages, which provided explanations for variations within KDP sites and across KDP and non-KDP locations, as well as allowed for testing the generality of the hypotheses emerging from qualitative work.

c. *Dataset of Reported Conflicts.* To assess patterns and types of conflicts, local newspapers were used to develop a dataset that broadly mapped conflict, levels of violence, and the nature of incidents in the research villages.

Source: Barron, Diprose, and Woolcock 2011, chap.3.

different sources and collection methods allowed for more robust conclusions than could have been obtained from using only quantitative or qualitative methods on the conditions under which KDP could or could not be part of the problem or the solution to local conflict.

Comparative research can also help in understanding the societal dynamics in a given context by comparing them to those elsewhere. The objective is to understand the commonalities, patterns, interactions, and motivations that underlie specific outcomes over time or across cases. Comparative analysis uses process tracing to pinpoint the mechanisms and dynamics that lead to specific outcomes, or that push outcomes in different directions despite initial conditions being equal, or that lead to similar outcomes despite variations in independent variables. Two examples are given in box 7.7.

Surveys can be designed or adapted to capture some information about societal dynamics. They have been usefully applied in contexts of violent conflict to get at important dynamics such as who is in conflict with whom, what are the impacts of the conflict, and what are the drivers of cohesion and resilience. Some developments have been made with surveys

BOX 7.7

Comparative Studies of Communal Violence

In the two studies described here, comparative research methodologies were used to better understand the factors that promoted ethnic peace or, conversely, increased ethnic violence between communities at the subnational level. Using case studies (medieval Indian Ocean trade ports and cities in India that experience communal violence versus ones that do not) and process tracing, the studies explore why some societies experienced fragility while others became robust.

Model of Inter-Ethnic Peaceful Coexistence
In his study *Maintaining Peace across Ethnic Lines: New Lessons from the Past*, Saumitra Jha sketches a model of the incentives that push agents to engage in trade in areas populated by locals and nonlocals. The model is applied to trading ports in medieval (17th century) India, where Hindus and Muslims developed norms and had incentives for peaceful coexistence. Using the logic of Hindu-Muslim cooperation in medieval ports from the empirical study and drawing from his theoretical framework, Jha offers broader lessons about why ethnic tolerance is fostered in some cases, and ethnic violence results in others. He concludes that (a) complementarities, rather than competition, must exist between groups; (b) the sources of ethnic complementarity should be costly to replicate or expropriate; and, (c) to maintain peaceful coexistence, an effective mechanism to redistribute the gains from trade must be in place, so that there are no glaring wealth inequalities.

Toward a Theory of Ethnic Peace: The Role of Intercommunal Networks in Civic Life
In the book *Ethnic Conflict and Civic Life: Hindus and Muslims in India*, Varshney (2002) tries to solve the puzzle of why some places, despite ethnic diversity, remain peaceful, whereas others experience recurring riots. Using the town or city as the unit of analysis, Varshney selected six cities in India—three cities that were riot-prone and three that were peaceful. These were arranged in pairs comprising a city where communal violence was routine and a city where communal violence was largely absent. To ensure comparability, demographic variables (roughly similar Hindu-Muslim percentages in the city), history, and cultural similarities, among others, served as controls.[a]

(continued next page)

BOX 7.7 (continued)

Based on research, surveys, and interviews conducted in the six cities, the study investigated the mechanisms that resulted in variations and commonalities across cases. It found that in cities with robust forms of civic engagement, particularly associational forms (business organizations, professional organizations, trade unions, sport clubs across communal lines), communal violence was less probable and peace was the most likely outcome even when there were tensions. In contrast, in cities without civic networks, or with only everyday forms of engagement (simple, routine informal interactions), organized gangs, politicians, or rumors were able to tear the social fabric apart and encourage communal violence.

Source: Jha 2007; Varshney 2002.

Note

a. Initial conditions were the same, but outcomes were different: The first city pair in the study, Aligarh and Calicut, had similar population percentages of Hindus and Muslims; the second pair in the study, Hyderabad and Lucknow, had similar population percentages, common histories of Muslim rule, and cultural similarities; and the third pair, Ahmedabad and Surat, shared history, language, and culture.

---

incorporating issues of conflict and violence. These include using open-ended questionnaires, fixed-answer categories, and standardized questionnaires with additional questions to better address specific issues, to name a few.[3] Given the sensitive nature of issues linked to conflict, violence, and fragility, surveys dealing with these topics should use more than one technique to ask essential questions to ensure that findings reflect actual priorities and concerns. Other creative applications of survey methods are discussed in box 7.8 and provide guidance for using surveys and questionnaires to probe and measure societal dynamics that are likely to affect fragility.

Finally, several indices have been built by think tanks and donors to assess levels of fragility. The CPIA, discussed earlier, is used by the World Bank for special resource allocations. Others are discussed in box 7.9. Most of these indices focus on governance, although some concern conflict and peace building. In some cases, they may include an assessment of societal dynamics or factors close to societal dynamics. Societal dynamics, however, remains marginal to the constitution of these indicators.

Clearly indices per se are not effective in capturing the depth of societal dynamics and how they affect situations of fragility, as they are usually

---

BOX 7.8

Adapting Survey Methods for Understanding Societal Dynamics

Purposively Designed Surveys. The field of micro-level analyses uses a small number of surveys that are designed to collect data and uncover conflict dynamics at the micro level. They include (1) ex-combatant surveys that focus on the experiences of former soldiers and rebels, their reasons for joining, and demobilization and reintegration; (2) genocide and atrocities surveys that focus on profiles of perpetrators, the fate of victims and type of violence suffered; (3) displaced people surveys that focus on reasons for return or preference to stay displaced and livelihood choices; and (4) postconflict reconstruction surveys that focus on the impacts of peacekeeping operations, attitudes towards the legitimacy of using violence, and the possibility of renewed conflict.

Creative Use of Socioeconomic Surveys and Living Standard Measurement Surveys (LSMS). The main objective of socioeconomic surveys and LSMS is to "assess the effectiveness of policies and interventions aimed at improving living standards" (Households in Conflict Network 2010). They are not designed to measure conflict and violence and therefore do not usually include questions on the different dimensions of conflict and their links. Some surveys, however, have addressed that challenge by intentionally including a module, or at least a series of questions, on experiences with conflict and violence. For example, several LSMS contain security modules, or specific questions as part of modules, that deal with issues ranging from personal safety and crime as challenges for businesses, to security and war as reasons for migration or decisions not to return home.

Some surveys have creatively used data collected in conflict-affected areas to analyze the processes, interrelationships, and consequences of conflict and violence. For instance, in several cases, data collected in conflict areas, on topics such as livelihoods and the labor market, health, and demographic outcomes have been systematically used to make links with conflict and violence (labor market data with displacement; livelihoods with reasons for participation in conflicts; health and mortality with genocide) (Households in Conflict Network 2010).

---

focused at the macro level and provide a static snapshot of an issue. Their significance, however, is that they strengthen historical and social analysis by highlighting how a specific issue is standardized. That in turn can be used to determine how that issue "scores" in a country over time, as well as to aid cross-country comparisons when needed.

BOX 7.9

Sample of Indexes to Measure Fragility and Cohesion

For a detailed discussion of indexes that highlight the societal dimensions of fragility, refer to: *Users Guide on Measuring Fragility* (UNDP 2009). Also see box 7.5.

Ethnic Power Relations.[b] The Ethnic Power Relations (EPR) dataset, a collaboration of ETH Zurich and University of California Los Angeles, identifies all politically relevant ethnic groups in a country and shows their access to state power. It covers all countries in the world, from 1946 to 2005, and has data on more than 733 groups. It identifies ethnopolitical configurations and the degree to which representatives of each politically relevant group held executive-level state power, ranging from total government control to overt political discrimination. It also shows when an armed conflict was fought in the name of a particular group.

The Legatum Prosperity Index.[c] The Prosperity Index defines prosperity on the basis of wealth and well-being, that is, direct correlation between high GDP and happy, healthy, and free citizens. It assesses 110 countries (comprising over 90 percent of the world population) on eight subindexes, with 89 variables, each of which has a definite effect on economic growth and personal well-being. The eight subindexes are economy, entrepreneurship and opportunity, governance, education, health, safety and security, personal freedom, and social capital.

Notes

a. For details, see: *"Indices of Social Development"*, International Institute of Social Studies, Erasmus University Rotterdam, 2011.

b. For details, see Andreas Wimmer, Lars-Erik Cederman, and Brian Min, 2009. "Ethnic Politics and Armed Conflict: A Configurational Analysis of a New Global Dataset," *American Sociological Review* 74: 316–37. Also see the websites www.epr.ucla.edu and http://dvn.iq.harvard.edu/dvn/dv/epr.

c. For details, see www.prosperity.com.

Notes

1. The CPIA is used to allocate International Development Association (IDA) resources. The CPIA is a broad set of indicators comprising an average of 16 clusters and is based on assessments made by World Bank staff. The CPIA assesses the quality of a country's present policy and institutional framework. "Quality" refers to how conducive that framework is to poverty reduction, sustainable growth, and the effective use of development assistance. The CPIA ratings are used in the IDA allocation process and several other corporate activities.
2. World Bank evaluation of the NSP and Yemen Social Funds.

3. Open-ended questionnaires allow respondents to discuss openly priorities that they see as important, to raise issues voluntarily and ensure that their opinions are clearly expressed. The problem is that often the issues that emerge as first reactions are not their real concerns and views. Fixed answer categories give respondents the ability to choose but often they become confused about what the choices mean. Standard questionnaires, often with direct questions, are necessary, but they need to be complemented by additional questions to ensure that priorities and needs are expressed correctly.

References

Barron, Patrick, Rachael Diprose, and Michael Woolcock. 2007. "Local Conflict and Development Projects in Indonesia: Part of the Problem or Part of a Solution." Policy Research Working Paper 4212, World Bank, Washington, DC.

———. 2011. *Contesting Development: Participatory Projects and Local Conflict Dynamics in Indonesia*. New Haven, CT: Yale University Press.

Brück, Tilman, Patricia Justino, Philip Verwimp and Alexandra Avdeenko. 2010. "Identifying Conflict and Violence in Micro-Level Surveys". Households in Conflict Network (HiCN) Working Paper 79.

Davidheiser, Mark and Aniuska M. Luna. 2008. "From Complementarity to Conflict: A Historical Analysis of Farmer-Fulbe Relations in West Africa". AJCR, Vol. 8, No. 1, 2008.

Durlauf, S., and M. Fafchamps. 2004. "Social Capital," NBER Working Paper No. 10485, National Bureau for Economic Research, Cambridge, MA.

Easterly, William, Jozef Ritzen, and Michael Woolcock. 2006. "Social Cohesion, Institutions and Growth." *Economics and Politics* 18 (2): 103–20.

Jha, Saumtira. 2007. "Maintaining Peace across Ethnic Lines: New Lessons from the Past." *Economics of Peace and Security Journal*.

Kearns, Ade, and Ray Forrest. 2000 "Social Cohesion and Multi-Level Urban Governance." *Urban Studies* 37 (5): 995–1017.

Lovejoy, Paul E. and Stephen Baier. 1975. "The Desert-Side Economy of the Central Sudan". The International Journal of African Historical Studies, Vol. 8, No. 4 (1975), pp. 551–581. Boston University African Studies Center.

Mata, Javier Fabra and Sebastian Ziaja. 2009. *Users' Guide on Measuring Fragility*. German Development Institute/Deutsches Institut für Entwicklungspolitik (DIE) United Nation Development Programme (UNDP).

Mazzarella, William. 2004. "Culture, Globalization, Mediation." *Annual Review of Anthropology* 33: 345–67.

Rajulton, F., Z. Ravanera, and R. Beaujot. 2007. "Measuring Social Cohesion: An Experiment Using the Canadian National Survey of Giving, Volunteering and Participating." *Social Indicators Research* 80 (3): 461–92.

UNRISD (United Nations Research Institute for Social Development). 2010. *Defining and Measuring Social Cohesion*. London: RISD.

Varshney, A. 2002. *Ethnic Conflict and Civil Life: Hindus and Muslims in India*. New Haven, CT: Yale University Press.

Wedeen, Lisa. 2008. *Peripheral Visions: Publics, Power, and Performance in Yemen*. Chicago: University of Chicago Press.

World Bank. 2007. *Yemen : Towards Qat Demand Reduction*. Washington, DC. https://openknowledge.worldbank.org/handle/10986/7734

———. 2011. *2011 World Development Report*: *Conflict, Security and Development*. Washington, DC: World Bank.

CHAPTER 8

Designing Policies and Programs to Build Social Cohesion

Finding ways to intervene effectively in fragile situations is one of the most urgent challenges of development today. The study reported in this book has departed from mainstream approaches by viewing the problem of fragility as one not only of state capacity, but also of dysfunctional relationships in society. It has advanced the argument that fostering social cohesion—that is, improving the quality of relationships across groups—is an essential part of reducing fragility.

Viewing the problem of fragility from the perspective of societal dynamics opens up many possibilities for programming in fragile situations. In particular, this approach calls for targeting interventions beyond the state to address fragile relationships across groups in society, perhaps more easily said than done. The dominant approach to fragile situations—building core state capacities—is well established among donors and policy makers. The tools available to practitioners are designed to work with the state as the central actor in fragile situations. Expanding the focus to give more attention to societal dynamics will require adapting those tools, where possible, and developing new ones.

This book does not aim to resolve all the technical issues that will arise with that shift in focus. Overall, it probably raises more questions than it answers. But given the scale of investment in dealing with fragile situations and their effects around the world, these questions would seem worth raising for debate, and it is hoped that the book will contribute to that discussion. This chapter takes a first step toward implementing an approach that emphasizes societal dynamics by looking at some of the prominent instruments currently used in fragile situations and how they might be better applied to address relationships across groups in society. The discussion focuses on ways to address the two factors, described in the previous chapters, that seem key to building social cohesion: dealing with perceptions of injustice across groups and improving the quality of interactions between institutions.

Addressing Perceptions of Injustice across Groups

As discussed in chapter 4, reducing perceptions of injustice across groups reinforces social cohesion. When groups perceive that they are being treated unfairly, they may feel little inclination to build any kind of relationships with other groups. Those perceptions may correspond to measurable inequalities across groups, such as income inequality, but not always. Perceptions of injustice can also be related to feelings of being disrespected by other groups, whether because of culture, race, or other differences. These feelings of being treated unjustly or treated with disrespect can be immensely socially disruptive for society overall.

Understanding How Different Groups Perceive Fairness and Justice

Ideas about what is fair will vary across contexts and even between groups. Some groups may be more interested in equal outcomes, while others place more importance on the process used to arrive at the outcomes. A particular outcome can be perceived as fair by one group, but not another, because of the criteria the two groups use to evaluate it. In a given environment, people might observe different policy outcomes, such as service coverage, as equal between communities, but not necessarily perceive the overall environment as fair or just.

It is crucial to understand the meanings people assign to fairness and justice in a given context to be able to address those perceptions. Perceptions of injustice by certain groups are often deeply rooted in history, for example, in cases where one group lags behind others as the result of something that directly affected previous generations. Descendants of slave populations in many countries often lag in human development indicators and wealth. The same is true for certain castes in India and Nepal and for indigenous populations all over the world (see World Bank 2011b, on India). It can take generations for the descendants of slaves who were illiterate to reach the same level of education as the rest of the population. It can also take generations for descendants to integrate themselves into social capital networks, or to create their own, and achieve social mobility. In this way, history has a big role in creating an "authorizing environment" that makes certain behaviors and discourse legitimate, and it strongly influences both individual and group agency. Understanding these legacies helps place current social divisions in context.

It is equally important for practitioners to be aware that they bring to their work their own biases and perceptions about what is fair and just, and that they may not align with the perceptions of the beneficiary community. For that reason, it is crucial for interventions to be informed by a context-specific understanding of what justice and fairness mean to people, as well as the mechanisms they rely on to dialogue across groups, to resolve conflict, and to address other, related tasks.

The following sections discuss some ways to reduce the perceptions of injustice and unfairness felt by groups in society. Following on the discussion in chapter 4, the sections take a broader view of the concept of justice than is usual in the policy literature. Justice is viewed here as related not only to conflict resolution and the justice sector, but also to the overall environment in which people live and interact with one another. Addressing perceptions of injustice across groups requires more than just reforming justice mechanisms, although doing that is an essential component. It also has to do with creating an enabling environment in which people feel that their group is being treated fairly, according to their own ideas of what fairness means, while ensuring that that is compatible with other groups' ideas of fairness. The discussion below first focuses on adapting conflict resolution mechanisms to the experience of justice and fairness in a particular context and then moves to interventions that focus on the broader social and economic environment.

Conflict Resolution Mechanisms and Justice Provision that Respond to the Ways People Experience Justice and Fairness

The importance of supporting mechanisms that promote resolution of local conflicts and provide justice for communities is often underestimated. In most fragile environments, access to formal justice mechanisms is meager. In geographically remote regions or areas where the state has lost legitimacy, there may be very little state presence for conflict resolution, and partly as a result, legal processes may enjoy very little legitimacy. People perceive that formal legal processes take time and money, are often biased against poor and less-educated people, and at times are corrupt. Large-scale reforms of justice systems are necessary, but they take time and require a minimum of institutional and political stability.[1]

If the state is virtually absent from the area of conflict resolution, customary institutions usually fill the gap. The state's absence can undermine the internal cohesion of groups and further reinforce the sense of injustice and insecurity. The country case studies showed how heavily people relied on traditional, informal mechanisms for conflict resolution and justice.

Perceptions of injustice can be addressed more effectively when people have access to means of resolving conflicts that make sense to them, in the terms in which they assess fairness and justice. In contrast to the western conception of justice based on individual rights, most traditional justice mechanisms are driven by the need to maintain social order and the continuity of life in the community. The scope of the resolution of a conflict usually extends beyond individual perpetrators and victims to include their families. Redress may focus more on addressing the particular harm done than on punishment. The seriousness of an offense in traditional societies in East Timor, for instance, is measured by the potential disruption it causes to the social order. In that context, divorce or marriage against the social order can be a more serious offense than murder or theft. Inserting other conceptions of justice into these local dispute resolution mechanisms—for example, ones based on individual litigation—may be ineffective at best. At worst it can increase dissatisfaction and prolong conflicts.

To accommodate different ideas of what is fair requires starting from an analysis of the problems that people are facing and then engaging the most helpful elements of different justice and conflict resolution practices. Often justice reform begins with the question of how to adapt best practices—usually westernized, formal systems—in a particular context. Taking a societal dynamics approach requires asking, first, What are the types of disputes, or the problems obtaining access to justice, that people face here? From this point of departure, culturally appropriate measures can be designed. Doing that will necessarily involve engaging customary dispute resolution mechanisms in places where they are important for people. In the past, development practitioners have often been reluctant to engage customary practices because of cultural biases or from an often-legitimate fear of supporting institutions that violate human rights. However, completely marginalizing customary practices in favor of a western-style formal system has clear dangers. Isser (2011) highlights the importance of integrating customary justice practices into justice reform efforts, especially in traditional societies affected by conflict. She argues that imposing a western-style, formal justice system in such societies while ignoring existing, traditional practices and their functions can have perverse effects in undermining the legitimacy of the reform effort and can even lead to the weakening of mechanisms that are already in place, without establishing adequate alternatives. Ultimately, such an effort can result in even less access to justice for some communities.

Integrating different conflict resolution systems requires accepting a certain amount of hybridity in the justice system. Some groups will prefer to approach state institutions to resolve conflict, and others will seek out customary mechanisms. For many people, the choice of state or customary institutions is not all-or-nothing but will depend on the type of dispute at issue. For those contexts, Isser (2011) offers some specific orientations. First, it can be helpful to articulate clearly the types of matters that are expected to be resolved via the formal legal system and its accompanying procedures. Similarly, defining the relationship of customary authorities with state structures can help reduce redundancy and address problems

---

BOX 8.1

Assessment of Local Conflict Resolution and Justice Provision in the Central African Republic

In the Central African Republic, the government understood that the formal justice system was not reaching the population outside of large urban centers. It was obvious that to build peace and reduce fragility people needed to feel that their day-to-day grievances and conflicts where being responded to.

A qualitative assessment of the types of local conflicts that were handled by various authorities showed that land and intrafamily conflicts, especially conflicts between husband and wife, were the most prevalent, followed by ones related to accusations of witchcraft. Next most prevalent were economic issues. The study showed that only in very few cases were conflicts resolved through the formal justice system, which people did not find appropriate for their needs. The qualitative work showed that the local chiefs were by far the most active resolvers of local conflicts and that they were probably the most trusted by the population. However, very few projects or programs were supporting the chiefs in that role.

Source: World Bank 2012.

of overlapping jurisdictions. Finally, states should develop an overarching framework that governs how they engage with customary systems.

Justice reforms must be informed with a contextual understanding of the local population's conception of justice and its social logic. The absence of a good understanding of customary practices, including their function and rationale, can make justice reforms unfit for the local context and offensive to local values. To discourage practices that violate human rights, justice reforms should offer workable alternatives. Reformers should make it a point to strategically employ some aspects of customary structures, at least in initial stages. The intention should be to provide practical solutions to problems in the immediate term, without trying to achieve full compliance with all rule-of-law principles. Such an incremental approach, which respects customary traditions and incorporates both punitive and restorative aspects in its articulation, can provide necessary legitimacy to the reform effort, opening doors for broader engagement. Efforts should be made creatively and incrementally to encourage customary systems to give greater voice to women, without challenging the legitimacy of the system (Isser 2011).

Reform measures should engage traditional authorities in ways that do not disrupt the legitimacy they hold in local communities, but which allow communities to hold traditional authorities accountable. For example, reforms could create mechanisms by which local communities periodically reaffirm traditional authorities' legitimacy, or make provision for the traditional authority's decisions to be appealed to a broader representation of the community, such as a group of elders. Such measures can reduce the traditional authorities' arbitrariness and provide greater legitimacy to the state's engagement (Isser 2011).

Creating an Environment Where People Feel They Are Treated Fairly and Respectfully

Providing effective and context-appropriate means for conflict resolution is but one part of addressing perceptions of injustice across groups; it is also important to address people's perceptions of the overall social and economic environment. Perceptions of injustice often arise from the sense that the disadvantages that groups face are structural in nature. In contexts of great social inequality, people from disadvantaged groups come to feel that no matter what they do as individuals, they will not be able to surmount the structural obstacles that their group faces. Even those individuals who are able to achieve some social and economic mobility may still identify strongly with the disadvantaged group and be motivated to act on its behalf.

Action to address such group-based inequalities should be taken in a visible and perceptible manner. Directed action can help send a strong signal to the affected groups, and other groups, that things are going to change. The types of actions to be taken will depend on the causes of the perceptions that need to be addressed. Many times the action will involve improving service delivery to populations that have not had adequate coverage in the past. In other cases, more inclusive systems may need to be built to increase tolerance for languages or cultures that have historically been excluded (see following section). Whatever the measures to be taken, it is important to accompany them with public campaigns or consultations, in which the state can explain the rationale behind the new policies and obtain feedback on potential unintended consequences.

As we have said, acting to correct perceptions of unfairness requires understanding the criteria that various groups use to assess situations as fair and unfair. The criteria may include need, equity and contribution, and identity and history, as described in chapter 4. Government officials and country leaders might not have a clear understanding of how these perceptions are playing out at the local level. Development organizations tend to assume that perceptions of unequal treatment are chiefly related to lack of access to basic services or employment. However, much research done in fragile environments and some of the fieldwork carried out for this study showed that issues related to land and water tend to be important for people, as are security and conflict resolution, and often come before health and education. What is morally acceptable in behaviors and attitudes is also very important for communities. For instance, attitudes toward elders (Central African Republic, Liberia), having the means to be able to marry (Yemen), and having access to local authorities (Haiti) were ranked high in focus groups. Acquiring an understanding of perceptions of fairness and justice requires asking particular questions aimed at discerning how people experience these concepts in specific contexts.

Action to address perceptions of injustice may mean giving a particular group preferential treatment to address past injustices. For example, in a postconflict situation, governments and donors often begin reconstruction by focusing on the areas that suffered the most direct damage to infrastructure and services. However, it may also be worthwhile to include some programs that benefit groups that incurred less damage, if doing so can help to address perceptions of injustice. It can yield long-term benefits in a sustained peace because it addresses the roots of future conflict. Very often, such actions must be accompanied by important explanatory campaigns that feature justifications by politicians and active mediation at the local level. In many cases, the justifications can be related to the fact that the marginalized groups are of foreign origin, or that they are newcomers who have benefited from the wealth of a territory that historically belongs to a different group.

The evolving experience of Disarmament, Demobilization, and Reintegration, or DDR, programs offers some useful insights in this regard. Initially, many DDR programs targeted services to former combatants, on the theory that it was important to address the needs of this vulnerable group so that they did not act as "spoilers" of peace agreements. However, it became clear that the interventions were perceived as preferential treatment, or even as rewarding that group for engaging in violent conflict. Other groups deeply affected by the conflict, especially women and children, were given less attention, which widened social divisions in some communities. In response, many DDR programs now target assistance to entire communities, according to the needs that those communities define, so that DDR can contribute to greater cohesion (World Bank 2009).

Efforts to address perceptions of injustice that are based on differences in service coverage for various groups need to be based on assessments of how the groups perceive the matter of access to services. Social mapping exercises can be useful to assess how best to get services to particular groups. This can be complicated, however, by the fact that data on ethnic, religious, or cultural attributes may not be available in the country or region. Indeed, many governments worry that collecting data by ethnicity or religion might reinforce separate identities and undermine attempts to build cohesion. Governments often resist sociocultural mapping out of fear that it will make unequal treatment between groups more obvious and might reinforce group competition for resources and attention. Mapping can, however, be undertaken using proxies, so that it does not explicitly refer to people's sociocultural characteristics.

In addressing inequalities in service provision, it is important to balance effectiveness and perceptions of fairness. It is practically impossible for states to provide the same services to all citizens, for a number of reasons, and that poses important technical problems that have to be addressed. Some excluded groups might live in areas where, from an economic perspective, investments and provision of services are expensive and not cost-effective. That is very often the case with populations who live in mountainous or dense forest areas. Provision of services in such areas is much more expensive and is not cost-effective in terms of human development outcomes, especially when the population is scattered and small. A different problem occurs when discriminated groups are mixed into the overall population or have regrouped in small pockets in large urban centers.

In some contexts, area development approaches have been particularly successful in addressing perceptions of injustice and building social cohesion through service provision. For example, experience working with displaced and host populations in Lebanon, Pakistan, Tanzania, and Zambia (see box 8.2) using area development plans shows that targeting both refugees and their hosts in areas affected by displacement is an effective way to mitigate the negative impacts of a long-term refugee presence and to build on the positive contributions of refugees to host communities. This type of approach can improve the daily lives of the displaced and their hosts during the displacement period and perhaps also prepare refugees to find sustainable solutions to displacement (Puerto Gomez and Christensen 2010).

Another promising approach is Targeted Development Assistance (TDA), which UNHCR, UNDP, and other bilateral and multilateral agencies have implemented in recent years (UNHCR 2006a). These initiatives are based on the recognition that even in a refugee crisis, development opportunities are available that can benefit both the refugees and the host population, as well as prepare the refugees for sustainable solutions, including return, settlement in a country of asylum, or settlement in a third country.

Finally, employing participatory processes in service delivery can go a long way toward striking a balance between effectiveness and fairness. Such processes can give marginalized groups a stronger sense of participation in the broader society. There are many reasons why providing top-down services without any role for the local population can reduce the effectiveness of services and damage the population's sense of fairness. Without participation, less opportunity and means are available to adapt the services to the needs of the beneficiaries and to reflect the cultural and social particularities of the group. These issues are discussed in more detail later in the chapter.

Promoting Policies to Accommodate Diversity and Promote Tolerance to Reduce Perceptions of Injustice

Chapter 4 discussed the ways that rigid boundaries around group identities can entrench perceptions of injustice and lead to greater fragility. That can

---

BOX 8.2

The Zambia Initiative: Supporting the Constructive Role of Refugees in Local Economies

In 2000, the Zambian government complained about security, infrastructure, environmental, social, economic, and service delivery challenges in western Zambia due to the prolonged presence of more than 100,000 Angolan refugees, some self-settled and others living in camps. UNHCR and the Zambian government consulted and designed an area development program that became known as the "Zambia Initiative" (ZI).

Launched in 2003, the initiative was designed as a multisector rural development program to benefit both refugees and their host communities. The program's main objectives were poverty reduction among nationals and empowerment of refugees and receiving communities through community-based development programs (UNHCR 2006b). Development interventions included various sectors, such as education, health, agriculture, infrastructure, forestry, and water resources. Although the initiative focused on refugees who were not likely to repatriate, it also supported refugees who wished to return by providing services, skills, and work experiences that could facilitate a return to their country of origin.

Development investments and encouragement of refugee self-reliance and joint ventures began to turn a negative refugee situation into something positive for all parties. As small economic ventures began to emerge, government teachers and health workers began returning to their duty stations, as the previously neglected, remote western region came to be seen as a place with development action. The improved level of coexistence with locals and increasing self-reliance of the refugees also led to improvement in the security situation.

The Zambia Initiative had at its outset all the ingredients to become a flagship operation, demonstrating how a good displacement policy and a holistic area development program can turn refugee presence into a benefit for all. An evaluation of the ZI considered its approach a good practice to support constructive roles for refugees in local economies and to identify places in which the burden of the government hosting refugees can be turned into opportunities. Strong national ownership and donor support for local development projects were key factors in the implementation of the ZI (Watabe 2007).

As a piloting experience, the ZI also confronted many operational challenges. First, limited government capacity at the local level constrained the execution and monitoring of development projects. The lack of systematic participation by communities and people affected by displacement in the local planning and decision-making processes

(continued next page)

BOX 8.2 *(continued)*

limited the extent to which their specific needs could be incorporated into national development plans. Second, consultation activities at the community level did not effectively include the most vulnerable groups, such as women, youth, and the elderly. Third, the lack of a clear framework to put the initiative into operation impeded a more consistent identification of the roles and contributions of external partners, particularly activities that could support the transition from emergency relief to development assistance. The initial successes slowly faded as (1) turnover of key policy figures in the government brought a gradual change from visionary to more traditional refugee policies, and (2) the international humanitarian agencies were reluctant to include traditional humanitarian handout-type programs targeting refugees only in the ZI, thus working counter to the approach of the initiative. The experience also showed how important it is to have visionary and courageous policy makers willing to make bold decisions at the right time.

Source: UNHCR 2006b.

occur particularly with excluded groups, who find seemingly insurmountable barriers to mobility into a more privileged group. The process of strengthening the boundaries around group evolves over time: as the identity lines between the in-group and out-group harden, the out-group experiences more social cohesion internally but isolates itself further and further from others. The boundaries are thus hardened by the social interactions, positive and negative, between groups. As Taylor (1994: 25) describes,

> our identity is partly shaped by recognition or its absence, often by misrecognition of others, and so a person or a group of people can suffer damage, real distortion, if the people or society around them mirror back to them a confirming or demeaning or contemptible picture of themselves.

The perception that one's group is treated unfairly can fester in the collective psyche and can mobilize even those members who have individually managed to attain social and economic mobility. Sometimes the process has been evolving for centuries and has become self-reinforcing. In those contexts it is difficult for a convergence of interests to form across groups.

Accommodating diverse identities can go a long way in addressing group-based perceptions of injustice. Today, identity is increasingly building along cultural and religious lines. In the 19th and 20th centuries, class identity was a prominent factor in conflicts and political violence. Today, however, religious and cultural identities are more important. Managing demands for identity recognition is important to reduce risks of conflict and violence. Today it is generally recognized that assimilation of various groups is not the best way to handle internal tensions in countries; rather, it is more effective to accommodate different groups' cultural, ethnic, and religious beliefs as much as possible. Increasingly the international community and the local community integrate cultural rights. The *2004 Human Development Report* (UNDP 2004: 1) directly links the management of cultural diversity with the recognition of cultural rights:

> Cultural liberty is a vital part of human development because being able to choose one's identity, who one is, without losing respect of others or being excluded from other choices is important in leading a full life. People want the freedom to practice their religion openly, to speak their language, to celebrate their ethnic or religious heritage without fear of ridicule or punishment or diminished opportunity. People want the freedom to participate in society without having to slip off their chosen cultural mooring.

Policies to accommodate various identities must address a variety of themes and sectors to be effective. Marc (2010) details three main components of these policies: (1) supporting political participation; (2) fighting discrimination; and (3) reducing cultural exclusion. Supporting political participation usually includes spatial devolution policies when cultural differences correspond to a territory and corporate decentralization when minorities do not have a specific territorial location. The latter consists of reserving seats in the parliament or creating special mechanisms for specific groups to govern their own communities or to use their customary institutions for making decisions and resolving internal conflicts. Fighting discrimination consists of legal provisions to ensure that equal rights are accorded to, and actually respected for, different groups; implementing affirmative action in service delivery or recruitment to the civil service; and others. Reducing cultural exclusion consists mostly of acknowledging specific cultural rights, so long as doing so does not infringe on others' individual rights. It also facilitates the exercise of individual rights by people that might be at risk of persecution because of their culture and way of life. For instance, some states have allowed nomadic populations to keep an address in a place where they do not reside so as to receive information and some of the social benefits they are entitled to. In most cases it is the combination of these different policies that is the most effective. However, some sectors are more critical than others in ensuring recognition of diversity.

BOX 8.3

Multicultural Education Reform in Papua New Guinea

In 1993, the Department of Education of Papua New Guinea implemented education reforms that introduced native language instruction for the first year of school. By 2001, 369 indigenous languages were introduced in the program, and a third of elementary school children began education in their native tongues.

Although the success of the program in improving overall education levels in the country is largely anecdotal at this point, it has demonstrably increased education access and resulted in lower dropout rates, particularly among female students. Lower secondary school enrollments doubled, and upper secondary numbers quadrupled over the decade following the introduction of the reform. The reform has improved social cohesion by providing a sense of belonging to the multitude of tribal groups making up the country.

Source: Litteral 2004.

Integrating cultural diversity in the education, health, land management, and justice fields is particularly important for creating a sense of fairness.

Steps can be taken to develop the social infrastructure that can accommodate diversity in society, starting with more inclusive language and education policies. Language and education are central in the recognition of cultural identity. That a person is able to learn the mother tongue, even if it is not the country's official language, is powerful recognition of cultural identity. As Kymlicka and Grin (2003: 11) write, "When a language group fights to preserve its language, it is never just preserving a tool for communication: it is also preserving certain political claims, autonomous institutions, cultural products and practices and national identities." It has also been proved that conducting lessons in a student's native language benefits cognitive development and improves their ability to learn other topics, including the majority language (Mehotra 1998).

Until recently, adopting a single national language was seen as one of the bases of a nation state. Today more and more countries have been able to build cohesion while using more than one language. Canada, Spain, and Switzerland, are three examples (also see the text box on the experience of Papua New Guinea). Even if they do not adopt multiple official languages, governments can send a very strong symbolic message of recognition and inclusion by publishing books, educational tools, administrative forms, and even official state documents in minority group languages. Not only can it further the inclusion of the group, but it can also facilitate children's education and help people access information and services.

Opening up education systems to minority languages is one of the first steps toward greater recognition of various groups' identities, and it is also widely recognized as a way to achieve better overall education outcomes (Marc 2008). Introducing a minority language in schools also requires that the education system take cultural differences into the classroom by attracting teachers from the minority group, that it reduce segregation among various schools (that is, separate schools for minority children), and that it adapt teaching methods and provide outreach to parents. Teachers need to receive training on how to integrate children of different ethnic backgrounds in a classroom. Training is especially important when some children suffer from a disadvantage at school because their parents are from a lower caste; because they are nomads and their father can be away for a long period; or because of something else specific to their group that will make the children feel different (Marc 2008).

Recognizing language by itself is insufficient to ensure the recognition of a group's identity, however. Recognizing its positive contribution to the nation and its history and ensuring that teaching methods and classroom organization are respectful of the group's culture are also important. Recognizing a group's contribution to the nation as a whole goes a long way in helping a group to feel part of a country. History books and school curriculum have a very big role to play here.

Projects that support an inclusive view of the country's history and encourage teachers to teach in ways that respect minority culture can also help to reduce fragility. This does not mean reinventing the past but describing it in a balanced way, trying to explain various groups' positions, avoiding stereotypes in explaining the histories of various groups, and involving stakeholders in redrafting the history curriculum. Teachers must be trained in the use of the new curriculum, and its appropriate use must be monitored through school inspections (Roberts-Schweitzer 2006). Besides the curriculum, very often teachers need to change the way they teach, and classrooms must be organized in a way that respects different values. Even the most mundane details can be important, for example, providing separate toilets for boys and girls to respect cultures that value gender separation, or changing the attitudes of teachers toward parents from a different sociocultural background.

Many countries have also found it useful to build monuments, museums, and cultural centers and to generate an official dialogue that acknowledges the contributions of certain groups to the nation. That approach has been actively used in the United States to support inclusion of the African American population. In cases in which minorities have been oppressed, or even massacred, integrating various groups' histories into education and official documentation is a very important source of cohesion. Many of the convergences and divergences in societal dynamics are played out around interpretations of history and culture. History and culture are much used to legitimize or delegitimize one group or another, and therefore the official history is an important force for both exclusion and inclusion.

Universal human rights should not be infringed upon as the cultural rights of minority groups are reinforced. It can be tricky to reinforce policies and programs that nurture cultural diversity and recognize the norms and values of one group, if those can be seen as conflicting with the values and beliefs of other groups in society. Efforts of this kind must be sensitive to the majority group, so as not to provoke a backlash or generate more tension and discrimination. That is particularly important where there has been a long history of discrimination.

Recognizing collective cultural rights must be balanced with protecting individual human rights. Cultural rights allow for individuals to express their identities as they wish, provided that those expressions do not violate the rights of others. Expressions can include collective obligations, such as undertaking certain rituals, dressing in a certain way, or eating specific food. Gender relationships are particularly sensitive, such that practices recognized for some groups could infringe on other groups' norms regarding appropriate relationships between men and women. This is a major issue when *sharia* law is recognized in societies in which other religions are dominant or ones that are more secularized. A balance among the rights of different groups can be achieved via interventions at different levels, primarily by ensuring that various participatory structures at the local level include representatives of minority groups, whether they be parent-teacher associations, health boards, or, if they exist, local governments.

Healing Trauma across Groups

Chapter 4 described how trauma can affect groups' relationships with other groups and harden divisions. Several structural factors reinforce the impacts of trauma and are particularly relevant here.

First, ongoing violence and insecurity do not allow traumatized people and groups the chance to heal, and that can exacerbate the trauma. In some cases traumatic events become master narratives, or "chosen traumas," which depict them as direct attacks on group identity (Volkan 1989; 2006). That contributes to a deepening sense of injustice against other groups and, in the worst cases, can be used to mobilize violence or revenge against other groups. For that reason, it is crucial to address the problems of insecurity for traumatized groups. An example from Aceh is described in the box 8.4.

BOX 8.4

Improving Overall Security to Address Violence and Trauma in Aceh

Three decades of civil war in Aceh, Indonesia, claimed up to 30,000 lives and caused US$10.7 billion of economic damages and losses (MSR 2009). The impact of violence on communities' mental well-being is shown by two comprehensive studies conducted by the Institute of Medicine (IOM) and Harvard Medical School shortly after a peace agreement brought the war to an end in 2005 (Good et al. 2006). The studies show just how profound the effects of the conflict were on civilians in Aceh. The first assessment randomly sampled 596 adult respondents in 30 villages in three high-conflict districts. Seventy-eight percent of the respondents reported having lived through combat experiences, 38 percent had had to flee from burning buildings in their community, 41 percent reported that a family member or friend had been killed, and 45 percent reported having their property confiscated or destroyed. Twenty-five percent of the men and 11 percent of the women reported being tortured, and 36 percent of the men (14 percent of women) were attacked with a gun or knife.

Those experiences led to pervasive psychosocial trauma of a level similar to that observed in postconflict Bosnia or Afghanistan. The relationships between the number of traumatic events experienced and both depression and posttraumatic stress disorder were highly significant. The youngest (17–29) and oldest (54 and above) were at the highest risk. The second study, conducted six months later in July 2006, extended the research to another 11 districts in Aceh. It found that even in "lower conflict" areas, the numbers experiencing traumatic events were very high.

A comparison of the two studies also shows the impact of improved security on psychological symptoms. In the first study, in February 2006, 47 percent of the respondents reported seeing perpetrators of crime and violence (*pelaku kejahatan*) as a continuing stressor, 30 percent reported experiencing physical or psychological attacks or threats (*penyerangan*), and 21 percent reported robbery (*perampokan*) since the peace agreement. Despite the cessation of formal conflict, continued insecurity remained a challenge to the recovery of individuals and communities (Good et al. 2006). By the

(continued next page)

BOX 8.4 *(continued)*

time of the second study, conducted in July 2006, security had drastically improved. The results suggested that with increased security and reduced levels of stressors, general psychological symptoms and collective anxiety were reduced significantly. Signs of trauma related to past experiences had not disappeared, but individuals were able to start moving forward (DelVecchio et al. 2007).

Source: Pouligny 2010.

Second, the loss of livelihood often associated with traumatic events, especially violence, becomes part of the experienced trauma. Displaced populations, particularly, lose part of their identity when they are forced to leave their place of residence but also lose access to their means of making a living. They may find themselves in new environments that may be hostile to them, where they lack the needed skills or social networks to enter the job market.

In these cases it is important to find ways to restore people's livelihoods. Such efforts will undoubtedly ignite political tensions, especially in cases of displaced populations, as they may be seen as creating incentives for groups to remain where they are not necessarily wanted. Some projects have succeeded by looking for ways to address the needs of the larger community within which the affected group is located, so as not to be seen as favoring an affected group. Such initiatives can also be more effective if they mobilize affected groups in ways that integrate them into the broader society and into economic networks.

Groups in which many members have experienced trauma, such as those forcibly displaced and victims of mass violence, need to see not only that their lost assets and livelihood are restored as much as possible, but most of all that the broader society considers them positive contributors to development. The sense of recognition and inclusion is essential for healing and for avoiding the perpetuation of trauma. For that to be achieved, participatory processes, by which the victims are not provided handouts but are engaged in productive activities and services, as well as in decision making, are essential. Ensuring that displaced people, and in particular internally displaced people, are not discriminated against and can enjoy the same rights as the rest of the national population is also important.

When violence happened inside a community in which victims and perpetrators will live together, community-based reintegration mechanisms can offer some solutions. These systems can foster social trust and community reintegration, in particular, in the aftermath of violence. This is particularly important in view of the frequently high proportion of violence that is committed at the heart of the community, in the immediate environment, or even within families. This "intimate violence" or "intimate crime" has been documented in contexts as different as Bosnia-Herzegovina, Cambodia, Democratic Republic of Congo, Liberia, Peru, and Sierra Leone (Pouligny 2002). But the violence is not only intimate; it is sometimes also popular in that it may enlist the participation of thousands of ordinary people, and even greater numbers of people may become its direct beneficiaries.[2] Victims, perpetrators, and bystanders often continue to live in the same communities, or come back to their former community, as in the case of former combatants, both children and adults. This continued coexistence, though possibly inevitable in some circumstances, may be marked by residual fears, animosities, and tension, all legacies of the violence.

Various methods of traditional reconciliation and healing can also improve cohesion by aiding community reintegration. These methods are much more effective when the community initiates them without external interventions. Traditional healing mechanisms (see box 8.5) can also have major drawbacks when they are sponsored by donors or NGOs without a deep knowledge of the healing traditions of communities and an understanding of the specific context. They can actually undermine customary authorities and norms. They are also essentially intracommunity mechanisms that do not resolve broader intercommunity needs for reintegration and healings.

Supporting restorative justice and peace and reconciliation mechanisms can also be effective to ensure that victims are recognized and justice is done. Even so, experience with peace and reconciliation commissions has been mixed; they can become very political and therefore difficult to support.

Improving Interactions among Institutions

Chapter 5 discussed the interactions between institutions as another important influence on social cohesion in society. One of the defining features of fragile settings is that institutions connect only weakly with one another, or connect in antagonistic relationships that undermine their effectiveness.

In resilient situations, institutions provide safe spaces for interests to converge across groups, reducing fragility. One of the most important functions of state institutions is to facilitate dialogue among groups in

BOX 8.5

Northern Uganda: Traditional Acholi Healing, Justice, and Reintegration Mechanisms

Traditional healing mechanisms have both great potential and some limitations. In northern Uganda, traditional Acholi rituals such as "stepping on the egg" (*nyouo tong gweno*) and, to a lesser extent, "drinking the bitter herb" (*mato oput*) currently play a key role in reconciliation and reintegration of ex-combatants or abductees in to their communities. Both rituals also include important healing dimensions.

"Stepping on the egg" is the ritual most commonly used for those who return home after a long absence. It is a welcoming ritual meant to cleanse a person of the ills that he or she may have contracted while traveling. The ceremony involves "the returnee stepping on an egg (*tongweno*) placed on a 'slippery branch' (*opobo*) and a stick with a fork (*layebi*), traditionally used to open granaries. The egg is said to symbolize purity. 'The egg has no mouth, and cannot speak ill of others.' The egg also symbolizes that which is 'soft,' 'fragile,' suggesting a restoration of innocence. The *opobo* is a soapy, slippery branch, which helps to cleanse the returnee from any external influences he or she might have encountered in the 'bush' that might be calling them back. The *layebi* is a symbol of welcoming a person back into the home, where the family members will once again share food together" (Harvey 2006). This ritual is considered a precondition before any reconciliation ceremony.

Ceremonies of this type have been organized by Ker Kware Acholi, the organization of traditional Acholi leaders, to reintegrate former Lord's Resistance Army (LRA) fighters. In the context of the conflict between the LRA and the Ugandan government, it is widely thought that abductees need no more than the simple cleansing ceremony, but that ex-combatants also need *mato oput*, "drinking the bitter herb." The ceremony is adjusted, however, to deal with each situation, including those of individuals who are "reintegrated" in a camp for internally displaced persons (IDP) instead of their home (Hovil and Quinn 2005). Beyond reintegration, the ceremony helps process some of the traumas that people have suffered. It has been reported to markedly affect children's ability to reintegrate fully. In contrast with Western models of addressing trauma, which emphasize psychotherapeutic recounting and remembering experiences, these rituals act to create a rupture with that past. "Stepping on an egg" symbolizes taking on a new life (McKay and Mazurana 2004).

The ritual of *mato oput* is intended to reconcile social divisions resulting from intentional or accidental killing. It is performed between the clan of the perpetrator and the

(*continued next page*)

BOX 8.5 *(continued)*

clan of the victim. It is therefore mainly a justice and reconciliation mechanism and has been discussed most widely in that context. The ceremony of *mato oput* comes at the end of a long process of confession, mediation, and payment of compensation to reconcile two clans after a murder has occurred between them. The ceremony itself has various forms across different clans, but common characteristics include the slaughter of two sheep, which are cut in half and exchanged by the clans, and the drinking of the bitter herb *oput* by both clans to "wash away bitterness." This dimension is the one considered to have important healing components and thus to be an integral part of psychosocial recovery (Liu Institute 2005; Allen 2006).

The ceremony of *moyo piny* involves the sacrifice of goats to appease ancestors and to cleanse an area of the evil spirits that are believed to dwell in places where war-related massacres have occurred. These ceremonies have been held at battle sites, at sites of deadly ambushes, and in fields and compounds where mass murders took place (Baines 2007).

All of the traditional rituals suffer serious limitations as instruments of reconciliation and justice. Among them is the fact that they are locally specific and designed to restore intragroup harmony more than intergroup relations. Their role in supporting healing processes, however, is largely acknowledged by existing studies, which highlight the positive potential of traditional rituals and beliefs, not as competitors with other approaches, but as complementary to them (Latigo 2008).

Source: Pouligny 2010.

---

society and provide a framework for those interactions. When the state fulfills that function well, it can help harmonize the efforts of other institutions, so that they do not work at cross purposes. Often states have deepened divides in society by not doing that job well. For example, sometimes grassroots organizations are captured by political actors, information is withheld as a means of maintaining power, or different institutions are played against each other. Moreover, the state cannot do the job alone. Little can be decreed or decided from the top down to create space for positive interactions between groups. Civil society organizations have a role, as do customary institutions and the private sector.

This part of the chapter offers recommendations for building better connections among institutions, emphasizing strengthening the interactions between formal and customary institutions as a means of improving the state-society relationship. Four areas are of strategic importance: supporting institutions to mediate across groups in society; improving community-driven development programs; strengthening civil society's ability to connect groups, horizontally with one another and vertically with the state; and enhancing the state's capacity to engage productively with various groups in society.

Focusing on Local Governance and Community-Driven Development to Better Connect State and Nonstate Institutions

Intervening at the level of the community or municipality is essential to building resilience because it is at the local level that people interact and their behaviors and values are shaped and transformed. In addition, it is at the local level that people form their perceptions of justice and fairness and that informal and formal institutions connect. It is center-stage for day-to-day societal dynamics. Decentralization that empowers the institutions that operate locally can provide a space for groups to participate in their own development—space that might not exist at the central level. Decentralization is also a way to manage cultural and ethnic differences.

Community-driven development (CDD) should not be seen as something added to top-down programs to foster more community participation, but as an integral part of local governance. At the local level, people are trying to solve many problems. CDD should be an integral part of local governments, not a parallel activity. CDD, as a function of local governance, can reduce patronage and elite capture if well designed.

From the perspective of societal dynamics, local governance that includes CDD has a central job to do in building trust, creating a sense of justice and fairness, and creating connections between institutions. Local governance systems are essential to improving relationships between communities and the state and provide the basis for a sense of citizenship. In fragile environments, the central state system is usually too far away and its representatives too disconnected from local realities, to be able to create the trust that would establish a sense of rights and responsibilities in relation to the state. In the Central African Republic, the investigation carried out for the study clearly showed that the village chief, even if contested and lacking legitimacy, was still the institution that people would go to for resolution of most of their day-to-day-problems. It was also the institution that most donor programs were bypassing and the one most neglected by the central state.

In volatile contexts, more use could be made of CDD projects to manage local disputes and resolve conflicts through the process of collective action. Barron (2010: 14) writes, "CDD holds potential to encourage new forms of collaboration across conflict divides, which can improve trust and make communities less prone to fresh violence. In postconflict Aceh and Rwanda, CDD has been used to target specific conflict-affected groups."

CDD projects are not by themselves a solution to reduce large-scale violence and conflict; the evidence does not establish a causal relationship (Barron, Diprose, and Woolcock 2007). Some evidence indicates that, in the long term, CDD can facilitate collective action by mediating among various social groups and local institutions (such as traditional chiefs, customary justice institutions, and local secret societies), but it does not happen automatically and must be managed (Barron 2010). For CDD to bring improved interactions and help local communities strengthen their own institutions, while connecting effectively with state and civil society, CDD operations would need to be designed in quite a different way than they are, especially in fragile environments.

For the project reported in this book, the team conducted a rapid review of CDD projects in fragile and conflict-ridden environments. The review showed that CDD projects are often based on simple assumptions about what societal dynamics are and how institutions work; for instance,

- that communities are homogenous and that they reach decisions equitably, if only they are given the chance;
- that traditional and customary community-based institutions are weak and prone to elite capture, and that therefore new institutions need to be set up for decision making if people are to have fair and legitimate processes; and
- that the main benefit of CDD interventions is the creation of a stronger commitment to the delivery of basic services and to cost-effectiveness in that delivery.

None of these ideas, taken independently, is wrong, but if they are the only principles guiding the design of local development operations and are applied narrowly, they can generate ineffective participatory processes and reinforce fragility. The most common problems besetting CDD operations in fragile environments are (1) rifts with local governments, which tend not to benefit from CDD operations; (2) ignorance of customary institutions and traditional conflict resolution mechanisms that undermines the benefits of CDD or renders the process one that is not really "community driven," with little legitimacy for part of the community; and (3) failure to go beyond a narrow focus on basic service delivery to address the population's real needs. These problems turn CDD into essentially a project implementation mechanism. It is rarely seen as a way to strengthen and develop institutions over the long term and, in particular, to mediate between groups in society and connect local institutions to formal state and nonstate actors.

Some CDD operations have come closer than others in addressing the broader needs of communities and contributing to positive interactions between institutions. They include the Kecamatan Development Program in Indonesia, the National Solidarity Program in Afghanistan, the Poverty Alleviation Fund in Pakistan, the Kalahi-CIDSS program in the Philippines, the Rural Investment and Local Governance Project in Cambodia, and the Magdalena Medio Regional Development Project in Colombia, to mention only a few projects financed by the World Bank. A number of large NGO projects are also achieving this broader objective, such as the Agha Khan project in Northern Pakistan.

These experiences span a range of contexts and designs, but some lessons can be drawn. Probably the most important one is that CDD projects are most successful when they are designed based on a broad vision for local governance, such that they help establish a framework for local institutions to grow and establish bridges in a way that is inclusive and responds to the real needs of the population.

Building bridges between communities and the state involves, first, a solid understanding of the societal dynamics at play in the particular context. CDD projects should start by identifying the most pressing demands of the population to improve their livelihood, reduce tensions and conflict, and ensure a sense of security and justice. Of course, some of those needs are matters of access to clean water, health centers, and schools. But other issues have to do with identity and social networks and thus involve less-tangible, but no less important, project goals and outcomes. In most cases the fieldwork for our case studies showed that resolving local conflicts, especially ones concerning land and inside families, is as important as other priorities. Feeling safe and secure is another important goal. Being connected to the world outside the community is also important, particularly for youth, including for livelihood purposes. Local development needs to address these issues, and more CDD programs should be designed with an understanding of them in mind.

Second, making explicit links between state institutions and CDD projects can cement relationships that will continue over time. When relations with local government officials are institutionalized in CDD projects, it fosters the development of vertical institutional connections. Mansuri and Rao (2004) assert that creating downward accountability and upward commitment, by maintaining close links between government and the community, is the key to making participation work. One way planners can do that is to recognize institutional multiplicity and use CDD to facilitate mediations between social groups and local institutions, eventually building the basis of new institutions, if necessary. Mechanisms to give feedback to service providers, to local government, and so on, are also important.

Embedding conflict resolution into CDD design and implementation can help ensure that projects strengthen community relations in healthy ways. Mediation and conflict resolution mechanisms should be integrated in the design of interventions, as should the work of such mechanisms already existing locally. In the more successful CDD projects, mediators or facilitators are often active in the community to facilitate interactions between groups and institutions (Barron 2010). Specific procedures for redress in case the intervention is seen as illegitimate or as excluding some members seem to be key. Mediation should take place not only between individuals but between institutions. It might require that subgroups be organized to reflect divides in the communities, for example, women's groups, youth groups, or others.

CDD operations should finance much more than social or economic infrastructure. They should fund service operations as well to ensure that communities are involved in running them. They should support more liveli-hood activities; they should encourage projects across communities. Projects dealing with security should also be supported, as well as the operations of customary institutions and many more. All of this is certainly not easy, but the narrow financing span of most CDD operations has also been the reason why they have rarely influenced institutions and connections between them.

Finally, efforts to strengthen local governance and state presence at the local level should be closely connected to the efforts to bring about partici-pation and community development. Service delivery should be embedded in a framework for local governance that involves local government and the participation of local communities, with a place for both central state and customary institutions. Links between various institutions operating at the community level are also important.

CDD operations have too often been designed with a focus solely on service delivery and only rarely with a focus on long-term institutional development. This is often a missed opportunity. To contribute toward that development, programs should evolve and improve over time. Spe-cifically, they will need to build in mechanisms for understanding societal dynamics and mediating among institutions and groups that are present in the communities, and apply an approach that reinforces a sense of citizen-ship and connection with other communities.

Community Mobilization and Institution Building—The Pakistan Poverty Alleviation Fund

Launched in 1999, the Pakistan Poverty Alleviation Fund (PPAF) is an autonomous, private sector organization with a mandate from the government of Pakistan to alleviate poverty in the country. PPAF is designed to reduce poverty and empower the rural and urban poor in Pakistan by providing resources and services, especially to women. It is achieving that goal through an integrated approach that includes building institutions of the poor and providing them with microcredit loans, grants for small-scale infrastructure projects, training and skill development, and social sector interventions. The PPAF has already provided 1.9 million microcredit loans, supported 16,000 community infrastructure schemes with grants, and provided capacity-building for 232,000 individuals in skill development and managerial training.

The PPAF has established strong outreach at the village level by building relationships with more than 70 partner organizations, which in turn have organized more than 92,000 community organizations in 32,000 villages and rural and urban settlements, in 112 districts of the country. The PPAF has a strong focus on engagement and empowerment of the most vulnerable and marginalized. Partner organizations are given the responsibility to ensure that every community they work with also develops human and institutional capacity through the creation of community organizations that are led and managed by members. Organizations work with community leaders, tribal leaders, *sadars,* and landlords to reach the ultrapoor households in their communities. Communities are also required to support the formation and subsequent activities of women's groups, as well as youth-related projects and activities. The PPAF continues to sensitize its partner organizations and encourage them to facilitate links between community organizations and the various tiers of local government. Synergies developed between the community organizations and public sector programs are expected to help efforts to alleviate poverty. The PPAF and its partner organizations are positioning community organizations to leverage resources from local government programs as well.

Source: http://www.ppaf.org.pk/default.aspx.

Supporting Civil Society in Improving the Relationship between State and Society

Chapter 2 disputed the idea, common in policy circles, of the state as an autonomous actor capable of directing change in society. In contrast, it was asserted that the state is one actor among many in society and may not even be the most powerful actor in some situations. Rather than directing change, the state is engaged in a mutually dependent relationship with society, such that progress toward common goals involves a constant negotiation and renegotiation of power.

The dominant state-building approach to fragile situations underestimates the potential of civil society institutions to forge a sense of citizenship. History shows that in many cases the sense of citizenship is only built over time and through the interaction of groups with the state. Some of the interactions involve formally organized civil society organizations, which have as a unifying goal some sort of common public interest. Other civil society groups participate indirectly, by fostering associational life. As Posner (2004: 242) writes,

> Trust and norms of reciprocity are formed as a positive externality of collective activities undertaken for other purposes. It makes little difference whether the group itself was explicitly formed to promote effective governance or whether it was an informal organization set up to coordinate cultural activities, build membership in a particular religious group, or organize sports events. ... What generates the trust is the act of successful mutual corporation.

The state has a role, but it is emphatically not the only actor, or the most important one.

However, it is important to realize that not all civil society organizations necessarily contribute to social cohesion and citizenship. Some of the most cohesive groups exhibit what Moser and McIlwaine (2004) and others have called "perverse social capital," which works at cross-purposes with positive social goals. "Warlord gangs, Mafia organizations, and paramilitary groups are as much a part of civil society as churches and women's associations" (Posner 2004: 237). These groups are focused on their own narrow interests and thus would undermine cohesion in the longer term.

Civil society has a central part in connecting people to the state, but in fragile situations, that role is often eclipsed by donors' needs for project implementers. As discussed in chapter 5, civil society organizations are often the only—or at least the most effective—agents that can connect to communities in fragile situations. In some cases their human resources and infrastructure rival those of the government, and their relationships with communities are often closer. In the name of efficiency, donors often capitalize on that capacity by contracting with civil society organizations to deliver services to communities. Yet over the long term, this tendency can stretch the limited resources of such organizations and hinder them from playing their larger role in connecting the state with its citizens. Donors may train local experts from civil society organizations in vital service delivery work, only to have them lured away to work for international organizations, at higher salaries, creating a brain drain from local civil society.

With few human and financial resources at their disposal, civil society organizations in fragile situations are often vulnerable to co-optation by power elites. During the fieldwork for the study, people in many communities told stories of grassroots organizations emerging, and initially achieving some legitimacy in communities, only to be manipulated by power groups. Often that involved the group's becoming associated with a particular leader and ending by serving that person's political ambitions, rather than community good. This sequence of events not only deprived communities of needed organizations that might advocate for their interests, but also contributed to people's cynicism about leaders in general, as the cycle was repeated.

Civil society organizations, especially the most genuine grassroots organizations, should be encouraged to stick to their most important province of connecting individuals and groups across the fractures that exist in society and with the state. If donors defer to the priority of this role for civil society, it may require trade-offs in terms of service delivery, but it promises a much more enabling environment for service delivery in the long run. Donors can support civil society in this important function by creating an enabling environment for civil society activities. Posner (2004: 251) proposes that the main objectives of such a policy should be to (1) reduce the cost of social interaction and (2) undermine forces that oppose civil society. In this regard he argues that "donor support for communications infrastructure like telephones, newspapers, local radio stations, and even transportation infrastructure may thus be a second lever for promoting civil society."

A promising example of civil society organizations' helping to improve the state–society relationship is the Salvadorian Movement of Solidarity Development (MODES), in El Salvador, comprising 60 organizations. With support from the German Development Cooperation (GDC), MODES fosters constructive interaction among groups in society, with state institutions, and with international donors. A similar platform, also in El Salvador, is the Intersectoral Pro-Youth Coordination Point (CIPJES), consisting of youth organizations and NGOs. Both organizations provide a space for more constructive interactions between groups in society and the state.

In another example, the GDC also supported a pilot program of participatory local governance, using community radio as an instrument for communication and information exchange. The transmissions were in local languages, allowing all segments of the population access to the information conveyed. The project triggered a wide public debate on the value of community radio, and media in general, as a way of enhancing dialogue between local government and citizens. In addition, participants were encouraged to form local working groups around common interests and to engage in their municipalities collectively. The aim was to allow citizens to hold governments accountable. This use of information technologies helped increase civic engagement and improve the state–society relationship.

Governments and donors should support governments in building links among communities and between communities and the government. Practical measures in this regard include organizing civic action, especially for young people. They can also push for greater accountability on the part of the government at various levels, for example, through participatory budgeting, more transparency in resource allocation, and other measures. Civil society can also work at building horizontal relationships across groups, helping to heal divisions in society that hinder the state's ability to function effectively.

Governments also need training and "rules of engagement" if they are to work with civil society more effectively. As Colletta and Cullen (2000: 102) argue, "Training for government representatives in partnership skills and use of the media to provide information on civil society will also help further intercommunity and government-community relations." In fragile and conflict-affected situations, such assistance will have to be based on a context assessment broader than the ARVIN framework that the World Bank has been using since 2002.[3] The ARVIN framework looks at (1) the legal and regulatory framework, (2) the political and governance context, (3) sociocultural characteristics, and (4) economic conditions. In fragile countries, however, the analysis will also have to include broader issues obstructing citizenship participation and government accountability. More attention will also have to be paid to informal variables.

Donor engagement should be informed by a sound understanding not only of civil society organizations' stated functions but also of their potential impact on broader cohesion in society. For instance, civil society organizations that are exclusive and created along collective identities are less likely to build crosscutting social capital. For instance, Colletta and Cullen (2000: 73) found that although attempts were made to strengthen civil society in Rwanda in the 1980s and early 1990s, prior to the outbreak of conflict, their narrow service orientation prevented them from fostering relationships between groups that would reduce tensions. "Democracy, inclusion and tolerance did not automatically result from the groups' mere existence; these qualities need to be actively fostered." Donors engaging civil society as a way to promote social cohesion should always consider the inclusiveness of organizations.

The impact of donor engagement on an organization should be carefully assessed—including potential impacts in both the short and the long term. Posner (2004: 250) cautions against engaging too deeply with "political entrepreneurs," who may set up civic organizations in developing countries to reflect donor priorities "even when the groups that they have formed are nothing more than vehicles for 'shaking the donor funding tree' to secure salaries and perks for themselves and their close associates." In this regard, Posner argues that nonadvocacy groups, ones that were originally set up to promote interests independent of the donor agenda, tend to be safer organizations to engage. Those organizations' ability to sustain themselves without donor funding is also a positive criterion.

Strengthening State Capacity to Engage Positively with Society

Most state-building interventions in fragile situations today focus on building state capacity for performing basic functions, such as service delivery and security. Much less attention is given to enhancing the state's capacity to engage with society and create a relationship based on a sense of citizenship. Delivering services effectively can help, but it is not sufficient. In fragile situations, the relationship between the state and society is often tenuous, with people having only minimal allegiance to the state.

Fragile relationships between society and the state are exacerbated in places where the state has historically acted in ways that have deepened social divisions, for example, through predatory behavior, authoritarian policies, pitting groups against one another, exclusion of some groups, and so on. In many conflicts the state is one of the main perpetrators of violence, and the associated trauma can cause divisions that span generations, even centuries. Where that has happened, rebuilding trust is a long and difficult process. But experience from some societies that have achieved the transition out of fragility offers some helpful insights. The case of Colombia is instructive in this regard. There, the state has undertaken initiatives to restore state presence and rebuild the social contract with vulnerable populations, such as internally displaced persons (see text box).

BOX 8.7

Colombia's Victims Law and the Restitution of Land to the Displaced

A powerful constraint on economic growth, development, and inclusion in Colombia is the protracted armed conflict that has affected the country for several decades. Among the most affected by the conflict are the estimated 3.7 million internally displaced people (according to the Colombian Presidential Agency for Social Action and International Cooperation (Acción Social). Colombia ranks second worldwide in the number of internally displaced people (IDP), after Sudan. Most IDPs live in extreme poverty, having been forced to migrate to large cities after losing their land, savings, assets, livelihoods, and socioeconomic networks.

To respond to the situation, the administration of President Juan Manuel Santos passed a new Victims Law in 2011 that undertakes the restitution of IDPs, primarily with regard to land. The act is a major departure from past administrations' approaches, reinforcing the state as the provider of justice to the victims of conflict and addressing land rights, which have been a main trigger of past and current violence. The law also introduces the concept of collective reparation and recognizes the relevance of increasing provision of social services and livelihood rehabilitation in areas of return and integration of displaced people. The Colombian government has also prepared an ambitious rural development plan to promote formalization of property rights (among other things) in rural areas, as an essential complement to implementation of the Victims Law.

Through this legislation, the Colombian government aims to go beyond merely addressing the humanitarian needs of IDPs to restore and strengthen the social contract with displaced citizens and reestablish the state presence in the area of land ownership. The law intends to send a message that justice will be provided to victims of displacement and that land seizures will not be tolerated.

The World Bank has worked actively to develop institutional capacities to support implementation of the Victims Law, including undertaking the Protection of Patrimonial Assets of IDPs Project, through the State and Peace Building Fund. During the first phase of the project, methodologies, procedures, and tools for the protection of the land of displaced people were designed and tested in five violence-affected regions of the country.

Looking ahead, the process of restitution of land faces several significant challenges because of the complex nature of land restitution and the dynamics of the protracted conflict situation. Among the challenges are (1) the size of the population expected to benefit from restitution (about one million households); (2) the geographic area to be covered, since land dispossession has occurred in almost all municipalities in the country;

(continued next page)

BOX 8.7 *(continued)*

(3) the presence of armed groups in several regions; and (4) the existence of several (often competing) groups interested in the land. Among the key issues the project must address are the development of mechanisms for land restitution according to land rights and land dispossession; ensuring the security of victims and project staff; the creation of an inter-institutional land restitution network to restore the livelihoods of IDPs; and the design of an independent monitoring and evaluation mechanism, with the participation of the international community, among others.

Source: World Bank 2004.

The state might be captured by some social dynamics, operating according to rules of a specific group. It can be strongly influenced by some customary institutions, such as secret societies in Africa or clan organizations in the Middle East. In that case the state will not be able to establish credible links with individuals or groups that operate according to different rules. Unless the state strives to operate by rules that are neutral to different groups, it will not be able to establish a relationship with society that will be legitimate. However, changing these internal rules of operation will require time and pressure from new groups in society, such as the middle class, young graduates, or others who will voice different ways of operating. Supporting these groups in voicing their concerns in constructive and nonviolent ways is important to encourage a changing culture inside public service. An understanding of the public service culture is needed before reforms can be initiated.

State institutions tend to respond positively to high expectations. If people expect state entities to deliver public goods effectively, those state enterprises tend to do a better job. For instance, in examining pockets of effective institutions in countries with "weak governance" environments, Leonard (2010: 98) found that effective organizations are associated with interest groups "that have a conception of the state as a public good, rather than simply as a target of predation or a tool for gaining advantage over others." Similarly, a study by Butterworth (2010) of Timor-Leste found that Timorese society placed high expectations on the state in terms of service delivery after independence in 2000, as the antagonistic state–society relationship evolved into one of expectation that the state would fulfill its basic obligations to the public.

BOX 8.8

Inheritance of Public Service Jobs in Yemen

In one of the focus group with youth carried out for the study in Sana'a, M., a young, well-dressed man in his late 20s, stated directly, in front of a group of about 30 other youths from various backgrounds, that he was lucky because he could inherit the job of archivist that his father held in an important ministry in the government. He said that he thought this was a wise decision because his father could train him and provide him with all the knowledge he needed to do the job. The group in the room seemed to consider this legitimate. However, in another focus group with youth, carried out in Mukallah, many young graduates said that they would not be able to enter the civil service because many jobs, if not most, were already reserved for particular families and clans. They cited this as one of their most serious grievances.

Source: Authors' field research.

Conversely, if people expect that state institutions will be predatory or weak, their expectations also tend to be fulfilled. To use again the example of Timor-Leste, when the state failed to meet initial expectations, societal perceptions transformed into a very low opinion of the civil service, which in turn influenced weak performance.

> When public institutions are not functioning effectively and efficiently there tends to be a vicious circle of poverty and inequality in distribution of scarce resources: when governments waste the scarce public resources, officials in the public service in some developing countries have little incentive to do their jobs well with their low (and often irregularly paid) salaries. (Hellsten and Larbi 2006: 138)

When public (formal) institutions are not able to deliver services effectively, they are perceived as illegitimate, and the society often depends on alternative (informal) mechanisms to fulfill needs.

Policies to improve the state's capacity to engage society must be informed by the specific social, cultural, and political environment in which the public service operates. Tesky and Hook (2010: 7) warn that "a dense patterning of institutions, some formal and many others informal, underpin all state structures and state society relations and are ignored at great risk." With regard to Timor Leste, they argue that the public service "should be more accurately viewed as a 'social relation' than a set of institutions standing in isolation from society. The conclusion is that creating organizational capacity (including through civil service reform) depends less on institutional design than it does on creating a durable political settlement among elites" that takes into account these contextual factors.

It is important to signal a clear departure from the previous way of doing things, especially when the credibility of public organizations may have suffered because of poor performance. For this purpose, it may be useful to locate public sector reforms within a broader framework of governance reforms that has the support of the highest level of government. For instance, in South Africa in 1995, the African National Congress prepared a White Paper on the Transformation of the Public Service, outlining the regime's broad goals for transforming the public service. The document had the sanction of the highest level of government and enjoyed broad public support. Locating specific reforms (civil service, public finance management, etc.) within this broader framework allowed reform measures to enjoy credibility even at the point of introduction (Ramsingh 2008).

The reform process should engage citizens closely, giving them ownership of the changes. Greater engagement with citizens will also allow better incorporation of local values and norms. Manor (2007) uses empirical evidence to argue that organizations in fragile situations are more likely to succeed if they employ consultative and participatory mechanisms throughout their implementation, as that enhances the sense of ownership both of local communities and of government officials.

Delegation of authority through some form of decentralization is a crucial part of strengthening states' ability to engage groups in society. The UN's *World Public Sector Report 2010* argued that decentralization is a key strategy to ensure citizen participation. However, the report makes a distinction between vertical decentralization, where "central government hands down certain powers, functions and resources to local governments," and horizontal decentralization, where "governance responsibilities are spread more broadly across the society, and civil society organization." It emphasizes the importance of employing the second form, horizontal decentralization, which is more empowering to citizens. In 1994, during South Africa's postconflict recovery process, the government undertook decentralization reforms as a means of empowering communities. Under the law, municipalities were required to create an "Integrated Development Plan," with the participation of all stakeholders and the entire community. The country found that these forums also provided a structure for peaceful interactions among community members. The reforms that Kenya achieved in its water sector in 2002 are also attributed to the consensus-based, stakeholder-driven, and decentralized approach that was taken (Krhoda 2008).

Finally, it is important to design participatory mechanisms with a good understanding of the power dynamics and belief systems in a particular community. If not, those structures could perpetuate inequalities and exclusion. For example, in communities where displaced individuals are

---

BOX 8.9

Examples of Positive Engagement with Society

Bangalore Agenda Task Force (BATF) achieved successful municipal reforms that Robinson (2007) attributes to its close engagement with local NGOs and the private sector from the earliest stages of the reform effort. The reform process facilitated broad public participation through publicity campaigns, consumer surveys, and other means. The successful reforms led to improved operations, greater public accountability, and improved taxation and budgetary controls within municipal agencies. Robinson cites the accountability and transparency mechanisms put in place through active citizen engagement as key to the reforms' success. Similarly, he found that a scheme in Karnataka to provide better access to credit for rural women (Development of Women and Children in Rural Areas—DWCRA) benefited from close engagement with members of civil society and local communities. Robinson argues that both programs managed to mobilize the civil society and the private sector to influence public opinion, politics, and the policy process.

In addition to directly contributing toward specific reform goals, positive engagement with society can also contribute to improving state–society relations. Bruni's (2008) examination of Nicaragua's public sector reform experience demonstrates how citizen engagement could improve the overall public perception of government. Though the reforms themselves were not widely successful (because of "the failure to engage the legislative branch in the process"), the author found that the participatory and consultative aspects of citizen engagement helped "foster a broader definition of the concept of the state and of the public administration beyond the concept of government" (348). In fact, despite limited success of the reforms themselves, Bruni found that the efforts at consensus building through a participatory and transparent process improved people's perceptions of the level of corruption in the state administration and improved their expectation of better economic prospects. "The main impact of the campaigns was to change the public's perception of a fragmented public administration, to increase public expectations for a better personal economic situation in the future by 7.6 percent, and to change the attitude of the media towards Nicaragua's public life, thus decreasing the level of conflict and focusing more on development goals" (347).

Source: Bruni 2008.

not considered citizens, they are unlikely even to be mapped as community members, preventing their inclusion in any participatory decision-making process.

Notes

1. The *2011 World Development Report* describes various approaches to improving criminal justice and dispute resolution (World Bank 2011a: 153).
2. See Mamdani 2001. For a balanced picture of the extent of the massive participation in Rwanda genocide, see Strauss 2007.
3. The components of the ARVIN framework are association, resources, voice, information, and negotiation.

References

Allen, Tim. 2006. *Trial Justice: The International Criminal Court and the Lord's Resistance Army*. London and New York: Zed Books.

Baines, Erin K. 2007. "The Haunting of Alice: Local Approaches to Justice and Reconciliation in Northern Uganda." *International Journal of Transitional Justice* 1 (1): 113.

Barron, Patrick. 2010. "Community-Driven Development in Post-Conflict and Conflict-Affected Areas." Background Paper for the *2011 World Development Report*. Washington, DC: World Bank.

Barron, Patrick, Rachael Diprose, and Michael Woolcock. 2007. "Local Conflict and Development Projects in Indonesia: Part of the Problem or Part of a Solution." Policy Research Working Paper 4212, World Bank, Washington, DC.

Bruni, Michele. 2008. "Participation, Transparency, and Consensus Building in Support of Public Sector Reform: The Case of Nicaragua." In *Governance Reform under Real-World Conditions: Citizens, Stakeholders, and Voice*, ed. Sina Odugbemi and Thomas Jacobson. Washington, DC: World Bank.

Butterworth, David. 2010. *Opportunity and Obligation in Timor-Leste's Civil Service: An Anthropological View of the Informal Organization*. Washington, DC: World Bank.

Colletta, N. J., and M. L. Cullen. 2000. *The Nexus between Violent Conflict, Social Capital and Social Cohesion: Case Studies from Cambodia and Rwanda*. Washington, DC: World Bank.

DelVecchio, Mary-Jo, Byron Good, Jesse Grayman, and Matthew Lakoma. 2007. *A Psychological Needs Assessment of Communities in 14 Conflict Affected Districts in Aceh*, 4–6. Jakarta: IOM.

Good, Byron, Mary-Jo DelVecchio, Jesse Grayman, and Matthew Lakoma. 2006. *Psychological Needs Assessments of Communities Affected by the Conflict in the Districts of Pidie, Bireuen and Aceh Utara*. Jakarta: IOM.

Harvey, Barbara. 2006. "Breaking Eggs/Rebuilding Societies: Traditional Justice as a Tool for Transitional Justice in Northern Uganda." Paper presented at the Youth Symposium on Conflict, Poverty and International Interventions, Montreal, April 13.

Hellsten, S., and G. Larbi. 2006. "Public Good or Private Good? The Paradox of Public and Private Ethics in the Context of Developing Countries." *Public Administration and Development* 26 (2): 135–45.

Hovil, Lucy, and Joanna Quinn. 2005. "Peace First, Justice Later: Traditional Justice in Northern Uganda." Refugee Law Project Working Paper 17, Refugee Law Project, Kampala, Uganda.

Isser, Deborah, ed. 2011. *Customary Justice and the Rule of Law in War-Torn Societies*. Washington, DC: United States Institute of Peace.

Krhoda, George. 2008. "A Consensus Based, Stakeholder Driven, and Decentralized Approach to Building Social Coalitions for Water Sector Reforms." In *Governance Reform under Real-World Conditions*, ed. Sina Odugbemi and Thomas Jacobson. Washington, DC: World Bank.

Kymlicka, Will, and François Grin. 2003. "Assessing the Politics of Diversity in Transition Countries." In *Nation-Building, Ethnicity and Language Politics in Transition Countries*, ed. Farimah Daftary and François Grin, 3–27. Budapest, Hungary: LGI Books.

Latigo, James Ojera. 2008. "Northern Uganda: Tradition-Based Practices in the Acholi Region." In *Reconciliation and Traditional Justice after Violent Conflict: Learning from African Experiences,* ed. Luc Huyse and Mark Salter, 117–18. Stockholm: International Institute for Democracy and Electoral Assistance.

Leonard, David. 2010. "'Pockets' of Effective Agencies in Weak Governance States: Where Are They Likely and Why Does it Matter." *Public Administration and Development* 30 (2): 91–101.

Litteral, Robert. 2004. "Vernacular Education in Papua New Guinea." Background paper prepared for the Education for All Global Monitoring Report 2005, *The Quality Imperative*. 2005/ED/EFA/MRT/PI/30, UNESCO, New York.

Liu Institute for Global Issues. 2005. "Roco Wat I Acholi: Restoring Relationship in Acholi-Land: Traditional Approaches to Justice and Reintegration." Liu Institute for Global Issues, University of British Columbia.

Mamdani, Mahmood. 2001. *When Victims Become Killers: Colonialism, Nativism, and the Genocide in Rwanda*. Princeton, NJ: Princeton University Press.

Manor, James. 2007. *Aid That Works: Successful Development in Fragile States*. Washington, DC: World Bank.

Mansuri, Ghazala, and Vijayendra Rao. 2004. "Community-Based and -Driven Development: A Critical Review." *World Bank Research Observer* 19 (1): 1–39.

Marc, Alexandre. 2008. "Taking Culture into Account in the Delivery of Health and Education Services." In *Inclusive States, Social Policy and Structural*

Inequalities, ed. Anis A. Dani and Arjan de Haan. Washington, DC: World Bank.

———. 2010. *Delivering Services in Multicultural Societies*. Washington, DC: World Bank.

McKay, Susan, and Dyan Mazurana. 2004. *Where Are the Girls in Fighting Forces in Northern Uganda, Sierra Leone and Mozambique: Their Lives during and after War*. Montreal: International Center for Human Rights and Democratic Development.

Mehotra, S. 1998. "Education for All: Policy Lessons from High-Achieving Countries." UNICEF Staff Working Paper, United Nations Children's Fund, New York.

Moser, Caroline, and Cathy McIlwaine. 2004. *Encounters with Violence in Latin America: Urban Poor Perceptions from Colombia and Guatemala*. New York: Routledge.

MSR 2009. *Multi-Stakeholder Review of Post-Conflict Programming in Aceh: Identifying the Foundations for Sustainable Peace and Development in Aceh*. December 2009.

Noble, Cameron, and Craig Thorburn. 2009. "Multi-Stakeholder Review of Post-Conflict Programming in Aceh: Identifying the Foundations for Sustainable Peace and Development in Aceh," MSR, Aceh, Indonesia.

Posner, Daniel. 2004. "Civil Society and the Reconstruction of Failed States." In *When States Fail: Causes and Consequences*, ed. Robert I. Rotberg. Princeton, NJ: Princeton University Press.

Pouligny, Beatrice. 2002. "Building Peace in Situations of Post-Mass Crimes." *International Peacekeeping* 9 (2): 201–20.

———. 2010. "Resistance, Trauma and Violence." Background paper for *Societal Dynamics and Fragility: Engaging Societies in Responding to Fragile Situations*. Washington, DC: World Bank.

Puerto Gomez, Margarita, and Asger Christensen. 2010. "The Impacts of Refugees on Neighboring Countries: A Development Challenge." Background paper for *2011 World Development Report: Conflict, Security and Development*. Washington, DC: World Bank.

Ramsingh, Odetta. 2008. "The Challenges of Reconstructing the Public Service after Conflict: The Case of the Republic of South Africa." Paper presented at the 2nd Committee of the General Assembly of the United Nations, New York, November 13.

Roberts-Schweitzer, Elund, ed., with Vincent Greaney and Kreszentia Duer. 2006. *Promoting Social Cohesion through Education: Case Studies and Tools for Using Textbooks and Curricula*. Washington, DC: World Bank.

Robinson, Mark. 2007. "The Politics of Successful Governance Reforms: Lessons of Design and Implementation." *Commonwealth and Comparative Politics* 45 (4): 521–48.

Strauss, Scott. 2007. "Origins and Aftermaths: The Dynamics of Genocide in Rwanda and Their Post-Genocide Implications." In *After Mass Crime: Rebuilding States and Communities,* ed. Beatrice Pouligny, Simon Chesterman, and Albrecht Schnabel, 122–41. Tokyo and New York: United Nations University Press.

Taylor, Charles. 1994. "The Politics of Recognition". *Multiculturalism: Examining the Politics of Recognition.* Ed. Amy Gutmann. Princeton: Princeton University Press.

Tesky, Graham, and David Hook. 2010. *The Lived Institution: The Political Economy of Civil Service Reform in Timor-Leste.* Washington, DC: World Bank.

UNDP (United Nations Development Program). 2004. *The 2004 Human Development Report.* New York: United Nations Development Program.

UNHCR (United Nations High Commissioner for Refugees). 2004. *Economic and Social Impacts of Massive Refugee Populations on Host Developing Countries, as Well as Other Countries.* Standing Committee, UNHCR, EC/54/SC/CRP.5.

———. 2006a. *Convention Plus: Targeting of Development Assistance for Durable Solutions to Forced Displacement: Joint Statement by the Co-Chairs (FORUM/2005/8).*

———. 2006b. *The State of the World's Refugees: Human Displacement in the New Millennium* New York: Oxford University Press.

Volkan, Vamik. 1989. "Cyprus: Ethnic Conflicts and Tensions." *International Journal of Group Tensions* 19 (4): 297–316.

———. 2006. "What Some Monuments Tell Us about Mourning and Forgiveness." In *Taking Wrongs Seriously: Apologies and Reconciliation*, ed. Elazar Barkan and Alexander Karn. Stanford, CA: Stanford University Press.

Watabe, Masaki. 2007. "The Zambia Initiative, Potentials of New Trials Promoting Human Security." *Technology and Development,* No. 20, January. Tokyo, Institute for International Cooperation, Japan International Cooperation Agency.

World Bank. 2004. "Protecting the Patrimonial Assets of Internally Displaced Persons in Colombia." Social Development, PCF Occasional Note, NO.5/NOVEMBER 2004, World Bank, Washington, DC.

———. 2009. "Disarm, Demobilize and Reintegrate: Transforming Combatants into Citizens to Consolidate Peace," World Bank Institute, Washington, DC.

———. 2011a. *2011 World Development Report: Conflict, Security and Development.* Washington, DC: World Bank.

———. 2011b. *Poverty and Social Exclusion in India.* Washington, DC: World Bank.

———. 2012. "Understanding Access to Justice and Conflict Resolution at the Local Level in the Central African Republic." Social Cohesion and Violence Prevention Team, Social Development Department, World Bank, Washington, DC.

Background Papers Prepared for This Book

Paper 1. Identities, Social Justice, and Citizenship

Successful nations are those where state policies are congruent with the form of state (nation-states, state-nations, multicultural states, etc.). For instance, if state-nations act as nation-states without sufficient accommodation of subnational identities, there is a risk of civil war. Similarly, if states emphasize diversity while ignoring connection to the national state, that too will increase the risk of violence. The way identities are distributed across the polity also determines the likelihood of violence in a society. Cumulative identities, where all sources of identities (language, race, religion, cast, tribe, etc.) are arranged along the same dimensions, magnify differences. Conversely, crosscutting identities (where some sources of identity are shared by different groups) generate moderation. Even though identities by themselves might not be a source of conflict, they may serve as an instrument for collective action (including hostile retaliation) when confronted with systemic inequities, fear, or violence. Opportunities for civic engagement, for the collective good of communities broader than groups, can ameliorate factors that cause groups to initiate violence against other groups.

Paper 2. Intersubjective Meaning

"Intersubjective meaning" refers to a common understanding of the nature of the problems facing the society and possible solutions to them. For instance, in the case of the misuse of public resources, it matters whether key actors regard the giving of such resources to associates as corruption or as a social norm. Intersubjective meaning is logically and empirically prior to interests, incentives, and values. Analyses of institutional rules, without an accompanying assessment of their relation to embodied knowledge and shared practices, is likely to be of only limited use for getting institutions right. Fragility increases when intersubjective meanings associated with crucial social practices are not shared in a society and where they are in conflict with formal institutional rules.

Paper 3. Social Organizations and Institutions

Such factors as history, narratives and sources of legitimacy, identity, the balance between consent and coercion, and changes in informal institutions underlie the dynamics of informal institutions. The dualism of formal-informal thus presents a false dichotomy. Informal institutions, to a large extent, indicate the configuration of power and social conflict over distributional processes, and there is nothing intrinsic about informal mechanisms that makes them more prone to promote social cohesion. Instead that depends on distributive outcomes and the degree of inclusivity or exclusivity of informal institutions and the nature of coercive force used to enforce norms. Modalities of interactions between state institutions, formal nonstate institutions, and informal traditional institutions (e.g., in the form of strategic collaboration, delegations, or co-option) are factors that influence fragility or resilience in a society.

Paper 4. Resilience, Trauma, and Violence

The particular structure of the conflict and the prevailing security situation seem to have additional implications for the outcomes of trauma and resilience. Long-term and repetitive violence, intergenerational impact, and certain determinants associated with trauma (direct exposure to violence, duration of the event, role of the state, mobilization of trauma by political interests, disruption of livelihood) can accentuate the effects of trauma. Meanwhile, individual trauma can affect the collective through its impact on social relations and trust, transformed relationship networks, civic trust and collective action capacity, promoting the emergence of new social patterns, the loss and disintegration of cultural beliefs and values, and the legitimization of violence. Trauma affects state–society relations by transforming the expectations from the state. In particular, the notion of the control of the legitimate use of violence by the state is usually affected quite profoundly. Justice, livelihoods, and symbolic issues matter most for resilience in traumatized societies. Mechanisms to address trauma that build on justice, livelihoods, and symbolism can strengthen resilience and increase cohesion.

Paper 5. Youth, Gender, and Fragility

The socialization process, "the process by which people acquire the behaviors and beliefs of the social world they live in," is the central interface between youth and society. This process is different for young boys and girls. Many sources of socialization have a conservative bias favoring the internalization of existing forms of social cohesion, norms, and rules. Young people are not passive recipients of socialization but active agents influencing and shaping the process itself, as well as the outcome, depending on their agency. A socialization process that is rigid, controlled, exclusive, or conflicting is an element of fragility and may encourage youth to seek an alternative socialization process, often through the use of violence. Civic engagement and other support systems for youth are of central importance to reducing fragility.

Authors and Advisers of the Background Papers

Paper Topic	Principal Author/s	Advisers
Paper 1. Identities, social justice, and citizenship	Ashutosh Varshney, Brown University	Daniel Posner, MIT
Paper 2. Meaning systems	Michael Woolcock, World Bank Varun Gauri, World Bank Deval Desai, World Bank	
Paper 3. Social organizations and institutions	Pilar Domingo, ODI	Caroline Sage, World Bank Dirk Kohnert, GIGA Mary Amuyunzu-Nyamongo, AIHD
Paper 4. Resilience, trauma, and violence	Beatrice Pouligny, Georgetown University	Paul Francis, World Bank Pat Barron, Oxford University Barry Hart, Eastern Mennonite University
Paper 5. Youth, gender, and fragility	Sabine Kurtenbach, GIGA	Gary Barker, ICRW Kathleen Kuehnast, USIP Jennifer Olmsted, Drew University

Lead-Authors of the Country Case Studies

Country	Lead Author
Liberia	Paul Richards, Wageningen University and Research Centre
Indonesia (Aceh)	Edward Aspinall, Australian National University
Central African Republic	Roland Marchal, National Center for Scientific Research
Yemen	Elham M. Manea, University of Zurich
Haiti	Louis Herns Marcelin, University of Miami

Internal and External Advisors—Overall

Internal Advisers

Paul Francis, Consultant

Nora Dudwick, Senior Social Scientist

Graham Teskey, Senior Adviser

Michael Woolcock, Lead Social Development Specialist

Varun Gauri, Senior Economist

External Advisers

Frances Stewart, Director of CRISE, University of Oxford

Daniel Posner, MIT

Boxes and notes are indicated by *b* and *n* following the page number.

www.ingramcontent.com/pod-product-compliance
Lightning Source LLC
Chambersburg PA
CBHW061726270326
41928CB00011B/2130